RACHEL R

BOLD

SIX PRAYING WOMEN, ONE FAITHFUL GOD

A Study of Praying Bible Women

SIX-WEEK STUDY
WITH VIDEO ACCESS

BOLD

SIX PRAYING WOMEN, ONE FAITHFUL GOD
A Study of Praying Bible Women

© 2022 Rachel Risner
All rights reserved.

ISBN 978-1-953016-01-0

Unless otherwise noted, Scripture quotations are taken from THE HOLY BIBLE, NEW INTERNATIONAL VERSION®, NIV® Copyright © 1973, 1978, 1984, 2011 by Biblica, Inc.® Used by permission. All rights reserved worldwide.

Scripture taken from the Holy Bible, New International Reader's Version®, NIrV®, Copyright © 2001, 2005 by Biblica, Inc.™ Used by permission of Zondervan. All rights reserved worldwide.

Scripture quotations marked HCSB are taken from the Holman Christian Standard Bible®, Copyright © 1999, 2000, 2002, 2003, 2009 by Holman Bible Publishers. Used by permission. Holman Christian Standard Bible®, Holman CSB®, and HCSB® are federally registered trademarks of Holman Bible Publishers.

Scripture taken from the New King James Version®. Copyright © 1982 by Thomas Nelson. Used by permission. All rights reserved.

Scripture quotations marked NLT are taken from the Holy Bible, New Living Translation, copyright © 1996, 2004, 2015 by Tyndale House Foundation. Used by permission of Tyndale House Publishers, Inc., Carol Stream, Illinois 60188. All rights reserved.

Scripture quotations are from The Holy Bible, English Standard Version® (ESV®), Copyright © 2001 by Crossway, a publishing ministry of Good News Publishers. Used by permission. All rights reserved.

Scripture quotations marked CSB have been taken from the Christian Standard Bible®. Copyright © 2017 by Holman Bible Publishers. Used by permission. Christian Standard Bible®, and CSB® are federally registered trademarks of Holman Bible Publishers.

Scripture quotations marked MSG are taken from THE MESSAGE*, copyright © 1993, 2002, 2018 by Eugene H. Peterson. Used by permission of NavPress. All rights reserved. Represented by Tyndale House Publishers, Inc. (*paraphrase)

To order additional copies of this resource, write to Bonfire Books, 5586 Township Road 381; Millersburg, OH 44654; email rachel@rachelrisner.com; order online at www.amazon.com or visit www.rachelrisner.com

Cover art Rachel Risner, Cover photo Creative Market, goffkein.pro

Printed in the United States of America

Bonfire Books
5586 Township Road 381
Millersburg, OH 44654

DEDICATION

This study is dedicated to all women who are ready to pray **bold**.

MEET THE AUTHOR

Rachel Risner isn't exactly a motormouth, but when it comes to sharing what she's learning about God through the women in the Bible, she's got plenty to say. Studying their stories has changed her life, and she can't keep the life-changing truth to herself.

Rachel is an author and the wife of John Risner, lead pastor at MCA, The Church on the Hill, right in the heart of Ohio's beautiful Amish country. Her days as a mom of eight are filled with math lessons, potty training, soccer practice, ministering, and—when she can—sneaking away to clack at the computer or poke her nose into a good book (or better, *the* Good Book). She writes online at rachelrisner.com. *Bold* is her second women's Bible Study. Her first is entitled *Significant.*

TABLE OF CONTENTS

BOLD

SIX PRAYING WOMEN, ONE FAITHFUL GOD

AUTHOR'S NOTE

Friend! I am thrilled to have you along for the ride, journeying with me through the scriptures and stories of Bible women who prayed. My own desire and prayer is that this study would draw your heart closer to God, transforming us both to be more like Him. I have taken care in my writing to do my best to stay true to God's word and to use reliable commentaries to assure the most possible accuracy in its interpretation. But I am fallible. Anytime a human teacher is involved there is room for misinterpretation and error. I urge you to hold **God's word alone** in the highest regard. Only the Bible is without blemish. Because of this, I encourage you to grapple with the words in this text. Do not accept these teachings flippantly, but examine them for yourselves, using scripture as your measuring rod for truth. Know God's word for yourself and seek Him through your own serious study. Blessings to you as we embark on this journey together! It's time to pray **Bold**.

This, then, is how you should pray:

Our Father in heaven
hallowed be Your name,
Your kingdom come,
Your will be done,
on earth as it is in heaven.
Give us today
our daily bread.
And forgive us our debts
as we also have forgiven
our debtors.
And lead us not into
temptation,
but deliver us
from the evil one.

for yours is the kingdom and the power
and the glory forever.

Amen.

INTRODUCTION

By Rachel Risner

And pray in the Spirit on all occasions with all kinds of prayers and requests. With this in mind, be alert and always keep on praying. Ephesians 6:18

God delights in the holy boldness that will not take "no" for an answer. – R.A. Torrey

Come to the table

Anyone hungry? You too? I think my stomach might be growling. Pull up a chair. You'll fit in for sure.

The table at my house isn't high-falootin'. In fact, my kids joke that we are low-falootin'. You won't find bone china, dessert forks, linen napkins, or any foreign-sounding delicacies (unless fettucine alfredo counts—ha!).

There will be plenty of vegetables, some bread, and some meat—food that nourishes and sticks to your ribs. There may be some crumbs on the floor, left by the sweeper-in-training. There will probably be an elbow—or six—on the table. You might even hear an unexpected burp escape someone's mouth (hopefully followed by an, "Excuse me!") We won't put on airs.

There will be spilled juice and laughter. There will be truth and love and joy in the midst of crumpled napkins and dribbled food scraps. It will be real, and it will be beautiful.

A little like this study.

There's no pretense here.

As I write women's Bible studies, I'm not aiming for flowery words and scholarly prose—you won't find the ideas in these pages tied up neatly in bows. There's no pretense here. I'm not here to impress anyone.

God's word is real. It's down-to-earth and when we look at it closely, we see our own bone-deep flaws clearly. So that's what you'll find when you pull up your chair at the table here.

In the pages of this study, we'll feast on God's word. And be real about what that reveals about our hearts.

Why?

You thought this book was about praying bold prayers—and it is. But before we pray our own bold prayers, we must be fed. We need to chew on teaching about prayer. And what better to feast on than God's word itself?

My dream for this book is that it be the meat-and-potatoes spiritual food your soul craves. That once you feed on it, your tired soul will be revived and energized to pray your own bold prayers, inspired by the very prayers we study in these pages.

Not because God needs us. He can work on His own without us.

But He lets us join in!

Friend, it's a joy to join in His timely work of praying bold prayers—and I don't want us to miss out.

As we work through the pages of this study and, more importantly, the verses of scripture—we will see time and time again how God moved in mighty ways in the lives of women who prayed bold prayers.

And now it's our turn.

A Call to Pray Bold when Life Leaves You Dry
Have you ever felt like your prayer life is dry?

You crave being closer to God but just feel distant. You've prayed and prayed and prayed but wonder whether your prayers are even making a difference. Are you really where you want to be in your prayer life?

> In the pages of this study, we'll feast on God's word. And be real about what that reveals about our hearts.

In scripture we find women who went through the same struggles we face:

- **Running** to false comforts, instead of running to God.
- **Captive** to their circumstances.
- **Stuck** in situations of defeat.
- **Suffering** heartbreak and facing spiritual starvation.
- **Trapped**, needing the freedom and forgiveness only Christ can offer.
- **Desperate** for divine direction—to be led in the right paths.

But they brought their burdens boldly to God, crying out to Him in their need, and boy, did He deliver.

We'll learn to pray boldly with kingdom purpose, prayers that move our hearts, grow our faith, and shape our lives.

Friends, I'm so glad you're joining me for *Bold: Six Praying Women, One Faithful God*.

In this study we'll learn to pray boldly with kingdom purpose, prayers that move our hearts, grow our faith, and shape our lives. Prayers that God uses to bring about His will.

Because just like Hannah and Miriam, just like Deborah and Mary, we're praying to the God who sees us and knows us by name, the God who shakes heaven and earth to give us the impossible victory, the God who provides for our every desperate need—friends, it's time to pray bold.

Bold Prayers from Bold Pray-ers

There's something inherently bold about prayer.

Think about it this way: someone like you or me—someone flawed and weak and hopeless without God, approaching the Almighty, All-powerful, Omnipresent God of the universe, the Creator of it all, the Beginning and the End, with her own thoughts and words and requests.

When you put it that way, it seems pretty gutsy, right?

If you're a take-the-bull-by-the-horns, confident, self-assured woman, the call to be bold is right up your alley. You're probably thinking, "Praying bold prayers! All right! Let me at it!"

But maybe you're content to watch the action, rather than instigate it. If so, the call to boldness might make you squirm.

Or maybe you fall somewhere in between.

At any rate, the reality is that we're all called to boldness in prayer—whether we feel like it or not. God commands us to pray all types of prayers, at all times (Ephesians 6:18).

We all need to pray. Always.

And if we need to be praying just as much as we need to be breathing, or we need our hearts to be beating, then we sure might as well learn all we can about what the Bible says about prayer.

So here we are, ready to learn. And I'm here right by your side, not because I am an expert pray-er—far from it! But because I need to learn just as much as you, just as much as any woman. In order to learn how to do this bold, essential, constant act of prayer, we must look to the examples of prayers in scripture.

So, let's dive in! What better time than now? And who better to learn from than the best pray-er himself, Jesus! Of course, we will also look to the women of scripture whose prayers and lives we can pore over, to learn about God, to learn about praying, and to learn the truths of scripture. I am pumped, and I hope you are too!

Prayer 101

Before we dive right into the thick of our study, let's make sure we're all on the same page when it comes to prayer basics.

Let's do a quick review—a "Prayer 101" course.

First of all, what is prayer?

Prayer is simply time with the Lord. It's talking with Him—either out loud or in your spirit, silently. And it's also listening to Him. Sometimes it's even just being still with Him, waiting for Him to nudge your spirit.

Does listening for God mean we're expecting an audible voice? Not necessarily. Though God spoke aloud to people in scripture,

> And pray in the Spirit on all occasions with all kinds of prayers and requests. With this in mind, be alert and always keep on praying for all the Lord's people.
>
> Ephesians 6:18

and certainly may still today, oftentimes He speaks to us in more subtle ways. Our part is to quiet ourselves to listen.

Step 1: It all starts with a relationship. The first step in any Christian's walk with the Lord is responding to God's invitation to a relationship. God has invited each of us to draw close to Him through accepting His son Jesus's gift of His life in our place. Romans 10:9-10 puts it simply. See it in the margin.

Giving Jesus control of your life, admitting your need for Him and believing He was raised to life to cover your sins is key to beginning a new life in Christ. If you haven't taken this step, there's no time like the present!

Do it today; you won't regret it. Talk to Him and tell Him you're ready to begin walking with Him—it's the most important prayer you'll pray! And it is the first step on the path to a life of praying bold prayers.

You could pray something like, "God, I want you to forgive my sins. Take control of my life and be my Savior and Lord."

If you've just made Jesus Lord of your life for the first time right now, please reach out to a Christian friend and let them know! If you don't have friends who follow Christ, find a local church and get involved—being part of a community is a great way to get started!

Step 2: Pray anytime, about anything. The Bible doesn't just suggest that we pray—it commands us to pray. Why? We can't know God's purposes completely, but prayer is good for us. It connects us to a loving, powerful God who is able to meet all our needs. With that in mind, why wouldn't we pray?!

Come to God at all times, with all things. This takes humility and diligence.

And it doesn't hurt to go to the scriptures and see how Jesus Himself taught us to pray. If you want to learn how to pray in the way scripture teaches, you've come to the right place!

> If you declare with your mouth, "Jesus is Lord," and believe in your heart that God raised him from the dead, you will be saved. For it is with your heart that you believe and are justified, and it is with your mouth that you profess your faith and are saved.
>
> Romans 10:9-10

But first, a thought about what prayer is not...

If you picked up this book expecting a worksheet to fill in, a script of exact words, prayers to memorize for various occasions, or a specific formula to follow—I have to burst your bubble. This isn't it.

While highly structured prayers can be one good tool in your prayer arsenal, that's not going to be the focus of this study. My hope is to equip you in a way that's more holistic.

As we study the lives and prayers of these six women, here is what we see: prayer is a matter of the heart. Our hearts must desire to open up to God, to look to Him, to be with Him. Then our prayers will flow from there.

After all, our prayers involve speaking with the Lord, and Jesus has said, "What you say flows from what is in your heart" (Luke 6:45 NLT).

Does this mean that we come to God with our ducks in a row, everything neat and tidy?

Hardly—you'll see that soon enough as we look at Hagar's life and prayer in Chapter One.

Prayer is not reading a script, it's not a 1-2-3 step-by-step formula, it's not mindlessly reciting words by rote. It's a heart that beats to be close to God. It's life. It's breath.

> Prayer is a heart that beats to be close to God.

In this study we will dig deeper than just the words of these women; we'll peer intently into their lives—their backstory, their thoughts, their feelings, their actions—to get the fullest, richest picture of their hearts' longing for God.

That's where we find our own hope—heart change.

It's not only about the words we say. It's not only about our theology—our ideas about God. Because prayer is a matter of the heart.

How to Use This Book

This book is designed with you in mind! It is an interactive, workbook-style, six-week study for you to embark upon with friends, with a Bible Study group, or individually.

It can be done alone, but your experience will be enriched if you invite at least one friend along for the journey, and keep each other company along the way.

Each of the six weeks, or chapters, delves deeply into the life of one of the praying women in scripture.

Whether they are women whose stories you are familiar with or not, I encourage you to ask God to help you see their stories with fresh eyes. The word of God is alive and active, and it speaks truths into our lives that we don't want to miss!

Each of the six women we'll study illustrates an aspect of the Lord's Prayer—the one Jesus taught us in Matthew 6. You'll see firsthand how they lived it out.

For each week, there are five days of study homework—designed to do individually before meetings, if you are doing the study with a group.

Six complementary video teachings are available to stream at rachelrisner.com that correspond with each of the six weeks of the study. You can also find them at my (Rachel Risner's) YouTube channel. They are to be watched after completing that week's homework.

At meetings women can discuss both the videos and the material found in this book. Group leaders may decide if they would like women to watch videos ahead of time, individually, or if they will watch together at gatherings.

May I encourage you to be purposeful in carving out time for your "homework," soul-nourishing time with the Lord. Doing the five assignments per week will take some diligence and intentionality, but you will find the time you spend pays dividends—time in God's word is never wasted.

> You will see firsthand how the women in scripture lived out the Lord's Prayer.

Take your time. Linger over passages and give yourself a chance to take it all in. Underline, circle, highlight, and dog-ear your book. Whatever it takes to make your journey memorable!

Some groups enjoy going at a slower pace—that's fine! Just remember that the study is designed to be done in this order:

1. Complete assigned chapter—five days of homework— individually.

2. Watch optional teaching video from rachelrisner.com or Rachel's YouTube Channel. This can be done before meetings or together at meetings, whichever your group decides. Viewer Guides are included in the back of this workbook, starting on page 269.

3. Meet together—this is the fun part! Gather to discuss what you're learning—both from the teaching videos and the workbook, and best of all, from scripture!

Exciting Things are Ahead

Over the next six weeks we'll walk through the lives and prayers of real women in scripture to see how God moved mountains and provided in unimaginable ways in response to their bold prayers. We'll learn along the way all about our great God and how we can pray our own bold prayers.

We'll see:

Hagar—who spoke in the wilderness to the fatherly God who saw her, who knew her by name. And we'll learn to have our own daughter-of-the-king, heart-to-heart relationship with the God Who Sees us.

Miriam—whose obedience to God's law instead of Pharaoh's positioned her to see God's mighty hand part the waters to set her people free—making the impossible, possible, in a way only God could. She became a worship leader, singing about the mighty acts she's witnessed firsthand. We'll learn how to win our own power struggle once and for all by laying down our need for control and praising the One who holds the waters in His hands—positioning ourselves for bold prayers.

Deborah—the warrior-judge who went God's way instead of following the pull of the pagan culture around her, and saw God shake heaven and earth to give His underdog people a miraculous victory. She saw the battle won, and sang His Kingdom Come. We'll learn for ourselves the joy of joining in bold prayers of kingdom victory, and see God shake heaven and earth in our own lives to knock our enemy off his feet.

Hannah—a barren and heartbroken woman who was burdened by her own people's spiritual barrenness. She cried out in desperation to God to provide—and God came through big time. Sure of God's timely provision, Hannah gave her son Samuel right back to Him, to lead His people out of their darkness and foreshadow the bread of life, Christ Himself. We'll be encouraged to boldly bring our own gut-wrenchingly honest pleas before the God who delivers blessing pressed-down, shaken-together, and running over into our laps.

Mary Magdalene—desperate for deliverance from her demons and her sins, Mary Magdalene experienced freedom we find only in Christ. Given a privileged position of travelling companion with Jesus and the Twelve, Mary Magdalene was able to live her life as a bold pray-er —living forgiven. Last at the cross and first at the empty tomb, she'd be the first woman to see the risen Christ and be commissioned by Him to spread the good news. Her life teaches us how we too can live forgiven, with lives changed radically by Jesus in a way that drives us to bold prayer and bold living.

Mary the mother of Christ—humble, poor, and young, Mary didn't have much going for her—at least that's how it seemed. But God knew she had eyes for the bigger picture—the spiritual impact of the Messiah—and her part to play in His arrival. So, He gave her the honor of being His mother—the role coveted by Jewish women for thousands of years. And in her response, we see a woman poured out for God's use, her heart following hard the leading of the Lord—not into temptation, but delivered from evil. We'll learn how to be led by the Lord in His life-giving paths, and how following God's path means humble, bold prayers in our lives.

Friends, how can we not want to learn these precious stories from scripture? How can we not also hunger to talk with a God who sees us and knows us by name, a God who parts the waters with His mighty hand when it seems the enemy surrounds us, a God who shakes heaven and earth to give us the victory that seems impossible, a God who provides our every desperate need, a God who frees us from the evil slave master of sin, a God who leads us forward in triumphal paths? May we pray bold, so that with God's help we can live bold.

Because a life with Him is the only one that matters.

Let's do this. Let's learn together to pray bold.

I can't wait!

This, then, is how you should pray:

OUR FATHER IN HEAVEN
hallowed be Your name,
Your kingdom come,
Your will be done,
on earth as it is in heaven.
Give us today our daily bread.
And forgive us our debts,
as we also have forgiven our debtors.
And lead us not into temptation,
but deliver us from the evil one.

DAY 1 | WHERE DID SHE COME FROM?

DAY 2 | BORN TO RUN

DAY 3 | GOD OF THE WILDERNESS

DAY 4 | THE BLESSING OF REPENTANCE

DAY 5 | PRAYING TO THE GOD WHO SEES

WEEK ONE
HAGAR
YOU ARE THE GOD WHO SEES ME

Start **each day**'s
study right here!
**Read the main
texts in your
own Bible**
before diving in
to the workbook
reading.

JUST TO BE CLEAR

In scripture, the Lord
often changed
people's names.

For clarity's sake, we'll
be using "Sarah" and
"Abraham" in this
study whenever
mentioning those
people, even though
they were born "Sarai"
and "Abram." This is
why, as you read the
scripture passages,
you may see that
discrepancy.

DAY 1: WHERE DID SHE COME FROM? WHERE DID SHE GO?

*I will say to those called 'Not my people,' 'You are my people';
and they will say, 'You are my God.' Hosea 2:23b*

To pray is to let Jesus into our lives" – O. Hallesby

Too many times I've gone my own way and neglected to pray, stepping forward without God's lead.

Too many times I've carried my own burdens when God was waiting right there to bear them for me.

Too many times I've been held captive by my own needless fears, forgetting that I can call on the God who controls the seas and has the power to bring perfect peace.

Too many times I've run to other comforts, instead of running to the only One who can really comfort me.

No more.

I want to pray bold—when I encounter trouble, when I need to praise, when I face a battle, when I am brokenhearted, when I need forgiveness, when I don't know which way to go—I want to pray. And since you've got this study in your hands, I have an inkling you do too.

But how?

We're going to take a closer look at the real lives and prayers of women of the Bible, and we'll begin with Hagar. But before we pick apart her conversation with God and mine for precious truths, let's take a step back and set the stage.

Those of you who completed my women's Bible study *Significant*, have already been introduced to Hagar. As we studied the life of Sarah, the wife of Abraham in that book, we touched on Hagar, and the part she played in Sarah's story.

But now we'll shift our perspective from Sarah to Hagar, who has her own amazing story of God's faithfulness.

Hagar was not a traditional Israelite. She didn't have the same ethnic and geographical background as the family with which she lived, Abraham and Sarah.

Where was she from? Check out Genesis 16:1 in the margin (or your Bible) for the dirt on Hagar. According to this verse, what was:

Hagar's homeland:

Now Sarai, Abram's wife, had borne him no children. But she had an Egyptian slave named Hagar;

GENESIS 16:1

Hagar's occupation:

We'll dig more into the specific events of this story tomorrow, but for now, please note that Hagar was an Egyptian maidservant of Sarah. But how does an Egyptian end up living with Abraham and his crew?

Abraham and Sarah, God's special chosen couple, had gone looking for food. They had followed God away from their homelands, only to be faced with famine. It was time to find something to eat (Genesis 12:10).

Their journey led them to the land of Egypt with its rich soil and dependable Nile River. And while there, Pharaoh decided he had a thing for Sarah. She was a real head-turner, after all.

So Pharaoh blessed Abraham richly with lavish gifts. What, pray tell, did these gifts include? Circle each of the items in the list in Genesis 12:16 in the margin, taking special note of just how this list might relate to an Egyptian maidservant named Hagar:

Did you catch it? Right there, listed among the livestock Abraham acquired, we find the phrase, "male and female servants."

He treated Abram well for her sake, and Abram acquired sheep and cattle, male and female donkeys, male and female servants, and camels.

GENESIS 12:16

Hagar was Sarah's Egyptian slave, a lowly piece of property who would go on to have an unlikely prominent place in history.

Some scholars assert that Hagar would have despised leaving the sophisticated Egyptian society to be doomed to a nomadic life of wandering.

The scriptures don't tell us how Hagar felt about living with Sarah and Abraham initially. But we do know that she was Sarah's Egyptian slave, a lowly piece of property who would go on to have an unlikely prominent place in history.

Bought with a Price

Though we don't know how Hagar felt about her life with Abraham and Sarah, we do know how much she was worth to them financially. The Bible tells us the going price for a slave in ancient times. What was it, according to Exodus 21:32? Circle the amount in the verse that follows:

"If the bull gores a male or female slave, the owner must pay thirty shekels of silver to the master of the slave, and the bull is to be stoned to death." Exodus 21:32

We see this specific amount showing up elsewhere in God's word. Zechariah was paid the same amount—as a slam. God tells Zechariah to just throw the payment back in disgust. Check out Zechariah 11:12-13, and circle it here too.

"'I told them, 'If you think it best, give me my pay; but if not, keep it.' So they paid me thirty pieces of silver. 13 And the LORD said to me, 'Throw it to the potter'—the handsome price at which they valued me! So I took the thirty pieces of silver and threw them to the potter at the house of the LORD."

In Matthew 26 and 27, the thirty pieces of silver make another showing—as the price for Christ. See Matthew 26:14 in the margin.

Judas sold out Jesus for the price of a slave. The Priceless one, the Name Above All Names, the King of Kings—for the insignificant, insulting price of a slave.

Thirty shekels of silver, the price of a slave in ancient times, is worth about $200 today. The amount you'd pay for:

- A week's worth of groceries.
- A pair of shoes.

Then one of the Twelve—the one called Judas Iscariot—went to the chief priests [15] and asked, "What are you willing to give me if I deliver him over to you?" So they counted out for him thirty pieces of silver.

MATTHEW 26:14

- Tickets to a concert.

For a person.

Are you getting the idea here? The amount paid for slaves in ancient times is so insulting, so minimal, so insignificant, you might as well just throw it on the ground.

As a slave, that's Hagar's value. Just like Jesus.

And if you are wondering how this slave price would have compared to Abraham and Sarah's total net worth, let's do a little digging to find out.

What does Genesis 13:2 have to say about Abraham's assets?

Just how much silver and gold would Abraham have had? To put it into perspective, look at these two passages where we see some specifics.

- According to Genesis 20:16, how many shekels of silver did Abimelek give Abraham?

- Looking at Genesis 23:15, what was the price Abraham paid for Sarah's burial plot?

While these two verses occur later in Abraham's story, they help us to get a feel for just how inconsequential Hagar was to Abraham and Sarah. Abraham received a financial gift from Abimelek worth 30 times more than the going value of a slave. Abraham paid over ten times the slave price for Sarah's burial plot. Get the idea?

Compared to the abundant wealth and riches of Abraham and Sarah, Hagar was nearly worthless to Abraham and Sarah.

But not to her Heavenly Father.

Abram had become very wealthy in livestock and in silver and gold.

GENESIS 13:2

Compared to the abundant wealth and riches of Abraham and Sarah, Hagar was nearly worthless.

But not to God.

A LIFE-CHANGING IDENTITY CRISIS

I recently watched a documentary that illustrated just how much our father's identity influences our own identities. It told the true story of several grown adults who had believed they knew who their father was, only to find out decades into their lives that their biological father was someone else—a man of unsavory character.

And it wrecked them.

Even though nothing about their childhood experiences and memories had changed—they had still been raised by the same men who had been part of their lives all along—they experienced deep identity crises on receiving the news. Some struggled with depression, others even felt like taking their own lives.

While I can never truly understand how they felt upon finding out their biological fathers weren't who they'd believed them to be, it illustrated to me just how much of our identity is wrapped up in our earthly father's—they're intertwined.

It was a lightbulb moment for me to then realize **how important it is for us to identify as our Heavenly Father's daughters** as we come to the Lord in prayer. No wonder Jesus told us to pray with the posture of a daughter of the king! When we realize that our true identity is found in the fact that we are children of God, we can be unshaken. We can pray with the right perspective and confidence—knowing that He wants to hear us, we are precious to Him, and He's got our best in mind.

What a game-changer.

> Everything you are is a gift from a God who loves you fiercely and created you just right with His plans in mind

Hagar's Humble Beginnings Echo Our Own

Maybe you find it easy to relate to Hagar's lowly state as a maidservant. While we haven't been given or sold as a piece of property, we may share feelings of lowliness and unimportance.

We may feel like others only value us for what we look like, or what we can do for them. The good news? It's not about what you look like, what you do, or how much value others place on you—but about finding freedom in God's love for you.

As daughters of our Heavenly Father, we have great worth in His sight, no matter what others think.

When you realize everything you have and everything you are is a gift from a God who loves you fiercely and created you **just right** with His plans in mind, you can live *free*!

Free from discouragement about striving and not succeeding according to your own standards (because they're just that, *your* standards!).

Free from trying to measure up and feel worthy, and acknowledging it's God who gives you worth and abilities. He's the one responsible for your value—not you!

Look up Matthew 11:29 in your favorite translation and copy the verse below. What does it tell us to do?

> Walk with me and work with me—watch how I do it. Learn the unforced rhythms of grace. I won't lay anything heavy or ill-fitting on you. Keep company with me and you'll learn to live freely and lightly.
>
> MATTHEW 11:28-30, MSG paraphrase

Did you catch that? Jesus said that if we take His posture of gentleness and humility it will refresh us! It will make our lives easier!

But what about that slick CEO we admire so much? Isn't her life easy? Or the celebrity? The politician? Aren't their lives a breeze? Don't they have the happiness, fulfillment, and self-worth we desire?

Friend, we deceive ourselves when we admire those our culture esteems. We trick ourselves into thinking: "If I just had his success...."

"If I just had her looks and popularity..."

"If I just had their wealth..."

"If I just had those abilities..."

But let me tell you, Matthew 11:28-30 holds the key to all those "if I just..." situations. And it's so much simpler than we make it.

LOWLY LIKE JESUS

Christ Himself was despised. The prophet Isaiah foretold it, "He was despised and rejected by mankind, a man of suffering, and familiar with pain. Like one from whom people hide their faces he was despised, and we held him in low esteem."

Isaiah 53:3

Come to Jesus. Take what He offers with gentleness and humility. That's where you find peace and rest.

Not in striving to be enough, to have enough, to feel good enough, but in allowing Jesus to be your enough. To be enough for you. To rest in our identity as a daughter of the King.

Because life on our own is about as pathetic as the life of a slave woman—lowly, not worth much. Like Hagar. And a life of striving or telling ourselves "we're worth it" on our own leaves us empty.

Only our Heavenly Father gives us true worth—and this week we'll see just how remarkable this is in Hagar's life.

> WHAT'S IN A NAME?
>
> People and places in the Bible often have names whose meaning lends insight into their stories. Hagar is no different. Her name means, "flight."
>
> In other words, fleeing, or running away. As we study her story in this chapter, we'll see how God responded when Hagar lived up to her name.

If at First...

I've been watching my 18-month-old explore the world, and it's so much fun. One of her favorite things to do is climb—anywhere on anything—of course this keeps me on my toes. More than once she has managed to climb onto the dining room table where it is all too tempting to get her fingers in the butter dish or pour out the salt and pepper shakers.

But I've noticed something about her climbing—she doesn't realize those times when she's got no chance in France to actually get up on something. She still tries even in situations where there's no way she'll be able to get up.

She loves baths so one of her most frequent attempts is to get into the bathtub. She comes right up to the edge of the tub and

Allow Jesus to be enough for you.

hikes her little leg in the air—nowhere close to actually being able to get into the tub. It never fails—in her eagerness she always tries to climb in on her own.

But for all her trying, she'd never make it!

I think so many times, that's how we act. We try to handle things on our own, but **the first step to praying bold is realizing our own in-abilities and lack,** realizing we are God's children and that on our own we are no better off than slave woman Hagar.

When you realize how utterly dependent you are on God, your Heavenly Father, it puts you in a position where you are ready to bring it all to Him.

Hit the pause button and take a moment to reflect: where are you when it comes to this? Are you tempted to live like you're the one carrying the load and handling your responsibilities? **How might this be affecting your relationship with God?**

Or are you obsessing about your lack to the point of despair? Is this the type of humility that helps our relationship with God? Why or why not?

Make a quick sketch reflecting your perspective in the margin. Draw a stick figure that represents you. Just above your head, write words that represent your burdens—the responsibilities or feelings you're bearing on your own. Circle them, and draw an arrow up from the circle towards the top of the page, representing giving them up to God—recognizing that He is the ultimate Burden-bearer.

Our worth rests not in how we look or what we achieve. We are daughters of our Heavenly Father. And that truth is a beautiful gift.

We'll see this play out in the life and words of Hagar. We'll see the beauty of coming to the God who pursues us, helpless as we are on our own.

> There is beauty in coming to the God who pursues us.

We'll learn that, ironically, it's our humility that enables us to come boldly to Him. And we'll gain the confidence we need—not from arrogantly telling ourselves we're worth it, but from running to the God who is more than all we will ever need.

> Knowing that our worth rests squarely in Christ alone gives us both the boldness and humility to pray.

Spend some time with the Lord in prayer:
- Confess your own humble state—that without Christ you are nothing, but that in Him you have everything you need.
- Thank God that your worth doesn't come from your performance, that you don't have to earn your way to Him.
- Pray that the Lord would prepare your heart to learn from the life of Hagar how to run to Him this week.

Takeaway Truth— *"The lowly he sets on high, and those who mourn are lifted to safety." Job 5:11*

MAIN TEXT
Genesis 16:1-6

DAY 2: BORN TO RUN

The righteous person may have many troubles, but the LORD delivers him from them all. Psalm 34:19

Pray when you feel like praying. Pray when you don't feel like praying. Pray until you do feel like praying. – Elisabeth Elliot

Sometimes we feel born to run.

On my high school cross country team, I remember those races when it was scorching hot and a big hill loomed ahead. I loved a challenge—this was what I trained for. Other runners tended to flag when faced with intense conditions and extreme uphills, but I thrived on them. As I passed opponent after opponent on the incline, my lungs were screaming, my muscles were pumping, and my body was pushed to the limit. As the race-day adrenaline rushed through me, I felt on top of the world.

But there are other times I've felt born to run in ways that weren't life-giving—they were life-squelching. Like when someone criticized me, and I made sure I didn't listen to anything else they had to say. Or when their actions hurt me, and I went out of my way to make sure they weren't ever close to me again. Or when I was sure I'd mortify myself with embarrassing behavior and chose crawling away to hide instead of facing a difficult situation. All too often, I run from my hardships; I run from my problems.

In the comedic movie What About Bob?' main character Bob Wiley is told by his therapist to "take a vacation from your problems." If only it were so easy!

While there are times when stepping back from a situation and biting our tongues is the godly choice, other times God calls us to press into the difficult conversations, relationships, and situations in life.

But, boy, is it easy to run.

And that's where we find Hagar today. Right smack-dab in the middle of her own tough situation and ready to hit the road. Let's peek in on what happens in Genesis 16:1-6. Take a moment and read the passage in your own Bible now, if you haven't already as the day's main text.

We'll do a quick recap of the background of this familiar story to make sure we're all up-to-speed.

When God didn't seem to be fulfilling His promises to Sarah and Abraham according to their own timeline, Sarah got the not-so-bright idea of copy-catting the culture around them and using Hagar as Abraham's concubine, a sort of second wife, to bear the son God had promised Sarah and Abraham.

> Often God calls us to press into the difficult conversations, relationships, and situations in life.

The LORD had said to Abram, "Go from your country, your people and your father's household to the land I will show you. 2 "I will make you into a great nation, and I will bless you; I will make your name great, and you will be a blessing. 3 I will bless those who bless you, and whoever curses you I will curse; and all peoples on earth will be blessed through you."

GENESIS 12:1-3

He slept with Hagar, and she conceived. When she knew she was pregnant, she began to despise her mistress.

GENESIS 16:4

Why was it so important that Abraham and Sarah have a child? Look at Genesis 12:1-3. Circle all the reasons Abraham and Sarah needed offspring to fulfill God's plan (in the margin).

For Abraham and Sarah, having descendants was the whole point. God had told them to leave their homeland, promising that if they did, their descendants would be great—leaving a legacy of blessing for the whole world.

But it's hard for your offspring to bless all of humanity when you don't have any.

Enter the struggle for Sarah. She couldn't have kids (or so she thought), so Hagar became the perfect solution!

"The LORD has kept me from having children. Go, sleep with my slave; perhaps I can build a family through her." Genesis 16:2

We can't get into Hagar's head and know exactly how she felt about this. Some speculate that this was an attractive situation for a servant like Hagar. If she succeeded in producing the much-wanted heir, then perhaps her status in the family would rise. Maybe this seemed like a golden opportunity.

Or it could be that this was not at all what she wanted. Maybe she saw her life playing out differently, and despised not having the power in this decision. Maybe it was just one more way to feel powerless.

Either way, things didn't exactly turn out rosy for Hagar. How did she feel according to Genesis 16:4?

The original Hebrew word for Hagar's feelings toward Sarah, likely translated "despised" in your Bible, can vary in severity from looking down on someone, to treating them with contempt, to cursing them. We're not sure exactly how these feelings of contempt from Hagar to Sarah played out between the two of them, but one thing's for sure. It wasn't pretty.

Things soured between maidservant and mistress. In a time when a main function of being female was producing offspring, a barren woman like Sarah was seen as defective. Hagar may have fallen prey to pride in her own ability to conceive while

BOLD: Six Praying Women, One Faithful God

Sarah could not. She quickly conceived while her mistress spent years trying, and failing. Hagar seemed to have forgotten her own humble beginnings. She despised Sarah.

According to the ancient customs found in the code of Hammurabi, a mistress in Sarah's situation had every right to reduce the heir-producing concubine to despised slave status (a point that Abraham acknowledged in Genesis 16:6, "'Your slave is in your hands,' Abram said. 'Do with her whatever you think best.'"). But just because culture condoned Sarah's abusive behavior didn't make it right.

Sarah, Abraham, and Hagar's lives were beginning to spiral out of control.

Sarah's poor decision to use Hagar as a concubine resulted first in Hagar's feelings of contempt, and now in Sarah's own retaliation and abuse. Everyone involved felt the sting of Sarah's wrath, according to Genesis 16:5-6.

What happened? In the margin passage, circle Sarah's biting words and poor choices, underline Abraham's spineless reaction, and put a box around Hagar's last-resort actions.

No sooner had Sarah given Abraham a good tongue-lashing than she turned her wrath on Hagar. Sarah's mistreatment of Hagar in the original language connotes browbeating, humiliating, oppressing, putting someone in her place.

But neither woman was willing to bury the hatchet.

Hagar found Sarah's abuse unbearable, and lived up to her name, "flight."

Used and Abused

You probably aren't being mistreated by a polygamy-instigating, abusive mistress, but **I think we can all relate to being wronged—or even just feeling like we've been wronged**.

Hagar found resentment for her mistress creeping in to their relationship.

Have you ever found yourself harboring similar feelings? Maybe you hustled and went above and beyond the call of duty, doing

Then Sarai said to Abram, "You are responsible for the wrong I am suffering. I put my slave in your arms, and now that she knows she is pregnant, she despises me. May the LORD judge between you and me."
[6] "Your slave is in your hands," Abram said. "Do with her whatever you think best." Then Sarai mistreated Hagar; so she fled from her.

GENESIS 16:5-6

THE SLAVE/MASTER POWER STRUGGLE

Ironically, the Hebrew word translated as *mistreated* in Genesis 16:6 that described how Sarah treated Hagar is the same word, *anah*, used for the way Hagar's people, the Egyptians, would mistreat Sarah's descendants in their own 400 years of Hebrew slavery in Egypt (Exodus 1:11).

Sarah would have done well to humbly swallow her pride and make the best of her relationship with Hagar.

more than what was expected of you at work, and you didn't get the praise you expected. Now you're feeling underappreciated, and you're stewing.

Maybe you've been working tirelessly, taking care of all of the unglamorous household duties that no one else touches with a ten-foot pole—the toilet cleaning, the meal-prepping, the dirty laundry, the fussy-toddler consoling—and no one seems to notice your exhaustion and your need for help. You resent the fact that everyone else seems content to leave the dirty dishes piled in the sink, and you take the position of a martyr.

Maybe even though you've bent over backward in a relationship, trying your hardest to make it work, the other person just can't seem to reciprocate and make their own effort at a healthy relationship. You just don't see any future for it. You're sinking into despair and you're ready to throw in the towel.

As much as we wish for picture-perfect relationships, in the real world, things are messy. And while we're allowed to have our own feelings, we also need to learn healthy ways of dealing with those feelings, and how to take responsibility for the ways we can improve our situation.

Earlier in my marriage, I often struggled with resentment toward my husband in our everyday life. One look around our house—filled with the mess of everyday life with small children—and all I could see was lots of work to be done. So how dare he take a nap on the couch on his day off?! (I think you see my problem here…)

I tend to be more of a hustler with a "git-er-done" personality, while my husband is the big-picture, visionary dreamer. God, in His incredible wisdom, has gifted us both to further His kingdom and bring Him glory. But I didn't always see that.

There were times I would resent my husband's (wise) tendencies to take much-needed rest, and grumble and gripe in my spirit about his "laziness." Couldn't he see all there was to get done?!

Now I see it—God has created healthy rhythms for our lives, and it's not always smart to work, work, work.

But even more importantly, whether others treat us in ways that are right or wrong, our reactions shouldn't spring out of feelings of resentment. We should communicate with kindness and address issues head-on, in a way that will build our relationships. There's no need to run from our relationship problems, or to harbor feelings of disdain in our hearts toward others.

Let's continue to learn from Hagar's mistakes.

When Hagar's resentment bubbled up enough to make both her and Sarah miserable, an avalanche of mistakes began on both sides. Sarah's berating of Abraham and abuse of Hagar culminated in Hagar's reaching her breaking point and heading for the hills.

I don't know about you, but I feel the same kinds of temptations Hagar struggled with regularly.

She was tempted to:

- treat others with contempt rather than humility
- run away and give up completely on tough relationships and situations

Let's make this personal. How about you? (You knew I wasn't going to let you off easy, right?). What difficult situation, circumstance, or relationship could use an attitude adjustment for you right now?

I know I'm tempted to serve others begrudgingly, to share my abundance halfheartedly, to pout self-centeredly, and to puff up piously.

Not good! I could use a healthy dose of humility to keep things in perspective and to keep less-than-ideal situations from getting even worse. Help me, Lord.

And I'm guessing I'm not the only one! Let's press on in our study of Hagar to glean wisdom for our lives. God is in the

God redeems difficult situations for His glory.

business of redeeming difficult situations for His glory. And God still has plenty to teach us from Hagar's messed-up situation. Let's press on through our week of studying her.

Even though Hagar's tendency was to react negatively and run from her difficult situations, we're going to learn this week that instead of running from those difficulties we face, we can run to God with them in bold prayer.

But first, we'll see the next development in Hagar's story.

And if you're getting antsy, thinking to yourself—yeah, yeah, Hagar was lowly and Hagar was resentful. But what in the world does that have to do with praying bold?! Don't get in a hurry— you'll see.

Because realizing just how low-in-status Hagar was, and learning the dynamics that were at play in her life, are both keys to unlocking some pretty amazing, blow-your-mind truths about her story. Have patience.

After all, we're about to get to the good part. We're about to get a sneak peek into Hagar's unprecedented face-to-face meeting with our amazing God and listen in on her bold prayer in response. I hope you make time for tomorrow's lesson. This is going to be good!

Instead of running from those difficulties we face, we can run to God with them in bold prayer.

> Life throws tough things our way, but resentment and running aren't the answer–bold prayer is.

Share a simple prayer time with the Lord:

- Ask God for help with your relationships so that resentment doesn't build in your heart.
- Pray that the Lord would give you grace and wisdom to deal with people and problems in your life—even when you feel like running from them.
- Thank God for the ways He will use this study to deepen your prayer life.

Takeaway Truth— *"The name of the LORD is a fortified tower; the righteous run to it and are safe." Proverbs 18:10.*

DAY 3: GOD OF THE WILDERNESS

MAIN TEXT
Genesis 16:7-10

A father to the fatherless...is God in his holy dwelling. God sets the lonely in families...but the rebellious live in a sun-scorched land. Psalm 68:5-6

Prayer not only empowers us to see God's hand move for us, but it also enables us to feel God's presence move within us. - Amanda Pittman

You might be wondering by now why we're studying an Egyptian maidservant. What does the life of a slave girl from pagan origins have to teach us? After all, she wasn't an Israelite. She wasn't part of the chosen people of God. Her son would be eclipsed by Abraham's other heir Isaac. If Isaac was the one who would go on to be Jesus's forefather, why bother with Hagar?

Hold on. Today you'll find out.

From the beginning of time, we know that women were in relationship with God. Eve was confronted by God after eating the forbidden fruit (Genesis 3:13). Noah's wife experienced God's mighty deliverance firsthand when she and her family were saved from the flood (Genesis 8:18). Sarah was included in God's promise to Abraham (Genesis 17:16).

But in Hagar's story, we get a rare peek into an intimate moment from a foreign woman in the ancient world, when she came face to face with God. You'll hardly believe it.

Making a Run for It

On day one of this week, we spoke at length about Hagar's humble state. To be a slave was to essentially be property—to be owned and controlled by someone else. We know that as far as people went, she was at the bottom of the pecking order. Worth only a paltry amount.

But in God's eyes Hagar was treasured.

On day two of this week, we learned that Hagar (like many of us) had moments when she needed an attitude adjustment. That her feelings of resentment were so strong they overflowed into her relationship with Sarah, who lashed out in anger as a result.

> In Hagar's story, we get a rare peek into an intimate moment when she came face to face with God.

So what's a helpless slave woman to do?

We learned that Hagar made like a tree—she leafed.

No one was standing up for her. No one was helping her. She was mistreated by her mistress and her master wanted nothing to do with the situation. Where else could she go?

Let's take a closer look at Genesis 16:7-10 and see where she ended up. What does verse 7 say about who found her and where she was?

The angel of the LORD found Hagar near a spring in the desert; it was the spring that is beside the road to Shur.

GENESIS 16:7

A SHUR ESCAPE

Where did Hagar flee, according to Genesis 16:7?

The angel of the Lord found her near a spring in the wilderness, on the road to Shur. Throughout the scriptures, the wilderness is a place away from everyday life where people have life-altering encounters with God. Over and over we read about characters who met God in the wilderness.

Who else had wilderness encounters with the Lord? Look up at least three of the following references:

Genesis 32:24-30

Exodus 3:1-4

1 Kings 19

Matthew 3:1-3

Matthew 4:1-11

Fearful Jacob wrestled with God in a wilderness camp on his way to be reunited with his incensed brother Esau. In his zeal, Jacob clung to God until he got his blessing, and his name was changed to Israel in the encounter.

Hagar was headed toward Shur. It just so happens that in Exodus 15:22 we learn that Shur was en route to Egypt. Hagar was heading back home, perhaps to find solace in the false Egyptian gods she grew up with. Sometimes when tough situations come, we head back to the familiar (false) comforts of the past—whether it be found in the fridge, a TV binge, a shopping spree, a toxic relationship, or a mind-numbing project. But God doesn't want us to run from those things He's called us to face, and when we're struggling the best place for us to run is straight to Him.

Reluctant Moses heard the Lord speak through a burning bush in the wilderness when God commissioned him to return to Egypt and courageously lead His people to freedom.

Suicidal Elijah fled wicked Ahab and Jezebel to the wilderness of Mt. Horeb, where he collapsed in desperate exhaustion. God spoke to him in a gentle whisper, telling him he was to go back from where he had fled, and equipping Elijah with the help he needed.

Radical preacher John the Baptist was the long-foretold "voice crying in the wilderness," preparing the way for Jesus and calling people to repentance and baptism, just as the prophet Isaiah predicted.

Jesus spent 40 days fasting in the wilderness following His baptism, barraged with temptation after temptation. Angels attended Him and He returned from the desert to begin His public ministry and His final years on earth.

Over and over in scripture, we see that the wilderness was a place of struggle and trial for God's people. It was a place of soul-searching, course-changing, and a place where people encountered the supernatural firsthand. Running to the wilderness in desperation for these individuals meant being met by God.

Look at your above list. What trends do you notice about the gender of the people in each of these wilderness encounters? How about their nationalities?

In the previous list, all of the famous supernatural wilderness encounters happened to Israelite men. But wasn't Hagar an Egyptian slave woman? What does the angel of the Lord's willingness to meet with Hagar in the wilderness reveal about God's character? Take the following pop quiz to test your understanding.

T or F God doesn't have time for humble slave girls.

T or F God only speaks to His own people, the Israelites.

T or F Hagar didn't know God.

If you answered False for all of the above, you've got it! We can learn from God's encounter with Hagar that God sees even the humblest of people—that includes slave girls neglected by their owners. We also see that even in Old Testament times non-Israelites had real relationship with God, sometimes being spoken to directly by Him.

God was attentive to Hagar's situation—even when Abraham and Sarah failed her. He noticed her and took the time to interact

One sidenote: As we read further in this account, it's important to understand that an encounter with "the angel of the Lord" is an encounter with God Himself. God is complex, and the angel of the Lord operates and speaks with the authority of our divine, three-in-one God (Exodus 3 is another example of this). There is a familiar sympathetic tone from Jesus when He cared for those who had been discarded. His treatment of the woman caught in adultery (John 8:1-11), for example, mirrors how the angel responds to Hagar. Although these women had been exploited, the Lord drew near with compassion and understanding. We can rightly understand exchanges with the angel of the Lord in the Old Testament as a physical manifestation of the eternal, unchanging, Most High God. So, for our purposes, I'll use the phrase "angel of the Lord" interchangeably with "God."

with her. And this interaction might just blow your mind as we take a closer look.

He Knew Her Name

When the angel of the Lord found Hagar next to the spring, what did He say to her (Genesis 16:8)? Record His words here:

"Hagar, slave of Sarai, where have you come from, and where are you going?"

GENESIS 16:8

Stop and notice the first word spoken to Hagar by the angel of the Lord. What is it? Circle it in your answer above.

When the angel of the Lord encountered Hagar, the first thing He did was **call her by name.**

In contrast, how was Hagar referred to by Abraham and Sarah? Circle how they refer to Hagar in the verses below:

Sarah (Genesis 16:2, 5) – "so she said to Abram, 'The LORD has kept me from having children. Go, sleep with my slave; perhaps I can build a family through her.'"

5 "Then Sarai said to Abram, 'You are responsible for the wrong I am suffering. I put my slave in your arms, and now that she knows she is pregnant, she despises me. May the LORD judge between you and me.'"

Abraham (Genesis 16:6) – 6 "'Your slave is in your hands,' Abram said. 'Do with her whatever you think best.'"

Compare the words you circled—from the Lord, Sarah, and Abraham. What do you see?

Even though her own master and mistress—the people with whom she lived, the household to which she belonged—didn't call Hagar by name, but instead degraded her and called her "servant," "maid," or "slave," (depending on your version) God dignified her by calling her by name.

Even though others degrade us, the Lord treats us with dignity.

Other places in scripture, God called His people by name as a gesture of reassurance of His intimate, personal relationship with them. See Isaiah 43:1-3 (ESV):

Even though others degrade us, the Lord treats us with dignity.

BOLD: Six Praying Women, One Faithful God

But now thus says the LORD, he who created you, O Jacob, he who formed you, O Israel: "Fear not, for I have redeemed you; **I have called you by name**, you are mine. When you pass through the waters, I will be with you; and through the rivers, they shall not overwhelm you; when you walk through fire you shall not be burned, and the flame shall not consume you. For I am the LORD your God (emphasis mine).

I've experienced this myself—the closeness of being known by name. I've also experienced the opposite—when someone whom I would have expected to know me by name, calls me the wrong name. It's off-putting, or even hurtful.

How about you? How does it feel when someone calls you by the wrong name? How about when they call you by your correct name?

Now hop back over to the Lord and Hagar's conversation in verse 8. You'll notice that He asks two questions of Hagar:

1. Where have you come from?

2. Where are you going?

This reminds me of Genesis 3, when Adam and Eve hid from God, and He called to them "Where are you?" (Genesis 3:9).

According to David's Psalm 139:1-3, would the Lord be unsure of where Hagar had come from or where she was going? Why? Underline the evidence for your answer in the margin verse.

Our all-knowing God certainly knew Hagar's whereabouts completely. So why ask her?

Perhaps for her own benefit.

We see Jesus using a similar technique to get people to ask for what they needed or wanted from Him in the Gospels (Matt. 20:32; Mark 10:36; Mark 10:51; Luke 18:41; John 1:38). Jesus knew what these people wanted from Him, and yet, He had them ask.

In fact, Jesus didn't mince words. He straight-up told us to spill our guts and tell God what we need. But why? Look for details in the Matthew 7 passage in the next margin to explain why:

You have searched me, LORD, and you know me. You know when I sit and when I rise; you perceive my thoughts from afar. You discern my going out and my lying down; you are familiar with all my ways.

PSALM 139:1-3

God is a good Father. He wants us to let Him in on our lives. He wants us to ask, to seek, to come knocking. He wants us to tell Him what we've been up to. He wants in on where we're heading—even though He already knows!

It's incredible to think that Hagar—a foreign slave woman, mistreated and degraded by her own mistress, on the run in the wilderness—would have this encounter...with God.

Realize this: if He desired to meet her in the desert, to hear her heart—even though everyone else treated her like dirt, even though she struggled with resentment and pain—then **He must want to hear you as well.**

So, pray boldly. Even though you know you are unworthy on your own. Even when you are not where you're supposed to be. Even when you are feeling ugly things—**He wants to hear from you.**

Caught Red-Handed

I often find my mischievous preschoolers up to no good. It's not uncommon for me to catch them red-handed—hand in the proverbial cookie jar.

And yet, when this happens, I ask what they've been up to.

It's not because I don't know—it's usually more than obvious they've been into the candy when I find the empty wrappers and see the chocolate smudges on their hands and faces—my asking is to hear it from them. When they've strayed, I want them to have the chance to make amends. I want them to 'fess up and repent.

In the same way, God loves to hear what we've been up to—whether good or bad. He longs to hear our hearts and draw us close. He realizes the healing power this has for our souls.

He knows, but He wants to hear it from us.

> God wants to hear from us—no matter how others treat us, no matter what we've done, no matter how far we've run—He wants to hear our hearts.

Spend a simple prayer time with the Lord:

- Thank God that no matter how others see you, no matter what others call you, He knows you and calls you by name.
- Praise the Lord for wanting to meet you, even in the wilderness.
- Pour out your heart to the Lord—telling Him where you're going, your plans for the future, and confessing where you've been. Know that He wants to hear it from you.

Takeaway Truth— *"He found them in a desert land, in an empty, howling wasteland. He surrounded them and watched over them; he guarded them as he would guard his own eyes…He nourished them with honey from the rock." Deuteronomy 32:10, 13 NLT*

DAY 4: THE BLESSING OF REPENTANCE

Where can I go from your Spirit? Where can I flee from your presence? If I go up to the heavens, you are there; if I make my bed in the depths, you are there. If I rise on the wings of the dawn, if I settle on the far side of the sea, even there your hand will guide me, your right hand will hold me fast.
- Psalm 139:7-108

MAIN TEXTS
Genesis 16:7-16
Proverbs 3:11-12

Some people think God does not like to be troubled with our constant coming and asking. The only way to trouble God is not to come at all. - D.L. Moody

And the lowly servant Hagar, without a family, without a home, abused (by Sarah) and neglected (by Abraham) by the people who were supposed to protect her, alone and pregnant, had finally found the One who cared about her enough to meet her in the wilderness—in the midst of her desperation.

Hagar wasted no time in confessing her situation to the Lord. There's no pretense, no pride now. She told the Lord what He

We follow a God who is steadfast, even when we waver.

"I am running away from my mistress"

GENESIS 16:8

⁹ Then the angel of the LORD told her, "Go back to your mistress and submit to her."

GENESIS 16:9

We sometimes get the idea that God wants only the best for us—and by the best we mean our own idea of the best.

already knew, "I am running away from my mistress" (Genesis 16: 8). Hagar came clean.

Our modern sensibilities tell us that running was the right choice for Hagar. When someone mistreats you, get out of the situation, and get out fast! But what we see from the Lord here looks more like the tough love of a father.

What does the Lord instruct Hagar to do in verse 9?

I don't think we should use this interaction as a reason to stay in abusive relationships, but I do think there's a lesson for us.

We sometimes get the idea that God wants only the best for us— and by the best we mean our own idea of the best! Our minds go to comfort, ease, financial blessing, smooth relationships, and instant success. But God often has bigger (and even better) plans for us.

While Hagar was cruising toward her homeland of Egypt and away from her nightmare-of-a-mistress Sarah, God's plan was for her to return, and (gulp) submit. Not going to be easy for a woman struggling with pride and resentment.

But remember how we learned that God the Father loves to give good gifts? Even though Hagar couldn't see it at the time, returning to Sarah and Abraham was part of God's plan to eventually shower her with blessing waaaaaay beyond anything she could have found in her homeland, alongside the powerless gods of her people.

So, what did Hagar do? Skip ahead to verses 15-16 of Genesis 16 and you'll see where Hagar ended up. What does it say?

Hagar went back to Abraham, and gave him a son. Instead of following her flesh and running back to the gods of her homeland, she changed the course of her life to follow Yahweh, the one true God who met her in the wilderness.

Proverbs 3:11-12 says, "Do not despise the LORD's discipline, and do not resent his rebuke, because the LORD disciplines those he loves, as a father the son he delights in." And while God hadn't necessarily rebuked Hagar for running from Sarah, He did tell her to course-correct, and go right back.

If this seems uncomfortable or unpleasant, remember that the proverb assures us that God's dealings with us are as a loving Father. When He works in our lives, it's for our good—even though it may not feel good at the time.

The writer of Hebrews explains it like this: "God disciplines us for our good, in order that we may share in his holiness. No discipline seems pleasant at the time, but painful. Later on, however, it produces a harvest of righteousness and peace for those who have been trained by it" (12:10-11).

Welcoming God's course-correction in our lives may not always be easy—but it's always good.

God's guidance is way better than GPS. I remember way back in our pre-smartphone days; we once borrowed a GPS system in order to travel. Never mind we had no idea how in the world to use it.

I was pretty excited to be relieved of my navigating duties, which at that point in time usually involved looking up directions on the MapQuest website ahead of time and copying them down by hand for the trip.

Something must have been wrong with the device we borrowed though. For some reason even though we were driving down the Interstate, it was convinced we were driving off-course through a field. It incessantly told us to we needed to turn around to reach our destination.

Thankfully, when God tells us to course-correct, we can trust He's never having an "off" day and giving us bad navigation advice.

But before we get too far ahead of ourselves in Hagar's story, there are some other important things to notice about her conversation with the angel of the Lord. Let's backtrack to take notice of these important details. You don't want to miss this—it's really good!

Welcoming God's course-correction in our lives may not always be easy—but it's always good.

The Angel foretells a bright future for the lowly maidservant Hagar—and the promises start in verse 10. What does the Lord promise her?

Lots of descendants! God promised Hagar lots of kids. In today's climate, we may not appreciate the gravity of this blessing—our culture has twisted our priorities so that we value not having children (or at least not having too many), but for millennia, to have numerous, thriving descendants was huge. It was universally accepted as a sign of God's favor and blessing.

Echoing similar promises to other Bible greats like Abraham (Genesis 17:2; 22:17), Isaac (Genesis 26:4), Jacob (Genesis 48:4), the Hebrews (Exodus 32:13), and the obedient of God's people (Deuteronomy 7:13), God made a covenant promise to Hagar that her descendants would flourish.

Lest you begin to think that's a promise to take lightly, let me point out a few shocking facts to you:

With over 2,000 gods in the ancient Egyptian pantheon, it may have blown Hagar's mind to think that there could be One true God who created and sustained the world—and He met with her.

God's promise of multiplying descendants was almost always made to men, and in regard to His people Israel. This promise was different—this covenant to multiply was made to a woman (!), and a lowly slave at that (!!).

God promised that Ishmael's descendants would have their own 12 princes (Genesis 17:20), a counterpart to the 12 tribes of Israel.

Hagar's experience with the Lord was an intensely personal one. How incredible that the first personal encounter and conversation exclusively between God and a woman was between an Egyptian slave and Lord of all?!

It is common that the tribes and nations who existed in Hagar's time did not thrive. The fact that her descendants are still a large people group today testifies to God's promise keeping. Backtracking a few verses, in Genesis 15:19-21 ten ancient people groups are listed (Kenites, Kenizzites, Kadmonites, Hittites, Perizzites, Rephaites, Amorites, Canaanites, Girgashites, and Jebusites), none of which survives today. But Hagar's descendants live on.

As we read on in verse 11, we see that the Lord tells Hagar she'll give birth to a son, strangely similar to Gabriel's proclamation, first to Zechariah and then to Mary in Luke 1 (verses 13, 31).

The name of Hagar's son Ishmael would be a constant reminder of God's faithfulness, as its meaning proclaimed "God hears." Though the future of Hagar's son would have its ups and downs, God had heard of her troubles, and responded with compassion to the plight of the lowly Egyptian slave woman. Hagar would be blessed.

His Eye is on the Maidservant

And it is from this lowly slave, struggling with pride, fleeing from abuse, called by name, blessed beyond anyone's expectations, that we see an example of a simple, sincere heartfelt cry to the Lord that we should emulate.

Hagar's faith-filled, bold words to the Lord are, **"You are the God who sees me!"** like a lost daughter, found by her heavenly Father.

Just as Jesus taught us to pray with the childlike posture of "Our Father." Knowing God as our Heavenly Father positions our hearts to pray right, like Hagar.

If Hagar, the foreign, forsaken slave woman, can experience a God who hears her, who knows her by name, whose intimate relationship wants her to divulge where she's going and where she's been, who calls her to right living, who blesses her beyond her expectations—then friend, so can we!

As we come to the Lord in prayer, let's position ourselves to pray prayers of childlike intimacy with a Father who sees us, hears us, knows us by name, challenges us to live right, and leads us into blessing when we do.

In those parts of your soul where you find yourself running to escape, take a moment to pray to the God who knows your name. Tell Him where you're going. Tell Him where you've been. He sees you. He knows you.

And as you pray, listen for how your Father, the God Who Sees You, is leading.

We know that with Hagar, God didn't lead her out of her challenges and difficulties. In fact, He told her to march right back in, with an attitude adjustment. Could God be saying something similar to you?

Hagar's faith-filled, bold words to the Lord are, "You are the God who sees me!"

Now to him who is able to do immeasurably more than all we ask or imagine, according to his power that is at work within us,

EPHESIANS 3:20

Take a moment to soul-search now. What areas of your life might need a change in direction?

Use the graphic below to organize your thoughts. Ask the Lord to show you areas of your life where you need course-correction and sketch or write words that symbolize those on the left. On the right, draw images or write words that represent the corrected path where your Heavenly Father is leading.

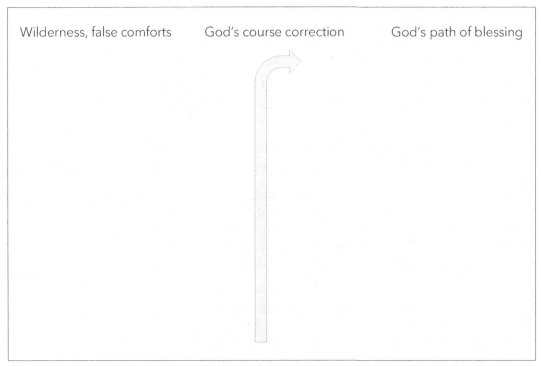

Wilderness, false comforts   God's course correction   God's path of blessing

God met Hagar in the desert. Life and hope would spring up from the sorrows of Hagar's past. The God Who Saw Hagar was enough! His fatherly love gave her the courage to go back to where He was calling her, to do what He was calling her to do—all the while proclaiming boldly how He had seen her and known her all along.

> God sees you—even in your wanderings,
> even in your pain—He sees you.

Share a simple prayer time with the Lord:

- Thank the Lord that He is the God who sees you.
- Ask God for the boldness to approach Him as your Heavenly Father.
- Pray that the Lord would give you a heart that is soft to His course-correction in any way you may need it—knowing that to go away from God means false comforts, but running to Him means a life of true blessing.

Takeaway Truth – *"In all your ways submit to him, and he will make your paths straight." Proverbs 3:6*

DAY 5: PRAYING TO THE GOD WHO SEES

MAIN TEXTS
Matthew 6:9-13
John 1:43-51

This, then, is how you should pray: "Our Father in heaven..."

-Matthew 6:9.

I pray because I can't help myself. I pray because I'm helpless. I pray because the need flows out of me all the time, waking and sleeping. It doesn't change God. It changes me. – C.S. Lewis

Hagar's not the only one whose example we should follow in coming to the God Who Sees Us—we have an even better example in Christ.

Throughout this study we're not only going to examine the prayers of women in scripture, but we're also going to view them through the lens of Jesus's important prayer—the Lord's Prayer.

We have an even better example in Christ.

Being a Christian is all about following in the footsteps of Christ, and our prayer life is no different. In Matthew 6:9-13, Jesus taught:

> *This, then, is how you should pray: "Our Father in heaven, hallowed be your name, your kingdom come, your will be done, on earth as it is in heaven. Give us today our daily bread. And forgive us our debts, as we also have forgiven our debtors. And lead us not into temptation, but deliver us from the evil one."*

Right off the bat, Jesus shows us the example of addressing God as Our Father.

Jesus referred to God as the Father often, both in His conversations with others, and with God Himself. For just a few of these examples, **let's play a little matching game.** Match the scripture reference in the margin to the way Jesus was referring to God as His Father.

John 11:40-42

Jesus prayed, "Father, I thank you that you have heard me" preparing to raise Lazarus from the dead, admitting the reason for saying it was for to inspire faith in those listening.

Mark 14:36

Jesus had an audible conversation with God, saying, "Father, glorify your name!" to which a voice from heaven responded, to the crowd's amazement.

John 12:28

As Jesus hung on the cross, He begged forgiveness for those who persecuted Him, and desperately cried out to God, "Father, into your hands I commit my spirit" as He breathed His dying breaths.

Luke 23:34, 46

Boy Jesus told His earthly parents that He'd been hanging out in the temple, calling it His "Father's house."

Luke 2:49

Jesus prayed, "Abba, Father...take this cup from me. Yet not what I will, but what you will" in the Garden of Gethsemane while His disciples took a snooze.

From these verses we glean that:

- God is a Father who **hears**
- God is a Father who is **glorious**
- God is a Father who **receives our spirit** when we die
- God is a Father who **desires us to join His work**
- God is a Father to whom **we can cry out** with raw emotions, in our hour of need

Our prayers have the right perspective when we take on the mindset of a child of God. We're not to see God as the unfeeling "Man Upstairs" or the wish-granting genie in a bottle. He's a good Father who knows us by name, who sees us, who wants to hear from us, and who cares about where we're going and where we've been. He may have some course-correction for us, but only because He cares.

Our prayers have the right perspective when we take on the mindset of a child of God.

Seeing and Being Seen

You can be bold in prayer because God sees YOU, God knows YOU! Not just as some woman, not just as someone's wife, or daughter, or sister, or a nurse, or a chef, or a lawyer, or whatever roles you play—God sees you! He sees me, Rachel Risner. He knows me by name. He knew Hagar by name. And He knows us deeper than we know ourselves.

There's something amazing about being seen, and being known, isn't there? Something wonderfully intimate and special.

Anyone who's taken a preschooler to the playground knows this. Little kids relish being seen. As my kids play, they often call out, "Mom!! Look at me!" as they glide down the slide, swing up high, or climb to a new height. We want to be seen.

John 1:43-51 records an encounter Jesus had with Nathanael that testifies to the power of being seen.

It happened at the very beginning of Jesus's ministry, when he was gathering His first followers. One of Nathanael's besties had told him about Jesus—that Jesus of Nazareth was the one everyone had been waiting for.

But Nathanael just couldn't believe it—he knew Jesus was from Nazareth, the wrong side of the tracks—how could He possibly be the Messiah?!

When Jesus saw Nathanael coming, He knew him already. Jesus called out, "Here truly is an Israelite in whom there is no deceit."

This was a head-scratcher to Nathanael, who'd never seen Jesus before. How could Jesus know him when they'd never met?

This question would be answered by Jesus's next words: "I saw you while you were still under the fig tree."

Immediately Nathanael's disbelief was washed away and replaced with faith as he proclaimed Jesus as the Son of God. Why? Because God knew him. Because before he'd even met Jesus, Jesus saw him.

Have you ever known anyone so well that you could finish a sentence for them, or answer a question the way they would, or

> When Jesus saw Nathanael approaching, he said of him, "Here truly is an Israelite in whom there is no deceit."
>
> 48 "How do you know me?" Nathanael asked.
>
> Jesus answered, "I saw you while you were still under the fig tree before Philip called you."
>
> 49 Then Nathanael declared, "Rabbi, you are the Son of God; you are the king of Israel."
>
> JOHN 1:47-49

Sometimes referring to God as a heavenly Father is troublesome for us. We've had times when our earthly fathers have let us down—or worse: abandoned or abused us. This distorts our view of fatherhood. And if this is your experience, my heart breaks for you. The truth is, God is not a man. He is a good father—better than any earthly father could be. I pray that the Lord heals your hurts and helps you to take your position as the daughter of a Father who loves you perfectly (1 John 4:18), and that the enemy's efforts to drag down your prayer life would be in vain. We call God our Heavenly Father because that's the example Jesus sets, not because He has the sinful flaws of our earthly fathers.

know exactly how they'd order their latte? Well, God's way of knowing us is so much deeper than how we want our coffee!

He knows our struggles and our successes. He knows our hopes and dreams. He knows our deepest desires and our most daunting fears. God knows our deepest pain, and He meets us there.

Who was Hagar—a lowly, pregnant, Egyptian slave girl roving in the wilderness without a home—for God to seek her out and speak with her?! And yet, God met her there, in the depths of her need, in the middle of her pain. The God of the universe saw her and spoke her name.

> Instead of running *from* God when challenges and problems come our way, let's run *to* Him—our precious God who sees!

Spend some time with the Lord in prayer: let's put this into practice right now! Today we'll end things a little differently, with time in scripture and prayer.

Practical, Bold Prayer Time

Now for a rubber-meets-the-road activity. You've been reflecting on Hagar's life, her encounter with God, and her prayer. It's time to put some of the attitudes and techniques you've learned from her time with the Lord in Genesis 16 into practice.

You'll remember that when Hagar first encountered the angel of the Lord, He called her by name. Before you begin composing your own prayers, pray through some scriptures about God knowing you. This will help to put you in the right frame of mind to pray to your Heavenly Father. Even an insignificant slave like Hagar could speak boldly to God—and so can you.

Just like God saw and knew Hagar and Nathanael, He sees and knows you. Take note especially what these verses have to say about your relationship to God—circle or highlight your thoughts. Perhaps you want to insert your name as you pray through them. Purpose to leave behind whatever distractions or worries are crowding for your attention and take some time to focus on God's word in these following verses (read along here, or in your own Bible):

But now, this is what the LORD says—he who created you, Jacob, he who formed you, Israel: 'Do not fear, for I have redeemed you; I have summoned you by name; you are mine. When you pass through the waters, I will be with you; and when you pass through the rivers, they will not sweep over you. Isaiah 43:1-2

Where can I go from your Spirit? Where can I flee from your presence? If I go up to the heavens, you are there; if I make my bed in the depths, you are there. If I rise on the wings of the dawn, if I settle on the far side of the sea, even there your hand will guide me, your right hand will hold me fast... For you created my inmost being; you knit me together in my mother's womb. I praise you because I am fearfully and wonderfully made; your works are wonderful, I know that full well. My frame was not hidden from you when I was made in the secret place, when I was woven together in the depths of the earth. Your eyes saw my unformed body; all the days ordained for me were written in your book before one of them came to be. Psalm 139: 7-10,13-16

Are not five sparrows sold for two pennies? Yet not one of them is forgotten by God. Indeed, the very hairs of your head are all numbered. Don't be afraid; you are worth more than many sparrows. Luke 12:6-7

A father to the fatherless, a defender of widows, is God in his holy dwelling. God sets the lonely in families, he leads out the prisoners with singing. Psalm 68:5-6

Which of you, if your son asks for bread, will give him a stone? Or if he asks for a fish, will give him a snake? If you, then, though you are evil, know how to give good gifts to your children, how much more will your Father in heaven give good gifts to those who ask him! Matthew 7:9-10

What do these truths speak to your soul?

You don't have to fear—you are His! He's with you no matter what you go through.

Anywhere you are, **He sees you**. He's known you from the very beginning—even within your mother's womb.

He knows every hair on your head.

He **cares for and defends you**, blessing you with good things when you ask Him. That's a Father worth running to!

Use some of the phrases you circled or highlighted above as a prayer to God, thanking Him for His special, Fatherly relationship with you and all the benefits that entails. Write your prayer below, or take a few minutes to write some of the scripture phrases that you find meaningful in pretty handwriting while you pray to God your Father.

BOLD: Six Praying Women, One Faithful God

After dwelling on your relationship to God as His daughter, share your past with Him. Tell Him where you have come from. Envision Him as the Father He is, wanting to know what's been happening in your life. Don't hold back, share it all with Him—even the things you've shared already this week. We know that fathers love hearing from their children, and we've seen from scripture that God is no different.

Now share with God where you're going. What plans do you foresee for yourself? How are you handling the situations and relationships that are on your mind right now? What seems best to you?

Offer up these plans to God, giving Him the chance to course-correct anywhere you might be out-of-line. Spend time listening to the Lord, and searching scripture for guidance and direction. Where might God be leading in the situations nearest and dearest to your heart? Ask God to comfort, guide, and convict you, if necessary, in order to get you on His path. Confess that you don't see exactly the future He has for you, but—if you can—proclaim with faith that you'll follow Him in obedience even when His way seems difficult.

End your prayer time by acknowledging the God Who Sees You—whether you feel seen or not. Thank Him for seeing you, for knowing you. Praise God that your relationship doesn't have to depend on your feelings.

And friends, cling with white knuckles to our main truth for this week:

To pray bold, we must run *to* our Heavenly Father, who sees us and knows us by name.

Takeaway Truth – *"They will be my treasured possession. I will spare them, just as a father has compassion and spares his son who serves him." Malachi 3:17*

> Allow the compassion of the Father to wash over you. He sees you. He knows you by name. Don't run *from* Him. Run *to* Him.

Pause for Praise: By diving deep into the account of Hagar's encounter in the wilderness with "the God Who Sees," we've learned that the best way to put ourselves into the proper posture for bold prayer is by running to the Father. Before you go on with your day, pause for some special time of praise with the Father. Allow your spirit to be caught up in worshipping Him for being the One you can run to. I suggest you watch the lyric video for Cody Carnes's "Run to the Father" on YouTube. If you prefer a more traditional style, try Stuart Townend's "How Deep the Father's Love For Us." Imagine yourself the lost sheep, found—the wayward daughter, now home. Seen. Known by name. Allow the compassion of the Father to wash over you. He sees you. He knows you by name. Don't run *from* Him. Run *to* Him.

Watching the weekly teaching videos from rachelrisner.com (or Rachel's YouTube)? Hooray!!

If you're a worksheet-fillin' note-taking, studious type (or even if you aren't) you'll find the video viewer guides for the teachings in the back of this book, starting at page 269. And find printable discussion questions to get the conversation started at rachelrisner.com/boldvideolessons.

This, then, is how you should pray:

Our Father in heaven
HALLOWED BE YOUR NAME
Your kingdom come,
Your will be done,
on earth as it is in heaven.
Give us today our daily bread.
And forgive us our debts,
as we also have forgiven our debtors.
And lead us not into temptation,
but deliver us from the evil one.

DAY 1 | THE POWER STRUGGLE IS REAL

DAY 2 | HOPE FLOATS DOWN THE NILE

DAY 3 | MOSES MESSES UP

DAY 4 | IN HOT PURSUIT

DAY 5 | A WORSHIP SET FOR THE AGES

WEEK TWO
MIRIAM
SING TO THE LORD

DAY 1: THE POWER STRUGGLE IS REAL

There is no one holy like the LORD; there is no one besides you; there is no Rock like our God. 1 Samuel 2:2

The more you get to know God and understand His holiness, the more you will begin to magnify God in your life, and then God will become the biggest thing in your life. – A. W. Tozer

> ⁶ Now Joseph and all his brothers and all that generation died, ⁷ but the Israelites were exceedingly fruitful; they multiplied greatly, increased in numbers and became so numerous that the land was filled with them.
>
> ⁸ Then a new king, to whom Joseph meant nothing, came to power in Egypt.
>
> EXODUS 1:6-8

Last week we took a close-up look at the prayer of an Egyptian (Hagar) enslaved to Hebrew masters (Abraham and Sarah). Fast forward a few generations and the tables had turned.

Abraham's grandson Jacob and his family had (much like his grandfather) travelled to Egypt when faced with a famine. Finding peace and prosperity there, thanks to Jacob's son Joseph, the family had settled for good—all seventy of them (Exodus 1:5). But the good times would not last.

Verses 6, 7, and 8 of Exodus 1 form the major plot twist that sets the stage for this chapter's study. What three major things occurred in these three verses:

Verse 6:

Verse 7:

Verse 8:

Alas, it was the end of an era. Joseph and his brothers all passed away, but their descendants' numbers grew like weeds. In fact, there were so many of them the new Pharaoh in town was shaking in his boots (or should I say sandals?). He was afraid God's people had become too immense.

> So they put slave masters over them to oppress them with forced labor, and they built Pithom and Rameses as store cities for Pharaoh.
>
> EXODUS 1:11

Pharaoh's response? Check out Exodus 1:11 in the margin. Circle Pharaoh's action steps when God's people seemed too mighty.

But God was about to show up in mighty ways—albeit through the most unlikely characters. Like a baby. And a tween slave girl. Throw in a blood-hungry tyrant, a pitch-covered basket boat, and a croc-infested river and you've got a story that's a real nail-biter—the kind of better-than-fiction story only God could write. Buckle up for the ride!

The Power Struggle is Real

Maybe right about now you're thinking, "OK, hit the brakes here. What does this history lesson have to do with my prayer life? I'm doing this study to learn about bold prayer, so why the deep dive into the olden days of Egypt? Why aren't you giving me a prayer script instead?"

And your question would be valid. But let me explain.

As I've combed through the Lord's Prayer and the lives and prayers of women in scripture, one thing has become crystal clear: prayer is about the heart. And when we hear stories of God's faithfulness in the lives of His people, our hearts can't help but be changed!

This week, we're learning how focusing our hearts on praising our Holy God—like Miriam did—prepares us for bold prayer.

Setting the stage for the work of God's hand in the life of Miriam helps us understand her response to our holy, mighty God's work in her life. The backstory gets us ready for the main event, the culmination of God's mighty holiness demonstrated in Miriam's life, to which she responded with a prayer of praise.

Dwelling on Miriam's walk with the Lord—from puberty to praise—molds our hearts to praise our Holy God in bold prayer. We need to recognize the holiness and power of God to put our hearts in the right posture for prayer.

The Hebrew people were about to witness a power struggle for the ages. Pharaoh fancied himself god-like and wanted to squelch the Hebrew people before they became too powerful. But it just wasn't working.

The more work Pharaoh required of God's people, the more they flourished (Exodus 1:12, in the margin). But just as the number of God's people increased, their favor with the Egyptians soured. What does Exodus 1:12 say about how the Egyptians regarded the Hebrews?

Prayer is about the heart. And when we hear stories of God's faithfulness, our hearts can't help but be changed.

Behold, the LORD rides on a swift cloud, And will come into Egypt; The idols of Egypt will totter at His presence.

ISAIAH 19:1 NKJV

But the more they were oppressed, the more they multiplied and spread; so the Egyptians came to dread the Israelites."

EXODUS 1:12

Sweat and Blood

God's people were growing in number, and the Egyptians weren't having it. What would Pharaoh do? According to verse 14, for what types of labor were the Hebrew slaves used? Underline your answers:

Harsh slavery and impossible demands were Pharaoh's go-to strategy. The Hebrews did the Egyptians' dirty work—construction and farming were outsourced to slave labor. Pharaoh demanded the Hebrews' sweat and toil. But that's not all. Pharaoh wanted blood.

Whose blood would Pharaoh target to weaken the enslaved Israelites, according to Exodus 1:16?

Baby boys. Powerful Pharaoh was threatened by baby boys. Sort of ironic, isn't it? Imagine the armies, chariots, horses, wealth, and power Pharaoh must have possessed, and yet, he knew the way to cut down his slaves was to target their offspring. He feared the potential of the next generation to overpower his reign.

The Bible teaches that not only born children, but unborn descendants are active in their forefathers' lives. It's a hard concept for us short-term thinkers to understand. But God isn't constrained by time. Check out Hebrews 7:9-10 (NKJV):

Levi wasn't Abraham's son. Not even his grandson. As the son of Jacob, who was the son of Isaac, who was the son of Abraham, Levi would have been Abraham's great-grandson. And yet, scripture talks about him paying tithes through his great-grandfather Abraham. I don't know about you, but as I'm writing my tithe check I don't ever think about my great-grandchildren tithing right along with me. It seems absurd.

And yet, God sees the whole picture. He knows that our lives aren't merely our own, but that we lead those coming after us, our descendants. Our lives are intertwined. God sees the generations to come, not just the here and now.

Pharaoh had a long-term view as well. But not for good, for evil.

Cut off the children of the Hebrews and you cut off their future. It was a sinister plan, but Pharaoh was up against a much greater power than an enslaved people. He was up against the people of the promise.

What did God's promise to His people say about those who'd oppose them? Circle the answer found in Genesis 12:3 (HCSB).

I don't know about you, but to me it seems that being cursed by the Almighty Creator of the Universe is the worst thing possible that could happen! Pharaoh didn't stand a chance keeping his power over God's people. His efforts would be squashed like a bug against God's power. Egypt's days as the slave masters of Hebrews were numbered.

What Pharaoh didn't realize when he ordered helpless Hebrew babies thrown into the unforgiving waters of the Nile, was that his struggle wasn't going to be against flesh and blood—it would be against a power much greater than his own.

Call the Midwives
Pharoah's plan was easy enough, right?

Wrong.

Not when God's people were involved. Ordering baby boys tossed in the river wasn't difficult, but getting God-fearing people to carry out infanticide wasn't so easy after all.

Who was first ordered to kill the baby boys? (Exodus 1:15-16)

Pharaoh's first resort was to call the midwives. He bet that Shiphrah and Puah could be bullied into taking lives rather than bringing them into the world. He was wrong.

What did they do, and why? (verse 17)

The Hebrew midwives knew better than to obey the barbaric orders of the king. Their allegiance was first and foremost to a God who gives life, who asks His followers to cherish children, not harm them.

Matthew 25:40 NIrV says, "What I'm about to tell you is true. Anything you did for one of the least important of these brothers and sisters of mine, you did for me."

I will bless those who bless you, I will curse those who treat you with contempt, and all the peoples on earth will be blessed through you.

GENESIS 12:3 HCSB

FLIGHT TO EGYPT

Pharaoh wouldn't be the only power-hungry ruler to kill young boys in cold blood. The incredible story is found in Matthew 2:13-23. Let's turn there in our Bibles.

What ruler ordered baby boys killed, according to verse 16? Why did he do this? (See surrounding verses, if necessary)

Just like in Moses's day, baby boys were targeted in the time of Jesus by blood-thirsty Herod. But just as God preserved His people from Pharaoh, so He would also preserve His son Jesus in Egypt. Powerful Herod didn't stand a chance against even-more-powerful God and His angels.

> The midwives feared God—this is even more remarkable when we realize they didn't have scripture to guide their way. In fact, their very obedience is why we have these scriptures of Moses today.

Surely the list of "least important" among people would include infants. And foreigners. And slaves. To the Egyptians, the Hebrew babies were all three. Easy targets. And yet scripture teaches that the last thing we should do is harm the least important. These are the ones we are called to love because in loving them, we love Christ.

The Hebrew midwives feared God—this is even more remarkable when we realize they didn't have scripture to guide their way. In fact, their very obedience is why we have the scriptures we're studying this week—Moses would grow to pen these stories himself, with the guidance of the Holy Spirit.

They knew that love for God meant obeying Him (John 14:15), even when God's ways were at odds with the commands of an earthly ruler. And God rewarded them for it (verse 21).

Riding the Struggle Bus

The days of enslavement in Egypt were fraught with misery for God's people. The Hebrews worked hard, but they weren't the only ones being held captive. Pharaoh was enslaved to his own hunger for power. And perhaps Pharaoh's slavery was even more miserable than the Hebrews'. After all, he'd never be delivered.

You see, the Hebrews—though slaves to Pharaoh—had a loving, mighty God as their ultimate master. Yes, their days on earth were filled with physical toil, but their eternal days would bring freedom and rest for God's people (Luke 16:19-31).

Not so, Pharaoh. A soul always hungry for more—more power, more wealth, more safety, more control, more anything—can never be at rest.

Pharaoh's paranoia at losing his power over the Hebrews, and the lengths he was willing to go to maintain his control, reveal his own slavery ... to sin.

Only in the God of the Hebrews could Pharaoh find his true peace and purpose, and ironically, it was against their God that he struggled so much. If only he'd been willing to leave behind the empty promises of the Egyptian gods and embrace the one true God, his paranoia could have been replaced by peace.

What a shame, I think, what a fool. It's so easy in this story to put myself in the place of the poor, righteous victims. The Hebrew slaves.

And surely we do need deliverance, and often we do suffer unjustly. But I do well to remember that Pharaoh's not the only fool around—not by a longshot. We stand so many years later knowing what a foolish endeavor Pharaoh undertook, opposing Almighty God.

And yet I can be so foolish myself.

I wrestle in my own power struggles with the God of the universe too. Sometimes I forget His holiness, His power, His wisdom, His authority, His peace, and His purposes are so much better, so much higher, than my own.

And waaaay too often my prayers to God include lines like:

"You want me to reach out to who?! No thanks!"

"You want me to give up what?! No way."

"You want me to go where?! I don't think so."

"You want me to serve how?! You don't understand."

And all too often I live like I don't need God's help, His strength, and His direction—with an, "I've got this" attitude. Oh boy.

I struggle against the God whose ways are the only way I can find peace. What a shame. I'm a fool.

What are some things God has asked of you that initially you resisted? Why? How did your power struggle turn out?

How thankful I am for God's patience with me—that when I engage in my own Pharaoh-like power struggles with God, He doesn't give up on me.

TALK IS CHEAP

It can be hard when we come upon passages where people are praised (like the midwives) who seem to have stumbled. After all, in Exodus 1:19 it seems like they're lying to Pharaoh, but the Bible makes it clear that lying is wrong. Psalm 34:13 says, "Keep your tongue from evil and your lips from telling lies."

Notice, they aren't praised for their dishonesty. Look at Exodus 1:21. What were the midwives rewarded for?

The midwives were rewarded for their faithful actions. We need to be careful in thinking that something is OK, just because a Bible character did it—especially when it's something that is clearly wrong in scripture. The bottom line: don't use the midwives' dishonesty to justify your own lying tongue; instead emulate their brave actions of obedience.

How merciful of Him to keep prodding me forward when I'm ready to turn tail and run from Him instead of walking the path He's calling me to tread.

Let Go, and Be Free

Those of us who grew up with the gold star for perfect Sunday school attendance know years later that God spoke clearly to Pharaoh through Moses: "Let my people go!"

But time after time, Pharaoh refused. He clung to his role as slave master with white knuckles. Oh no, he wasn't letting go.

Spend some time in reflection. Could there be something God is calling you to let go of? An attitude? A habit? A grudge? A pet sin? An idol? Record your thoughts below.

> Could there be something God is calling you to let go of?

So often when I feel like God is asking me to let go of something, I cling tighter still. "Surely God's mistaken on this one," I think. "He can't want to take this from me."

It's like rappelling. I remember rappelling down a small cliff as a kid at summer camp. The ropes instructor taught me to lean back into the harness, sitting almost, with my legs horizontal against the face of the cliff.

This seemed to go against all my childish sensibilities. Usually to stand safely, I needed to be feet down—vertical, not horizontal.

But to be successful at rappelling, we campers needed to listen to the instructor, not our own logic. We needed to let go of doing things the way it made sense to us, and trust the instructor.

I did, and boy was it fun. My feet bounced me off the face of the cliff like a trampoline-turned-sideways as the rope glided smoothly through my harness. I felt free—like I could fly.

I remember looking back up at the other campers attempting the rappel, once my turn was over. Some leaned back, listening to the instructor, going horizontal and gliding down the cliff face with ease—relaxed and smiling.

Others struggled.

The urge to stay vertical was too much. They couldn't relax and lean back in the harness. What happened was scraped knees and elbows, and an embarrassingly clumsy descent. They missed out on so much joy.

The next time God asks me to let go and to lean into His plans, I pray I will remember to relax into His purposes like I relaxed into the rappelling harness. I want to glide smoothly. I want to feel free.

> I'm a fool to struggle against God when real freedom is found in following Him - putting aside my power struggle positions me to pray.

I want to let go and to lean into His plans. I want to feel free.

Spend a few moments with the Lord in prayer:

- Pray that, like the Hebrew midwives, your life would be characterized by courageous obedience.
- Praise God for His holiness, surrendering to Him any power struggle you might be engaging in.
- Thank God for the freedom found in life with Him— that you no longer need be a slave to cruel sin, but that you can find freedom in your new, loving master— Christ.

Takeaway Truth – *And if you were free when the Lord called you, you are now a slave of Christ. 1 Corinthians 7:22 NLT*

DAY 2: HOPE FLOATS DOWN THE NILE

MAIN TEXT
Exodus 2:1-10

Sing the praises of the LORD, you his faithful people; praise his holy name. Psalm 30:4

I must never lose that sense of wonder and awe when I come into the presence of God. He is worthy of my praise, and it is the very act of praising him that changes my perspective and enables me to pray with power. –Marlene Bagnull

Today we'll recount more of Miriam's amazing story of walking with God—how His fingerprints were all over her life, even as a tween. And we'll continue to dwell on God's holiness—that "hallowed be His name."

As we study Miriam's story, our hearts will further be molded into ones ready to pray boldly, because we serve a mighty, holy God. Following her storyline will help us follow her footsteps in prayers of praise to our Holy God.

Storing Up Treasure

Let's look closely at Miriam's story to get all the details of Exodus 2 straight about our holy God's hand working in her life. See verse 2 of Exodus 2 in the margin or in your own Bible.

What did Miriam's mother Jochebed notice about baby Moses? Circle your answer in the verse.

> The woman became pregnant and gave birth to a son. She saw that he was a special baby and kept him hidden for three months.
>
> EXODUS 2:2 NLT

Moses was a special baby. Some versions of the Bible translate the original text as beautiful, some as fine. Some say goodly, others especially healthy, others fair or delightful. No question in Jochebed's mind: there was something different about this boy right from the start.

And because Moses was such a special baby, Jochebed would certainly hide him, keeping her precious babe from the deadly fate intended by blood-thirsty Pharaoh.

As I write this chapter, my own three-month-old baby daughter grins her gummy grin. She coos and smiles and her bright blue eyes melt my insides. All of the drool, spit up, stinky diapers, and night-time feedings—even the pregnancy morning sickness and botched epidural—are well worth the trouble as my mama heart can hardly bear her preciousness.

How could any mother place such a sweet, little, helpless child in a pitch-covered basket to float among the crocodiles? It turns my stomach just thinking about doing that to her.

And yet, I'm so glad that the faithful mother of Moses and Miriam did!

Just as the Hebrew midwives were willing to put their lives at risk to save little ones, so Moses's mother Jochebed defied Pharaoh's murderous decree—putting her own safety at risk.

The original Hebrew word translated as "hid" in Exodus 2:2 means hiding something precious—a treasure.

Look up the following verses where this same word is used in the Hebrew. What was hidden in these passages the same way Jochebed hid her treasure, baby Moses?

Joshua 2:4

Psalm 119:11

In the same way that Rahab courageously hid the spies and secured for herself and her household a ticket out of the destruction of Jericho, Jochebed courageously hid her squirming newborn for the first three months of his little life. And we too should do our own treasure hiding—of God's precious word in our hearts, so that we might not fall into sin.

Cast Your Son Upon the Waters

I can't imagine placing my sweet three-month-old in a basket to float on the dark waters of the longest river in the world, full of apex predators like hippos and crocs strong enough to kill a lion.

But Jochebed and Miriam knew God's power. They trusted the God who controlled the waters (Matthew 8:27), who had the power to shut the mouths of predators (Daniel 6:22).

The waters belonged to God.

Water would mean death for the Egyptian armies (Exodus 14:28), but for God's people His sovereignty over the water would be a demonstration of God's holy power and protection for His people.

Years later, Solomon would write about releasing the fruit of one's field onto the water, despite feelings of uncertainty. Read his wise words from Ecclesiastes 11:1, 5 (ESV).

Why can we let go and "cast our bread upon the waters" according to these verses?

But the woman (Rahab) had taken the two men and hidden them. She said, "Yes, the men came to me, but I did not know where they had come from.

JOSHUA 2:4

I have hidden your word in my heart that I might not sin against you.

PSALM 119:11

Cast your bread upon the waters, for you will find it after many days ... As you do not know the way the spirit comes to the bones in the womb of a woman with child, so you do not know the work of God who makes everything.

ECCLESIASTES 11:1, 5 ESV

We can entrust our treasure to God

The same God who formed baby Moses in the womb could be trusted to care for him—even amidst crocs, hippos, and river currents. When God led Jochebed to tuck her son in his basket-boat bed, she could rest in the certainty that God's sovereignty and power would preserve Moses for a salvation plan only God could accomplish. Jochebed and Miriam's part was to obey. They'd need to send baby Moses afloat on the water.

And just like she let go of her own precious babe, her hidden gem, so too can we entrust our treasure to God. We can let go of those things He calls us to let go of, knowing that He controls it all—nothing can happen outside of His sovereignty.

We too can show the courage of Jochebed and Miriam.

The Right Shipwright

I've often called the vessel Jochebed constructed to hold her precious babe a basket-boat. And it was constructed from reeds and papyrus. But if you've read Exodus 2 in the KJV or NKJV, you probably have some insight about this vessel that others of us may have missed. Note the word for the basket in this verse:

That's right—she built an ark.

Just as God delivered Noah and his family from the dangerous, deadly waters by keeping them afloat on an ark (Genesis 7:23), so would Moses be kept afloat on his own little ark of deliverance.

Did Jochebed build this ark because of a direct, verbal command from God, as Noah did (Genesis 6:14)? Or did she sense in her spirit it was the right thing to do? We don't know the answer to those questions, but we do know that the same faith that led Noah to build his ark of deliverance gave Jochebed the strength for her own task of ark-building.

And an important task it was. God had big things in store for baby Moses—for all of Jochebed's children—and she courageously rose to the occasion.

DRAWN OUT BY A SOFT HEART

Now it was Miriam's turn to be courageous. And she didn't disappoint.

Wise-beyond-her-years Miriam stood with a watchful eye on baby brother as he floated through dangerous waters.

Why did Miriam watch? Re-read Exodus 2:4-6 in the margin, or in your own Bible.

What happened when Pharaoh's daughter opened the basket (v. 6)?

Jochebed's hidden treasure had providentially been discovered by a woman with a tender heart. Though Pharaoh's heart toward the Israelites was hard, his daughter's was soft. When Moses cried out, she had compassion.

She felt sorry for him. Pharaoh's daughter spared precious baby Moses from his death sentence.

The Lord similarly sees us as His treasure. And in His mercy, He spares us. Malachi 3:17 of the New Living Translation says it like this: "'They will be my people,'" says the LORD of Heaven's Armies. '...they will be my own special treasure. I will spare them as a father spares an obedient child.'"

Friend, you and I have been treasured; you and I have been spared. Just as no ruthless Pharaoh and no hungry, irritable croc, and no dark waters would touch baby Moses, nothing can keep us from the powerful love of God. Why? How could God spare us? Because He didn't spare Christ.

Romans 8 lays it out plainly:

> He who did not spare his own Son, but gave him up for us all—how will he not also, along with him, graciously give us all things?... Who shall separate us from the love of Christ? Shall trouble or hardship or persecution or famine or nakedness or danger or sword? ... No, in all these things we are more than conquerors through him who loved us. For I am convinced that neither death nor life, neither angels nor demons, neither the present nor the future, nor any powers, neither height nor depth, nor anything else in all creation, will be able to separate us from the love of God that is in Christ Jesus our Lord (verses 32, 35, 37-39).

Because God didn't spare His Son, we're spared. Our own deliverance hinges on the gospel power of God (Romans 1:16).

⁴ His sister stood at a distance to see what would happen to him. ⁵ Then Pharaoh's daughter went down to the Nile to bathe, and her attendants were walking along the riverbank. She saw the basket among the reeds and sent her female slave to get it. ⁶She opened it and saw the baby. He was crying, and she felt sorry for him. "This is one of the Hebrew babies," she said.

EXODUS 2:4-6

For I am not ashamed of the gospel, because it is the power of God that brings salvation to everyone who believes: first to the Jew, then to the Gentile.

ROMANS 1:16

Then his sister asked Pharaoh's daughter, "Shall I go and get one of the Hebrew women to nurse the baby for you?"

[8] "Yes, go," she answered. So the girl went and got the baby's mother. [9] Pharaoh's daughter said to her, "Take this baby and nurse him for me, and I will pay you." So the woman took the baby and nursed him.
EXODUS 2:7-9

AFTER AWHILE, CROCODILE
Pharaoh wasn't the only deadly enemy baby Moses faced. Second only to salt-water crocs, Nile Crocodiles are the largest reptiles on earth. They're eight times deadlier than American Alligators. Reaching 20 feet long and with the strongest bite of any land animal, they're a force to be reckoned with. But even the fiercest of crocs are no match for the mighty power of the God who rules the seas and everything in them (Genesis 1:21).

Just as we have been spared by God's mighty hand, so too was baby Moses, under big sister Miriam's watchful eye.

Look again at verses 7-9 of Exodus 2. What happened next, thanks to Moses's sister Miriam's quick thinking?

Big sis to the rescue! Seeing an opportune chance for her family to care for baby brother, Miriam courageously spoke up to Pharaoh's daughter, offering to find a wet nurse for baby Moses.

And just like that, baby Moses went from being an endangered baby boy to being the adopted son of Pharaoh's daughter, nursed by his own mother—who was able to care for her son during his most formative years, while earning a wage to boot!

No more hiding baby brother Moses. What a relief that must have been for Moses's family! And how providential of our powerful God.

Even as a teenager, Miriam saw firsthand the powerful hand of God working around her, through her family, against all odds to save her baby brother—forming in her heart a boldness to praise our holy God.

And Moses would not only be saved, but trained for his important future with God. Read Acts 7:22. How did Moses's position as an adopted son of Pharaoh's daughter prepare him to successfully lead the people of Israel? Underline your answer.

"Moses was educated in all the wisdom of the Egyptians and was powerful in speech and action." Acts 7:22

The man who'd one day speak to God face to face, who stood up to stubborn Pharaoh, who led God's people away from everything they'd known, who received the Ten Commandments, and who recorded the very scripture we're studying right now—he learned to read and write from, you guessed it, the Egyptians. Pretty ironic, isn't it? The pagan Egyptians taught literacy to the very man who wrote the first books of the Bible.

But isn't that like our God, doing the miraculous in unexpected ways?

And we can't forget how the story really ends—not just with baby Moses preserved, not just with God's people being freed, not just with scripture being written, not just with the Promised Land being reached, but with our precious Savior Jesus Christ coming in the flesh through His people to save all mankind who would trust in Him—the once-for-all, happiest ending possible, our only hope, the Messiah.

MOSES THE MIGHTY

Though it's not stated in scripture, Jewish tradition records that when Moses was adopted by Pharaoh's daughter, Pharaoh had no sons, so Moses was being groomed to rule Egypt. Later Pharaoh would have a biological son, but Moses was still given a position of leadership among the Egyptians. He was said to be a great captain, thus the phrase in Acts 7:22, calling him "mighty in words and deeds" (NKJV).

Throughout scripture God's people often expected their leader to be a political one, but usually God had other plans (see also 1 Samuel 8; John 6:15). Moses's attempt to fix his people's situation by force was a dismal failure (Exodus 2:11-15).

Only God's way would prove successful for His servant Moses.

> **The pagan Egyptians taught literacy to the very man who wrote the first books of the Bible.**

Seeing God's protection of and provision for His people through Miriam and her family positions us to praise our holy God in bold prayer.

Spend a few moments with the Lord in prayer:

- Pray that, like Miriam and Jochebed, your life would be characterized by courageous obedience.
- Praise God for His powerful protection of Moses— despite the crocodiles, the waters, and Pharaoh. Thank Him that He's more powerful than any enemy or obstacle you may face.
- Thank God for the salvation God's people found because of Miriam, Jochebed, and Moses's obedience—and for the salvation we all experience as the story played out over centuries through the life and death of Christ.

Takeaway Truth — "Yet you are enthroned as the Holy One; you are the one Israel praises." Psalm 22:3.

MAIN TEXTS
Exodus 3
Numbers 20:1-13

DAY 3: MOSES MESSES UP

But you are a chosen people, a royal priesthood, a holy nation, God's special possession, that you may declare the praises of him who called you out of darkness into his wonderful light.
1 Peter 2:9

God is most beautifully praised when His people hear His Word, love His Word, and obey His Word. – Albert Mohler Jr.

Holy Ground and Bush that Won't Burn

There's something captivating about fire.

No, I'm no pyromaniac. I don't take undue delight in torching things, but at the same time, I am drawn to the crackling blaze of a good campfire. I can't help but watch.

One of the aspects of fire that's so fascinating is how fires consume—they burn anything combustible in their path. You can even hear the "whoosh" as flames spread in a sudden burst.

I remember during prayer in a candle lighting service, hearing that "whoosh." I think the woman in front of me had applied too much hairspray, and held her candle a little too close to her hair.

But today we'll study the miraculous bush that didn't burn—and what we can learn from it about God's holiness and our own boldness in prayer.

Hallowed is an old-fashioned way of saying holy, honored, and revered.

Context is crucial in expanding our understanding of the great narratives our awesome God wrote through His people's history. This is why in our study of God's work in Miriam's life, we first studied her world—the powers at play, the dangers and obstacles her family faced, and her role in preserving one of the most important men of God in the history of the Hebrew people.

Throughout this chapter we'll continue to learn about the experiences of Miriam's people with our mighty, saving, holy God. First let's take stock of what we've already learned, seeing how it can inform our prayer lives.

In the Lord's Prayer, Christ taught us to pray by saying, "This, then, is how you should pray: 'Our Father in heaven, **hallowed be your name'**" Matthew 6:9. *Hallowed* is an old-timey way of saying holy, honored, and revered—and that's just what Miriam experienced firsthand in her life.

She had a front-row seat to the work of a powerful God, worthy of all praise and honor—as He protected her baby brother from dangerous predators, spared baby Moses from Pharaoh's death sentence, and prepared Moses for power.

Miriam had positioned herself to witness the power of a holy God by living in obedience to Him. Despite the dangers she faced in disobeying the powerful Pharaoh's order, Miriam followed her mother Jochebed's courageous example of preserving Moses, the special baby.

Though she was only a teen at the time, Miriam kept careful watch of her baby brother, boldly speaking to Pharaoh's daughter at just the right time.

Her brother Moses grew to a position of power in Egypt. But his own attempt at solving his people's misery was a bust. You can study that in more detail in Exodus 2:11-15 (also see yesterday's "Moses the Mighty" section).

What happened when Moses tried to help his people in his own strength? See Exodus 2:14b-15 in the margin.

What did Moses feel, according to these verses?

Where did Moses go?

When Moses feared for his safety, he headed for the wilderness and sat by a well.

Sound familiar? It's strikingly similar to Hagar's fearful flight from Sarah (Genesis 16:7-13) where she had her own encounter with "The God Who Sees Me."

When we don't know what else to do, we flee to the wilderness, and God meets us there. That's just what Moses did. Moses's time in the wilderness would include his own encounter with

> Then Moses was afraid and thought, "What I did must have become known." When Pharaoh heard of this, he tried to kill Moses, but Moses fled from Pharaoh and went to live in Midian, where he sat down by a well.
>
> EXODUS 2:14b-15

God, whose holy ground proclamation "I AM WHO I AM" (Exodus 3:14) put Moses's fears in their place.

Moses had committed a hasty crime and feared for his life. But God wasn't done with the beautiful baby who'd grown into a rash man. God would meet Moses in the wilderness, once again orchestrating Moses's life by His mighty hand.

Review Exodus 2:23-3:1-10, note these important details:

What significant details do we find in Exodus 2:23-25? What might these facts have to do with Moses?

> 23 During that long period, the king of Egypt died. The Israelites groaned in their slavery and cried out, and their cry for help because of their slavery went up to God. 24 God heard their groaning and he remembered his covenant with Abraham, with Isaac and with Jacob. 25 So God looked on the Israelites and was concerned about them.
>
> EXODUS 2:23-25

What was the name of the place where Moses encountered God (Exodus 3:1)?

Why was Moses fascinated with what he saw (Exodus 3:3)?

Why was Moses instructed to remove his sandals (Exodus 3:5)?

So much time had passed since Moses lived in Egypt that he was now 80 years old. The first 40 years of his life had been spent in Pharaoh's palace, the second 40 as a lowly shepherd in the wilderness of Midian.

But the Pharoah he feared was now dead, and God's people still needed a deliverer. It was time for Moses to witness God's power and holiness right before his eyes.

On Mt. Horeb (this is also called Mt. Sinai in some versions) while Moses was doing his ordinary, everyday shepherding, God showed up.

The famous burning-bush encounter changed the trajectory of Moses's life forever. No longer in exile in Midian, the reluctant Moses would team up with brother Aaron, and along with their sister Miriam, lead God's people out of their captivity, against all earthly odds.

Notice in this encounter the link between God's demonstration of power (the burning bush), His holiness (the command to remove sandals because of holy ground), and a call to obedience (commanding Moses to lead His people).

This intertwined relationship between God's power, His holiness, and His people's obedience is a central theme in the story of Miriam, Moses, and the exodus of God's people from their slavery in Egypt—and a wake-up call for us.

Let's stop for a moment to remember the details from Miriam and Moses's life stories where evidence of the following three themes have been seen. They are woven throughout the narrative, like a three-strand braid. Fill in the circles with facts you remember:

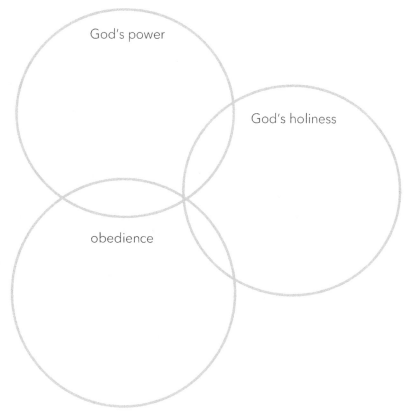

MOSES AND ELIJAH'S MOUNTAINTOP EXPERIENCES WITH A HOLY GOD

If you're like me and enjoy a good scripture rabbit trail, this sidebar is for you! (You're welcome!)

Moses had other experiences on Mt. Horeb/Sinai, in addition to the burning bush encounter with God. See for yourself in the following verses:

Exodus 17:6

Deuteronomy 5:2

In addition to his personal encounter with God, Moses would later experience the miracle of the water from the rock at Mt. Horeb, and he was given the Ten Commandments at the same place. Talk about a prime location!

But Moses wasn't the only one who met God on Mt Horeb/Sinai. Check out 1 Kings 19. Who else met God there?

When fleeing evil Jezebel, after sleeping under the broom tree, Elijah encountered God on Horeb. Not in the wind, the earthquake, or the fire, but in the still small voice.

Just as Moses was discouraged and hesitant when God met him in the burning bush at Horeb, so was Elijah. But God charged both of them to boldly lead, together with the help of others.

Moses and Elijah would appear on a mountain again, but this time with Jesus. Check out Matthew 17:1-3. Notice how God revealed His Holiness in Jesus during this mountaintop experience.

Maybe you remember seeing God's **power**ful hand in His deliverance of baby Moses safely to Pharaoh's palace, His **holiness** in the burning bush encounter with Moses, and **obedience** in the lives of Jochebed and Miriam.

Those are just some of the things you may have noticed. Continue to look for these fingerprints of God in Miriam's life as we dig into her story this week, returning to page 75 to record what you find.

Now let's use this narrative as a springboard to focus our own lives—specifically preparing to pray bold. If we want to declare the holiness of God, like Miriam, then we'd be wise to prepare our hearts.

Are you tuned-in to God's mighty power, the evidence of His holiness in your life? Does your awareness of His holy, matchless power drive you to obedience? Does it drive your prayers? Record your thoughts.

TO OBEY A HOLY GOD IS BETTER

Sadly, even Moses didn't always get it right. Years down the road, even after God saved Moses as a babe (Exodus 2), used him to call down plagues on the Egyptians (Exodus 7-12), gave Moses signs to perform (Exodus 4), Moses met with God Himself (Exodus 3, 19), and (spoiler alert!) God miraculously delivered His people through the Red Sea and provided for them in the desert—after all of God's powerful faithfulness Moses STILL failed to recognize God as holy. Oof!

Let's peek into the scriptures to see just what happened in Numbers 20, underlining the twelve words that come after the word, "because":

The Lord had told Moses and Aaron to speak to the rock to get water for the thirsty Israelites, but fed-up Moses struck the rock instead.

Then Moses raised his arm and struck the rock twice with his staff. Water gushed out, and the community and their livestock drank. But the LORD said to Moses and Aaron, "Because you did not trust in me enough to honor me as holy in the sight of the Israelites, you will not bring this community into the land I give them." These were the waters of Meribah where the Israelites quarreled with the LORD and where he was proved holy among them."

NUMBERS 20:11-13

Why? Because Moses didn't trust God enough to honor God as holy.

When we trust God, we obey Him—and that honors Him as holy. So, an important part of hallowing God's name is **obedience**.

Conversely, our disobedience proves we're failing to trust God and to honor Him as holy. Yikes!

Disobedience reveals lack of trust and respect.

But those of us who are parents or teachers or bosses get this, right? When those we're in charge of don't obey, it reveals issues of trust and respect. That's why we sometimes tell our children that the reason they should obey is "because I said so"—when a loving authority is in charge, obedience should be automatic.

It's why having to tell your daughter for the seventh time to unload the dishwasher reveals big problems—disrespect and lack of trust.

Psalm 4:4 (ESV) says, "Be angry, and do not sin."

It's hard to be angry and not sin. Think about classic anger situations: someone cuts you off in traffic and before you know it, you're feeling "road rage;" or the ref makes an awful call and before you know it, you're out of your seat yelling, "Come on! Get some glasses!"

But Moses failed to be angry without sinning. His angry disobedience led to dire consequences. The man whom God saved as a babe, who performed signs and wonders, who met with God Himself, who delivered God's people through the Red Sea—would not be allowed to enter the long-awaited Promised Land after all the years of wandering and waiting.

Why? Because his disobedience showed a lack of honor for a most holy God.

I wonder about us.

Can we be angry, and yet, not sin? We have so many things to be angry about as believers—God's name is disgraced as our culture uses it flippantly (Exodus 20:7), the unborn are treated like trash rather than valued (Matthew 25:40), God's word is misused as scriptures are twisted and contorted to mean any number of ungodly things (2 Peter 2:1), God's church is fractured and broken needlessly over trivial issues despite

Jesus's call to unity (John 17:21)—but does our righteous anger express itself appropriately?

If mighty man-of-God Moses can struggle with righteous anger resulting in sinful behavior, I'm guessing we can fall prey too. How might our anger as believers—appropriate as it may be—cause sin?

While our righteous anger might trip us up in any number of ways, a few possibilities come to mind:

- We can take on an antagonistic spirit against people whose theology or behavior seems ungodly to us, instead of speaking with grace (Colossians 4:6).
- We can begin to see other sinners who are loved by God as our enemies, rather than recognizing that our true enemy is Satan himself (Ephesians 6:12).
- We can spend an undue amount of time arguing scriptures rather than growing in our knowledge of them (Titus 3:9; 2 Timothy 2:14-15).
- We can act just like the world, fighting among ourselves (1 Corinthians 3:3).

These behaviors turn our righteous anger into soured living. When we allow our anger to turn into sin, it dishonors our holy God. The result is not only a compromised witness to the world, distraction from our true enemy, and missed opportunities for good, but consequences for us as well.

Just look at Moses.

After years of faithfully leading God's ungrateful people through the desert, he'd never reach the earthly Promised Land.

Think honoring God as holy is important yet? Oh yes, yes, it is.

So often our culture tells us to "go with your gut." From rom-com movies, to inspirational greeting cards, to commercials, to fairy-tale books for children—we can't get away from the message that our emotions and instincts are trustworthy.

Think honoring God as holy is important? It is.

> May our prayers not be empty words, but a true echo of our hearts and lives, lived in reverence to our holy God.

"Follow Your Heart" was even printed on my 18-month-old daughter's nightgown, above a picture of princesses.

Well, see how well that played out for Moses and the rock!

Unfortunately, our emotions can't be trusted, and our earthly heart cannot lead us. Jeremiah 17:9 says, "The heart is deceitful above all things and beyond cure. Who can understand it?"

I was doing a devotional with my six-year-old about obedience despite our fears, and he confided to me, "Mama, this summer, I was so afraid to obey my swim teacher and dunk under the water, but I knew God wanted me to obey her, so I did!"

If only we all had such a strong resolve to obey, no matter what our emotions were telling us!

We see in the story of Moses and Miriam a powerful God and the importance of recognizing His holiness and following in obedience.

Just as we hear in the Lord's Prayer, "hallowed be your name," may we also live according to His holiness. May our prayers not be empty words, but a true echo of our hearts and lives, lived in reverence to our holy God. In our anger, may we not sin.

My recognition of God's holiness should be evident in my obedience to Him, no matter what I'm feeling.

Spend a few moments in prayer:

- Ask the Lord to soften your heart for prayer by helping you recognize just how holy and powerful He is.
- Ask God to help you respond in praise to the evidence of His holiness and power in your life and in the world around you.
- Pray that instead of following your heart or going with your gut, you'd live in obedience to God, and in doing so honor Him as holy.

Takeaway Truth --"But blessed is the one who trusts in the LORD, whose confidence is in him. They will be like a tree planted by the water that sends out its roots by the stream. It does not fear when heat comes; its leaves are always green. It has no worries in a year of drought and never fails to bear fruit." Jeremiah 17:7-8

DAY 4: IN HOT PURSUIT

Sing to the LORD, all the earth; proclaim his salvation day after day. Declare his glory among the nations. 1 Chronicles 16:23-24

Fretting magnifies the problem, but prayer magnifies God.
–Joanna Weaver

Israel's Deliverer was a-Comin'

Miriam, Aaron, and the rest of the Hebrew people's long wait was over. God had heard their groaning and the day had finally come when the deliverance would begin.

Aaron received divine direction from God to fetch Moses from Mt. Horeb, where Moses had been called by God from the burning bush (Exodus 4:27). After four decades of Moses's exile in the wilderness, and the longsuffering patience of God's people, the time had come for action.

The brothers headed back to Egypt and gathered Israel's leaders, showing them the miraculous signs they'd been given for Pharaoh.

How did the nation of Israel respond? Why? Look up Exodus 4:31 to find out.

And they believed. And when they heard that the LORD was concerned about them and had seen their misery, they bowed down and worshiped.

EXODUS 4:31

The Hebrew people responded to God's words by bowing down in worship because they believed. I can only imagine there must have been a giant collective sigh of relief. After so many weary years of oppressive slavery under hard-hearted Pharaohs, deliverance was at hand.

Finally.

Aaron and Moses's meeting with the elders proved that God had heard the cry of His people, He had seen their suffering. As word of the plan spread, Miriam, along with the whole nation of Israel,

THE POWER PLAY

In day one of this week's study, we talked about the irony of the power struggle between Egypt's powerful Pharaohs and the One True God. Throughout our time in Exodus, we've seen a ruthless Pharaoh, willing to murder baby boys in order to weaken the Hebrews (Exodus 1:22).

We've also witnessed the cruel master the Pharaoh had become as the paranoia of the Egyptians grew, and the power struggle between God's people and their masters intensified (Exodus 1:12-14; 3:9). Moses's charge to let the Hebrews go would only cause Pharaoh to double down in his outrageous demands, asking the slaves to produce massive quantities of bricks without straw (Exodus 5:8-9).

How ridiculous Moses knew he would seem, going to Pharaoh and proclaiming that the God of these slaves, those whom Egypt had successfully oppressed for hundreds of years, demanded their freedom. Moses knew it was audacious to appear before one who was himself worshipped as a god and demand millions of his workforce be allowed to journey to the wilderness to worship another, their God.

couldn't help but respond by falling down in worship of their mighty, holy God.

Arm Wrestling with God

The Pharaoh, who was known in ancient texts as strong-arming his people (Exodus 3:8; 14:30; 15:9), was about to experience the work of a hand much mightier than his own. Choose at least three of these texts and notice the references to hands in each. Record your thoughts below:

Exodus 3:19 –

Exodus 6:1 –

Exodus 7:4 –

Exodus 9:3 –

Exodus 13:3 –

Exodus 15:6 –

God's mighty hand was about to act time and time and time again on behalf of His people—compelling Pharaoh to let God's people go, afflicting Egypt with plagues and acts of judgement, delivering His people.

Miriam, Moses, and Aaron were about to get a front-row seat to some of God's most legendary acts of power. The power struggle between God's people and Pharaoh was going to be over once and for all.

Buckle up. It's about to get good.

Might and Flight

Though initially Pharaoh was reluctant to let God's people go (after all, several years of free labor was a pretty good deal for him ...), the ten plagues, culminating in the death of his firstborn son, were just too much for him to bear. The God of Pharaoh's slaves had won.

Exodus 12:31-33 records Pharaoh and the Egyptians' breaking point. Read the passage, circling evidence of the Egyptians' urgency to rid themselves of God's people.

Going the Scenic Route

At long last God's people would leave the land of their captivity. Finally free from the bondage that held them for generations, they set out—in the middle of the night nonetheless—for freedom.

But if you read the main scripture text for today, you may have noticed that their journey was a difficult one from the get-go. God took His people on the scenic route to the Promised Land.

Why did He do this, according to Exodus 13:17-18?

Have you ever been in a hurry to get somewhere, only to hit a detour? Not fun! Now imagine waiting generation after generation for your journey to begin, and right away being led the roundabout way. Can we say frustrating?

But, as always, God had good reason for leading His people through the wilderness to the Promised Land. What was His initial reason, according to today's passage? Circle it in the verses.

Do you feel like God has you on the "scenic route" instead of the quickest path to where you'd like to go? Perhaps, like the Hebrew people, an unseen enemy lies on the direct path. Maybe

During the night Pharaoh summoned Moses and Aaron and said, "Up! Leave my people, you and the Israelites! Go, worship the LORD as you have requested. Take your flocks and herds, as you have said, and go. And also bless me." The Egyptians urged the people to hurry and leave the country. "For otherwise," they said, "we will all die!"

EXODUS 12:31-33

When Pharaoh let the people go, God did not lead them on the road through the Philistine country, though that was shorter. For God said, "If they face war, they might change their minds and return to Egypt." So God led the people around by the desert road toward the Red Sea.

Exodus 13:17-18

God is protecting you from an unnecessary battle, leading you safely in an easier, albeit out-of-the-way path.

As I write this, summer is turning to fall and greens are fading into oranges and reds and golds all around me. Last week, I fired up our furnace as the temperatures were getting chilly—but nothing happened.

Now, calling a furnace repair man isn't too big a deal, but I had already decided that we weren't going to spend any more money this calendar year on home improvement. We'd hit the limit of our budget and it wasn't wise to spend more. Plus, I had a busy week. It seemed like this hiccup was just One. More. Thing. (Maybe you can relate to this type of First World problem).

I had plans for my day and my bank account that were getting a detour.

After the obligatory pounding and examining, the repairmen came to me with bad news—it would be a costly repair. But their words were startling— "It's a good thing your furnace didn't fire up. The part inside that was supposed to be sealed was severely cracked. If it had run, it would have leaked dangerous carbon monoxide into your home."

A shiver ran down my spine. My daughter's bedroom is next to the utility room, and I shudder to think of what might have happened.

> Perhaps your desert road is actually a route of protection.

And suddenly, the broken-down furnace—the scenic-route detour—became God's protection instead of an inconvenience. Suddenly, what was once a source of discouragement became a blessing for which to praise God.

Perhaps your desert road is actually a route of protection too. Our struggle isn't in vain. Trust God's leading, even when it doesn't seem to make sense to you. Follow His guide, even as it leads you to the impossible-seeming shores of the Red Sea. Because sometimes that's just where you need to be led in order to see the mighty hand of our holy God part the waters and walk you through.

But I Do, But I Don't

In our house we have a running joke: "But I do, but I don't." It comes from asking one of our kids, during the toddler phase, if she wanted something. As in, "Do you want water or juice to drink?"

If you've taken care of toddlers, you know they are notorious for changing their minds. Just when you start to pour the water they asked for, they're sure they wanted juice instead. And they're sure to protest loudly so everyone can hear.

When asked why my daughter was so upset to be receiving the water she requested, I said to her, "Didn't you want water? That's what you said!"

"But I do! But I don't!" came the famous reply.

Read Exodus 14:5. You'll see Pharaoh have his own "but I do, but I don't" moment.

It's not only little ones who change their minds. So often we want both choices (or we don't want either) that it causes us to change our minds, just like a fussy toddler.

Pharaoh wanted the slave labor of the Egyptians, but he didn't want to deal with the plagues of their God. He wanted to be rid of the bother that went with keeping them, without giving up his workforce.

But he couldn't have it both ways.

And so, the chase was on.

Between a Rock, and a Hard Place, and a Deep Sea
Pharoah and the biggest, baddest army of his day bore down on God's people. So much for avoiding hardship.

No sooner had God's people finally left their days of slavery in Egypt behind than Pharaoh decided to pursue them after all. And the coast was anything but clear.

Exodus 14:1-3 shows God instructing Moses to lead the Israelites into a vulnerable location—where they'd be sitting ducks, right between mountains on either side, and headed straight toward the sea. They were easy targets. Weak people, in a pitifully poor location, up against Pharaoh's mighty army.

> When the king of Egypt was told that the people had fled, Pharaoh and his officials changed their minds about them and said, "What have we done? We have let the Israelites go and have lost their services!"
>
> EXODUS 14:5

Who came in hot pursuit, according to these verses?

Exodus 14:6-7

Exodus 14:8-9

Pharaoh's formidable army was made up of horses, chariots, charioteers, and troops. And big, bad, Pharaoh himself harnessed up his chariot and joined the chase. He wanted this done right, so he'd do the job himself.

He hadn't given up on his power struggle with the Israelite God after all—though he was about to experience God's ultimate power and glory, and he wouldn't live to tell the tale. "I followed God's people into the Red Sea and didn't even get a lousy t-shirt."

What was the reaction of the people of Israel when they saw Pharaoh's army pursuing? Look at Exodus 14:10-12 in your Bible or in the margin. Circle or highlight their reaction.

And so, the fearful, ungrateful Israelites began a long legacy of complaining against Moses, and ultimately against God.

Thankfully, Moses, Aaron, and Miriam were wise enough to continue their forward journey, leading the Hebrew people away from Egyptian captivity—no matter how impossible it seemed.

The Hebrews were following a God who makes the impossible, possible (Mark 10:27). And they were about to see it happen right before their very eyes.

You Need Only to Be Still

Even though Moses had an entire crowd of men, women, and children (not to mention livestock) hitting the panic button, literally between a rock and a hard place, he remained level-headed.

Moses answered the people, "Do not be afraid. Stand firm and you will see the deliverance the LORD will bring you today. The Egyptians you see today you will never see again.

**The LORD will fight for you; you need only to be still."
Exodus 14:13-14.**

What a gift! These verses contain so much that speaks to our fearful souls. Let's break it down:

Do not be afraid—with so much to fear (big bad Pharaoh's army, wilderness ahead, a million unknowns, no way forward)—it would seem that Israel had everything to fear, and yet Moses assured them they need not fear at all.

Stand firm—in such a vulnerable situation, how could God's people not be knock-kneed? When up against formidable foes, our tendency is to wilt in weakness, but God's people were to stand firm.

You will see deliverance—the whole gospel hinges on this: God delivers us! Surrounded by obstacles on every side, fleeing a powerful, cruel oppressor, God's people needed a mighty hand of deliverance! Especially powerful is learning that the Hebrew word used in this verse and translated as "deliverance" or "salvation"— is *yeshuw`ah*. Did you catch that? It's Yeshua—it's Jesus! The whole reason we do not need to be afraid, the whole reason we can stand firm is that we have Yeshua. We will see our salvation, our deliverance in Christ! Amen!!

The Egyptians you see today you will never see again—when God saves us from the power of death that once held us captive, we leave it behind for good! Just as the Hebrews didn't have to fear Pharaoh after God defeated him, neither do we need to fear the power of darkness and death because God has defeated it. Just as Pharaoh's army was swallowed up into their watery grave, "death has been swallowed up in victory" (1 Corinthians 15:54-55).

The Lord will fight for you; you need only to be still—Because of God's mighty hand, because of His victory, our part is to be still. Not that we don't move. God's people needed to step out into the Red Sea—but our tumultuous hearts need to be stilled. We can live in peace with a quietness of soul because God fights our battles. We need not cry out in complaint; we need not call out in fear. Even though the waters had not yet parted, even though the situation seemed impossible, even though the

> The whole reason we do not need to be afraid, the whole reason we can stand firm is that **we have Yeshua**. We will see our salvation, our deliverance in Christ.

natural reaction was to panic and complain—Moses encouraged the people to be at peace.

I can't help but hear a similar echo in Psalm 46:10:

It says, "Be still, and know that I am God; I will be exalted among the nations, I will be exalted in the earth."

Because of God's exaltation—because of His holiness, His glory, His might—because He is a great God, we can be still. We can be quiet in reverence, ready to pray bold with peace in our hearts when the enemy stares us down. Why? Because our God is stronger. He is mightier. He is greater. He is exalted. He is holy. Peace is ours.

Moses's four-sentence sermon preached volumes to God's people, as it does to us.

And now it was time to go. It was time to step forward in faith and see God move.

Because of a holy God, it was time to be bold.

> We can be quiet in reverence, ready to pray bold with peace in our hearts when the enemy stares us down.

Because of God's mighty hand of deliverance, I can trust His lead and pray bold with a soul that is still—even in the most difficult of situations.

Spend a few moments in prayer:

- Beg the Lord to soften your heart for prayer by helping you recognize His mighty hand of direction and deliverance.
- Ask God to help you respond in praise to the "scenic routes" of life, when it seems the road is challenging.
- Pray with a heart that's grateful for the God who fights battles on our behalf.

Takeaway Truth — "He says, 'Be still, and know that I am God; I will be exalted among the nations, I will be exalted in the earth.' The LORD Almighty is with us; the God of Jacob is our fortress." Psalm 46:10-11

DAY 5: A WORSHIP SET FOR THE AGES

MAIN TEXT
Exodus 14:15-15:21

Is anyone among you in trouble? Let them pray. Is anyone happy? Let them sing songs of praise. James 5:13.

In praise my soul ascends to self-forgetting adoration.
– O. Hallesby

A TIME TO PRAY, A TIME TO MOVE

The second half of Exodus 14 is just so good, it deserves another read. I hope you enjoyed your time there again today.

God wasn't the only one who was going to move—He wanted His people step forward in faith, even as the waters still covered the sea. What did God say to His people in Exodus 14:15?

There's a time to stand still (Exodus 14:14), a time to cry out to God (Ephesians 6:18), and a time to spring into action. Though we are to pray at all times (1 Thessalonians 5:17), sometimes we have to simultaneously pray and move forward in obedience.

> Then the LORD said to Moses, "Why are you crying out to me? Tell the Israelites to move on."
> EXODUS 14:15

Isn't it interesting that God told His people to get moving before He parted the waters? Sometimes we are called to go a certain direction, even though we can't see the way forward. But isn't it beautiful that before His people even stepped into the riverbed, God came around behind His people, between them and the enemy army, hemming them in safely (Exodus 14:19-20)? What a beautiful picture of the protective hand of God, keeping His obedient people in the palm of His hand.

Scan the verses of Exodus 14 again, paying special attention to the Israelites' experience crossing the Red Sea compared to the Egyptians'. Fill in the two following pictures with words or sketches, comparing the two crossings (for example, you may write "dry" on the path for the Israelites' crossing, while you might write "jammed chariot wheels" on the Egyptians' diagram):

Israelites' path through
the sea

Pharaoh's path through
the sea

It's fascinating to compare the experiences of the two groups—one travelling by the power of God on dry ground, with sturdy walls of water on either side, followed by God Himself in pillars of fire and cloud. A picture of peace and salvation, thanks to the power of God—for the same God who saved the beautiful baby Moses from drowning and danger in the Nile, saved His people from the deadly waters of the sea and the dangerous army that pursued them all night long.

But the Egyptians' fate would be completely different. For them, the journey to the bottom of the sea would be chaos. As they charged into the waters, their armies were thrown into a confused panic. Chariots, once a formidable force, now jammed and twisted uselessly. Men once strong and brave now begged to retreat. They knew too late the power of the God they battled. As the sun rose, the waters crashed down, and the once-great army was cut down completely. No one survived.

> The blood-thirsty Egyptians who'd tried to drown the Hebrew baby boys so many years earlier were now themselves drowned.

The blood-thirsty Egyptians who'd tried to drown the Hebrew baby boys so many years earlier were now themselves drowned by God. The tables had once again been turned.

And when the Israelites saw the mighty hand of the LORD displayed against the Egyptians, the people feared the LORD and put their trust in him and in Moses his servant.
Exodus 14:31

Can you imagine the relief and joy washing over the whole Israelite camp as God delivered them safely to the other side of the sea? The once-quieted people could now shout for joy. Their prayers became songs of praise to the mighty, holy God who'd brought them safely from slavery to salvation.

A Worship Set for the Ages

If you've ever seen the ending of a championship athletic game that's a hard-fought, underdog victory with a buzzer-beater winning shot and the overjoyed fans jump to their feet, screaming and storming onto the field—I imagine the victory song of the Israelites something like that, only way better.

I think they probably shouted out and jumped up and down in utter joy and relief when the waters finally closed in a watery grave over their enemies, a sign of the Israelites' complete deliverance and God's victory over their enemies.

Or perhaps the Israelites collapsed to the ground in exhausted exhilaration with absolutely no words.

Maybe they clung to one another, tears of joy washing their dusty faces. Either way, I think it's safe to say the experience of their deliverance through the Red Sea had to be like nothing else.

And in Exodus 15 we find the first worship song recorded in scripture. The Israelites sang out in praise of their Holy God— singing hallowed be His name (Exodus 15:11). The song is referred to as "The Song of Moses and Miriam," but who sang it, according to Exodus 15:1?

All the people of Israel together worshipped the Lord: Moses, Miriam, and the massive group of once-enslaved, newly freed travelers, heading for the Promised Land. Look closely at the words of this song of praise in Exodus 15.

What are the words or phrases that you notice regarding:

God's victory:

God's actions (pay special attention to the verbs):

> Their prayers became songs of praise to the mighty, holy God who'd brought them safely from slavery to salvation.

> Then Moses and the people of Israel sang this song to the Lord, saying, "I will sing to the Lord, for he has triumphed gloriously; the horse and his rider he has thrown into the sea.
>
> EXODUS 15:1 ESV

God's holiness:

The enemy's demise:

Who among the gods
is like you, LORD?
Who is like you–
majestic in holiness,
awesome in glory,
working wonders?

Exodus 15:11

It is filled with the language of **victory and power**: "triumphed victoriously" (NLT), "my strength and my defense," "The LORD is a warrior," "Majestic in power," "by the power of your arm," "The LORD reigns forever and ever."

And highlights **God's actions**: "He has hurled both horse and rider into the sea" (NLT), "Your right hand … shattered the enemy," "You threw down those who opposed you," "by the blast of your nostrils the waters piled up," "You stretch out your hand," "in your strength you will guide them," "by the power of your arm," "You will bring them in and plant them."

As well as **God's holiness**: "He is highly exalted," "He has become my salvation," "He is my God, and I will praise him, my father's God, and I will exalt him," "the LORD is his name," "the greatness of your majesty," "majestic in holiness, awesome in glory."

A THEME RUNS
THROUGH IT

Themes from the song
of Moses run
throughout scripture.

Here are a few
examples: God is my
salvation (Exodus
15:2; Isaiah 12:2), the
Lord is a warrior
(Exodus 15:3; Isaiah
42:13), He rules the
waters (Exodus 15:8;
Psalm 104:7), God's
victorious right hand
(Exodus 15:6; Psalm
98:1), the earth
trembles before Him
(Exodus 15:14; Psalm
96:9).

And don't forget the ultimate **downfall of the enemy**: "drowned in the Red Sea," "deep waters have covered them, they sank like … a stone," "they sank like lead," "the earth swallows your enemies," "nations will hear and tremble … anguish will grip the people, …chiefs … will be terrified, the leaders … will be seized with trembling, the people … will melt away; terror and dread will fall on them."

The Preeminence of Praise

The song of Moses and the Israelites is the first in a long-standing tradition of worship throughout the Bible. This habit of worshipping the Lord in song continued through scripture at crucial times like:

* David appointing the dream team of Asaph and other worshippers to sing before the Ark in 1 Chronicles 16:
  o *Sing to the LORD, all the earth; proclaim his salvation day after day. Declare his glory among*

the nations, his marvelous deeds among all peoples. 1 Chronicles 16:23-24.

- Jehoshaphat commissioning a worship team to go out in front of the army in battle, recorded in 2 Chronicles 20:20-22.
  - o Circle what happened when they praised, as recorded in verse 22: *As they began to sing and praise, the LORD set ambushes against the men of Ammon and Moab and Mount Seir who were invading Judah, and they were defeated.*
- When the temple was purified and dedicated, according to prophecy.
  - o This happened under King Hezekiah. There was singing in 2 Chronicles 29 (see verse 27-28, following). *As the offering began, singing to the LORD began also, accompanied by trumpets and the instruments of David king of Israel. The whole assembly bowed in worship, while the musicians played and the trumpets sounded.*
- Paul and Silas's prayers and worship preceded a miraculous earthquake prison break, resulting in the salvation of an entire family, and Paul and Silas's release from prison.
  - o *About midnight Paul and Silas were praying and singing hymns to God, and the other prisoners were listening to them. 26 Suddenly there was such a violent earthquake that the foundations of the prison were shaken. At once all the prison doors flew open, and everyone's chains came loose. Acts 16:25-26.*

Our praise can usher in the presence of God. It can defeat the enemy. It can consecrate in preparation for God's holiness. It can set prisoners free and bring salvation. Not because of us, but because of Him.

Reflect on your life. Have you experienced worship's key role in (fill in any experiences you've had):

Ushering in God's presence –

> Our praise can usher in the presence of God. It can defeat the enemy... Not because of us, but because of Him.

Ambushing the enemy –

Dedicating the temple – (hint: 1 Corinthians 6:19)

Setting free and bringing salvation –

> There's power in praise. That's why we should follow Christ's example in the Lord's Prayer—Our Father in heaven, holy is your name.

There's power in praise. That's why we should follow Christ's example in the Lord's Prayer—Our Father in heaven, holy is your name.

Our words of praise are key in setting the stage for effective prayer, according to Jesus's example. After all, if He—though He Himself was God—showed us to pray by first glorifying His heavenly Father, how much more should we begin our prayers with a posture of praise?

We learned last week about the intimate closeness we can have with God as a result of our father/daughter relationship with Him—that He knows us by name and cares enough about us to want to hear from us. God wants to know how we are, where we are, and where we've been.

Now we learn an equally important principle: God's powerful holiness.

In praising God for His might, His power, and His holiness at the outset of our prayers, we position ourselves for a right attitude and perspective in prayer.

We'll be less self-focused and more likely to realize just how powerful and awesome a God we're talking to. **This bolsters our faith and emboldens our prayers.**

What an amazing paradox Jesus's opening to the Lord's Prayer is: how could it be that a holy, mighty God, most worthy of praise, could also be a God who knows us well—who wants to hear from us, who cares about us more than we know?! I have an inkling that we can't even fully understand how both of these can be true—and yet they are. Our God is familiar, and yet, our God is holy. Amazing!

Praise at the End of the Age

The Song of Moses and Miriam from Exodus 15 is noteworthy as the first recorded worship song in scripture—but did you also know Moses is credited with a similar song at the end of the age?

Scripture is bookended by another seashore sing-along. A song with the words of Moses, of David, and of Jeremiah (Psalm 111:2,3; Deuteronomy 32:4; Jeremiah 10:7; Psalm 86:9; 98:2).

With the song of praise found in Revelation 15 at the end of the age, scripture comes full circle. This song of Moses and the Lamb speaks of God's holiness, His mighty deeds, His righteous acts, and His dominion over all.

Read the song, noticing the themes that echo throughout the ages from the story of Miriam's journey with God through the sea, to the worship session by the glassy sea at the very end of the age.

Slave Girl to Prophetess & Worship Leader

God's fingerprints had been on Miriam's life from the days of her youth. With God's help she had obediently protected her baby brother as his basket boat navigated dangerous waters under her watchful eye.

She had assured his connection and rootedness to the Hebrew people and his nurture by volunteering their mother as a nursemaid at the opportune time. Miriam's part was instrumental in preserving and raising up Moses as the deliverer of God's people.

Miriam's faithful obedience would again be key in the salvation of God's people. According to Micah 6:4, what was Miriam's role? Who sent her?

Micah 6:4 says, *"I brought you up out of Egypt and redeemed you from the land of slavery. I sent Moses to lead you, also Aaron and Miriam."* According to this verse, Miriam was sent by God to help deliver His people. And we're just about to uncover how.

And I saw what looked like a sea of glass glowing with fire and, standing beside the sea, those who had been victorious over the beast and its image and over the number of its name. They held harps given them by God and sang the song of God's servant Moses and of the Lamb:

"Great and marvelous are your deeds, Lord God Almighty. Just and true are your ways, King of the nations. Who will not fear you, Lord, and bring glory to your name? For you alone are holy. All nations will come and worship before you, for your righteous acts have been revealed."

After this I looked, and I saw in heaven the temple—that is, the tabernacle of the covenant law—and it was opened … And the temple was filled with smoke from the glory of God and from his power.
REVELATION 15:2-5, 8

> [19] For when the horses of Pharaoh with his chariots and his horsemen went into the sea, the LORD brought back the waters of the sea upon them, but the people of Israel walked on dry ground in the midst of the sea. [20] Then Miriam the prophetess, the sister of Aaron, took a tambourine in her hand, and all the women went out after her with tambourines and dancing. [21] And Miriam sang to them: "Sing to the LORD, for he has triumphed gloriously; the horse and his rider he has thrown into the sea."
>
> EXODUS 15:19-21 ESV

Let's take a closer look at verses 19-21 of Exodus 15 (ESV):

Now, like a journalist, fill in the "5 W's and the H" of verses 20-21 (I'll start for you):

Who - Miriam

What -

When -

Where -

Why -

How -

I think the news headline would be something like: Miriam leads Hebrew women in dancing, proclaiming praise of God after unlikely deliverance and enemy-crushing defeat.

And notice: she exalts God. She proclaims Him high and holy.

This was huge.

God raised up Miriam to help lead His people out of slavery and into victory. The teen who bravely disobeyed Pharaoh's decree, who courageously spoke up to Pharaoh's daughter, now alongside her brothers was raised as a prophetess and the first worship leader.

The once-slave girl who was oppressed by the cruel hand of Pharaoh, but delivered by God's mighty hand now took an instrument of praise in her own hand, and burst into a song of prayer and praise.

After the monumental victory God's people had just won in defeating the Egyptians once and for all, it was time to praise.

Repeating the words of the ancient song Moses had just penned, Miriam gathered the women and the instruments in a worship service for the ages. The women danced, they sang, but most importantly they praised the God whose power, might, and holiness had delivered them from their formidable foe.

I can't help but think that our everyday worship becomes lackluster. In our cluttered lives we easily forget the power of our awesome God, and the evidence of His faithfulness in our lives. But we must remember the power of praise.

BOLD: Six Praying Women, One Faithful God

Read 1 Samuel 18:6 that follows. In this verse, the women's behavior echoes that of Miriam and the Hebrew women in Exodus 15:20-21. Circle the similarities you see.

Notice the similarities? Victory! The gathering of women! Singing! Dancing! Timbrels! What monumental victory were these women celebrating? Turn to the previous chapter, 1 Samuel 17 to find out.

This group of singing, dancing, tambourining (I don't think that's a word—but it should be!) women were celebrating triumph over the giant! They were praising God in joyful response to Goliath's fall.

And just like these women who had heard of the beheading of behemoth Goliath, just like the women who saw the unforgiving, dark waters of the Red Sea crashing over their slave masters— we too can cry out in jubilant praise!

Why? Because our own giants have been slain! Our own slave masters have been rendered powerless! We are freed from the dark powers of sin that have ruled our lives—whether it be fear, addiction, greed, hate, selfishness, jealousy—none of it can hold power over us once our lives are ruled by the God of Heaven's Armies.

No longer need we fear the slave master of sin—God has delivered us! He has drowned it in the sea. No longer need we fear the giants who once threatened to rule us! One greater than David—his descendant Jesus—has defeated and decapitated our giants once for all!

And so we learn from Miriam's example to praise. Praise God for the victories of the past. Praise Him for His power and might. Praise Him for who He is, for what He does, for what He has yet to do. Praise the holy God who fights for you. Don't hold back your praise!

Your prayer life will be transformed if you learn to praise. You will unlock a new boldness in your prayers. No longer will you be dwelling in your old fears, no longer will you be subjected to your former bondages—there's freedom in the power of praise!

When the men were returning home after David had killed the Philistine, the women came out from all the towns of Israel to meet King Saul with singing and dancing, with joyful songs and with timbrels and lyres.

1 SAMUEL 18:6

Praise Him for who He is, for what He does, for what He has yet to do. Praise the holy God who fights for you. Don't hold back your praise!

> Praising our holy God prepares our hearts to pray,
> turning our eyes from ourselves to our God.

Spend a few moments in prayer:

- Ask the Lord to open your eyes to His work around you, and praise Him for what you see and what you don't see.
- Ask God to help you respond in praise to the enemy-crushing victories He has already won—victory over sin and death on your behalf through Jesus!
- Meditate on God's holiness—exalt Him!

Takeaway Truth – *"This, then, is how you should pray: 'Our Father in heaven, hallowed be your name.'" Matthew 6:9*

Friend, latch on to the main truth we learn from the life of Miriam, and don't let go:

To pray bold, we must glorify our Holy God, who fights for us, and delivers us.

Pause for Praise: By diving deep into the account of Miriam's life—her faith, her obedience, her deliverance, and her song—we've learned that the best way to put ourselves into the proper posture for bold prayer is by not only running to the Father, but also glorifying Him as holy. Turning our hearts to God in praise takes our focus off of ourselves, and puts it right where it belongs—on our incredible God. Looking back and seeing how His mighty hand has moved on our behalf draws our hearts to Him and inspires us to praise! Before you go on with your day, pause for some special time with the Holy Father. Allow your spirit to praise Him for being the Holy One. I suggest you watch the lyric video for Leeland's "Way Maker" on YouTube. If you prefer a more traditional style, try Reginald Heber's "Holy, Holy, Holy." Allow yourself to be lost in the majesty of the One who makes a way when there seems to be no way. Think on His perfection, His power, His omnipotence, His goodness, His eternal nature, His victory! He is the Incomparable God—there is none like Him!

Our Father in heaven
hallowed be your name,

YOUR KINGDOM COME

Your will be done,
on earth as it is in heaven.
Give us today our daily bread.
And forgive us our debts,
as we also have forgiven our debtors.
And lead us not into temptation,
but deliver us from the evil one.

DAY 1	MOUNTAINS HIGH, VALLEYS LOW
DAY 2	STEPPING INTO KINGDOM PURPOSE
DAY 3	MIGHTY TO SAVE
DAY 4	A SONG OF KINGDOM VICTORY
DAY 5	KINGDOM VICTORY TODAY

WEEK THREE
DEBORAH
RISING LIKE THE SUN

DAY 1: MOUNTAINS HIGH, VALLEYS LOW

God reigns over the nations; God is seated on his holy throne.
Psalm 47:8

Relying on God has to begin all over again every day
as if nothing had yet been done. – C.S. Lewis

Dismal Failure

We all love a good fail video, right?

A fisherman awkwardly waving his arms and tumbling overboard; a teen botching a way-out-of-their league bike stunt; a birthday cake toppling to the ground into a messy pile of icing and crumbs—we love them so much that the Fail Army YouTube channel has over 16 million subscribers. Their top 10 most-viewed videos have over 523 million views altogether! We're slightly obsessed with watching other people's disasters play out before our eyes.

God's people had their own share of fiascoes—we will learn this all too well this week. Unfortunately, Israel's fails aren't nearly as amusing as a Fail Army video. Their consequences were much more serious than a ruined birthday cake.

In chapter two, we learned about how our mighty, holy God delivered His people out of slavery through the miraculous parting of the sea—drowning their cruel slave masters once for all. Through this mountaintop experience, **we learned that praying like Miriam means recognizing the power and holiness of God.**

Before that, we zoomed in on the story of Hagar, the lowly, Egyptian slave. Through her encounter with God as she fled her own cruel mistress, we learn that our **God is a loving father— a God who sees us, who cares for us, who knows us by name.**

Our mighty, holy God—who has the power to part waters and squash our adversaries like bugs—He is also the God who loves us intimately, who cares to hear our hearts, who knows us by name.

> Our mighty, holy God— who has the power to part waters and squash our adversaries like bugs—He is also the God who loves us intimately, who cares to hear our hearts, who knows us by name.

But there's more to the success of our prayer lives than positioning ourselves as the dearly-loved daughters of a holy King who is matchless in might.

So for our next step in learning to pray, we return to the perfect prayer, spoken by the perfect Pray-er—the author and perfecter of our faith, Christ Himself.

Return to the Lord's Prayer in Matthew 6. According to verse 10, what should be the focus of our prayers?

Your kingdom come, your will be done, on earth as it is in heaven.

MATTHEW 6:10

But before we tackle our next subject—praying kingdom-minded prayers—we'll do a speedy recap of Israel's history between the times of Miriam and Deborah.

A Roller-Coaster Ride Through History

From the amazing victory of the Hebrew people over their captors at the shores of the Red Sea, the people of Israel would sink to new lows in their roller-coaster time of wilderness wanderings.

Despite supernatural provisions of manna and quail, Israel would be tempted to worship false Gods (Exodus 32). They would succumb to temptation, doing things their own way rather than God's (Numbers 20).

But they would again experience victory over their foes as they crossed the Jordan under Joshua's leadership to enter their long-awaited Promised Land. With the help of courageous Rahab, and once again the mighty hand of God, His people would defeat the formidable men of Jericho, leaving their once-strong city walls in ruin.

Finally, God's people inhabited the land promised to their father Abraham so very long ago.

And here, we find ourselves on the cusp of Deborah's rule. One would expect after so many miracles, so much provision, and so many second chances, the people of Israel would be ready for lives of victorious obedience to the one true God.

One would expect after so many miracles, so much provision, and so many second chances, the people of Israel would be ready for lives of victorious obedience.

After tasting firsthand both the hardship of a life of disobedience and the sweet victory of walking with God, it would seem like a simple choice—to live according to God's plan.

But what should have been an easy choice proved to be a strong temptation to God's people as they were once again sucked into the vortex of going their own way in sinful rebellion.

Joshua had breathed his last (Joshua 23-24), but not without first charging Israel with two important tasks. What were they? Find them in the margin verse and record them below:

1.

2.

Now then,' said Joshua, 'throw away the foreign gods that are among you and yield your hearts to the LORD, the God of Israel

JOSHUA 24:23

In his famous, "Choose for yourselves this day whom you will serve" and "but as for me and my household, we will serve the LORD" speech (Joshua 24:15), Joshua warned the Israelites against serving other gods, whether it be the gods of their ancient ancestors before Abraham (24:2) or the gods of Egypt (24:14) or even the gods of the Canaanites, whose land they'd inhabit (Joshua 23).

He warned that if Israel were swayed by the gods of the land, they'd surely be in trouble. What would happen, according to Joshua 23:12-13?

You'd think such a warning from a godly man like Joshua would really sink in.

If the Israelites weren't careful to keep themselves from being sucked into temptation of the culture surrounding them, their future would be bleak. They'd be enslaved once again, trapped, and would lose the blessing and power of God on their side. Aligning themselves with false gods meant death, according to Joshua (23:16).

You'd think such a warning from a godly man like Joshua would really sink in.

Think again.

God's people would be sucked into rebellious disobedience. Again. The dawn was breaking on one of the darkest times in the history of God's people—the days of the Judges.

Talk About Your Fixer Upper

Judges 1-3 is a CliffsNotes version—a teaser trailer of what's to come during the time of the Judges. It's an overview of Deborah's era. Brutal defeat by enemies, cycles of disobedience, wicked idolatry—the outlook was pretty grim.

Just like that, the Israelites once again went from an amazing victory—finally setting foot in the Promised Land—to defeat.

Where did they go wrong? Do some sleuthing in the following verses to figure out their slippery slope to disaster. Look for a common theme, circling the verb that appears in all of these verses:

Judges 1 (NLT):

19 The LORD was with the people of Judah, and they took possession of the hill country. But they failed to drive out the people living in the plains, who had iron chariots.

27 The tribe of Manasseh failed to drive out the people living in Beth-shan, Taanach, Dor, Ibleam, Megiddo, and all their surrounding settlements, because the Canaanites were determined to stay in that region.

29 The tribe of Ephraim failed to drive out the Canaanites living in Gezer, so the Canaanites continued to live there among them.

30 The tribe of Zebulun failed to drive out the residents of Kitron and Nahalol, so the Canaanites continued to live among them.

31 The tribe of Asher failed to drive out the residents of Acco, Sidon, Ahlab, Aczib, Helbah, Aphik, and Rehob

32 Instead, the people of Asher moved in among the Canaanites, who controlled the land, for they failed to drive them out.

33 Likewise, the tribe of Naphtali failed to drive out the residents of Beth-shemesh and Beth-anath. Instead, they moved in among the Canaanites, who controlled the land.

Failed.

The Israelites failed.

Failed.
The Israelites
failed.

They failed to drive out the evil influences from among them. Joshua had warned them what a dangerous prospect it was to live among idolaters, and yet Israel was not willing to go the distance to drive out the evildoers right next door.

Big mistake.

The message could hardly be clearer to the Israelites. Read the words of the angel of the Lord to the people in Judges 2:1-3, circling or highlighting God's promises and actions, underlining their disobedient acts.

Israel was like a child placed in time-out following a defiant outburst, now suffering the consequences.

God had warned them to drive out and destroy the negative influences that would draw them away from their faithful God, but they had failed. And now, the people would not have God's help. Instead, what would they have? Put a box around it in verse 3 in the margin.

Instead of a powerful God paving the way for them in their Promised Land, Israel would be plagued by their enemies, a continual temptation—a lure away from God, a ceaseless trouble.

This wasn't God's plan.

God had planned to prosper His people. He planned to make a way for them. To help them thrive.

They knew this was coming. God's people knew the expectations He had for them. This was no Jack-in-the-box surprise—ever since the days of Moses the expectation had been clear: drive out the Canaanites and destroy their idols (see Numbers 33:50-56).

Why? Because otherwise God would bring upon His own people the fate of the Canaanites (Numbers 33:56).

I don't know about you, but I don't want to be on the receiving end of God's discipline. No, thank you!

And yet that's exactly where the Israelites found themselves in the days of the Judges—worshipping the gods of their evil neighbors because of their own lack of obedience in failing to drive them out. Foolishness!

Idolatrous and disobedient. These are the people Deborah was called to rule. This is the kingdom she inherited. Despite God's power and faithfulness, His people were repeatedly disobedient. Talk about a lousy situation.

Yikes.

Ever found yourself in a less-than-ideal situation, like Deborah?

Maybe you do right now. It could be a sin-cycle in your own life that you just can't seem to break free from—is it really so bad to lose your cool when you're frustrated? (Spoiler alert—yes.)

Or a financial debt-hole you can't seem to crawl out of, even though charging all those bills seemed like a good idea at the time.

Or maybe a relationship you've damaged by your hasty words— even though she really deserved it (right?). Maybe you've made a mess of things.

Or it could be that your less-than-ideal situation is nothing of your own doing. Sometimes a medical diagnosis, a relationship issue, a crummy life circumstance is out of our control—but we seem to find ourselves plopped right in the midst of it anyhow. How will we respond?

What is a less-than-ideal circumstance or situation you've found yourself in (could be now or in the past)? Take a moment to reflect on your response to the hardship you've faced. Have you taken your trouble as an opportunity to trust God? Have you looked at your circumstance from a kingdom perspective? Record your reflections in the margin.

I can think of times when I've failed miserably to have a godly response to adversity. When our family was up against financial uncertainties, it was my opportunity to trust God. Guess what: I failed to walk in faith.

Too often during that time I lay awake at night worrying— foolishly acting as if the solutions to my problems rested solely on my shoulders. Even though God was right there, walking me through it—only a whisper away.

Now I see clearly God's hand providing for us all along—how silly of me to allow my uncertain situation to suck me into

Even though Deborah found herself leading people who were prone to bad decisions, her prayers and purposes were kingdom-minded.

faithless fears. Dare I trust my bank account more than the God who made it all?! Ridiculous!

And just like that, I squandered my chance to live in victory in my earthly promised land, trusting God's provision.

Thankfully we don't see this kind of freak-out-in-response-to-lousy-circumstances from Deborah.

We'll see this week that even though Deborah found herself leading people who were prone to bad decisions, her prayers and purposes were kingdom-minded.

Despite her difficulties, Deborah's dependence on God shone through. No Debbie downer here. Her confidence in God was unflagging.

And though she found herself in an unlikely position of power, her realization of the One who was truly in power was key to her own success and the success of her people.

Stay tuned. This is going to be good.

> Though our pasts are marked by both our failures and successes—our mountaintop experiences with God, and our dismal failures—God calls us to follow Him faithfully from this day forward.

Spend a few moments with the Lord in prayer:

- Reflect on God's faithfulness in times past—that just as He delivered and provided for His people long ago, He does the same for us today.
- Confess the times you've stumbled and fallen short despite God's goodness to you.
- Commit to following God in obedience from this day forward.

Takeaway Truth — *"If my people, who are called by my name, will humble themselves and pray and seek my face and turn from their wicked ways, then I will hear from heaven, and I will forgive their sin and will heal their land" 2 Chronicles 7:14*

DAY 2: STEPPING INTO KINGDOM PURPOSE

Those deceived by worthless things lose their chance for mercy.
Jonah 2:8 (CEB)

Most of us talk too much when we pray, ... If prayer is a conversation with God, how can we hear what He has to say if we're talking all the time? - Bob Buford

Fools and Folly

I have to admit that God's people seem like real boneheads here. If you reviewed the main text, you know what I'm talking about.

I mean, come on—how much clearer could God's instruction be? Go into the land, and drive out the godless people there. If not, you'll be sorry.

Easy peasy.

But as we learned in yesterday's lesson, time after time after time, God's people failed. Big time.

Like I said, bonehead move, Israelites.

And yet, their behavior gives me pause.

Proverbs 26 says if we repeat our mistakes, we're like dogs going back to their vomit. Yuck! We've been raising a pup with a weak stomach and I can tell you—that's just gross.

> As a dog returns to its vomit, so fools repeat their folly. Do you see a person wise in their own eyes? There is more hope for a fool than for them.
>
> PROVERBS 26:11-12

I've done foolish things in the past. I've allowed myself to fall into sinful behaviors and attitudes. And though I have had victories—though I've entered into God's promised land for me through salvation in Christ—have I done my part to drive out the enemies of God lurking in that promised land? To separate myself from ungodly influences and temptations?

Have I removed those snares, those enemies, those lures that surround me? Or am I all-to-comfortable cozying up with the idolatrous culture that I live in?

What about the shows I watch? The too-gossipy conversations I have? The selfish decisions I make with my bank account? The indulgent ways I spend my time? Am I really better at godly living than the Israelites of so long ago?

Do my decisions reflect the Lord's priorities, His rule and reign in my life? Or am I too busy satisfying my own appetites to chase after God with hungry abandon? Oof!

Take a minute to reflect on your own life. Have you ruthlessly eliminated anything that might lure you away from your devotion to God?

> Catch for us the foxes, the little foxes that ruin the vineyards, our vineyards that are in bloom.
>
> SONG OF SONGS 2:15

In Song of Songs 2:15, we read of little foxes ruining the vineyards of love between the lovers. Seemingly innocent little foxes.

But we know that sometimes sin and danger creep in, looking like cute, harmless, furry creatures—but end up causing more destruction than we ever imagined.

In what turned out to be a bad rerun, a recurring nightmarish cycle of disobedience, idolatry, and defeat—Israel neither conquered those who inhabited their land nor obeyed God. What may have seemed like a not-so-big deal to them ended up having huge consequences.

Sisera The Fox

If the lovers in Song of Songs needed to drive foxes out of their vineyards, the people of God even more so needed to drive out big bully Sisera.

> So the LORD sold them into the hands of Jabin king of Canaan, who reigned in Hazor. Sisera, the commander of his army, was based in Harosheth Haggoyim. ³ Because he had nine hundred chariots fitted with iron and had cruelly oppressed the Israelites for twenty years, they cried to the LORD for help.

Who was Sisera, and what did he have and do, according to Judges 4:2-3 (Look in the margin, or your own favorite Bible)?

BOLD: Six Praying Women, One Faithful God

Sisera was Canaanite King Jabin's big-time commander. He had control of 900 iron chariots—formidable weapons—the tanks of their day.

Not only that, he was cruel. Sisera bullied God's people. They had escaped the clutches of the Egyptian Pharaoh, only to fall prey to new oppressors.

How could God let this happen to His beloved people? Check Judges 4:1 (in the margin or your Bible) for the answer.

The Israelites did evil. Again.

Like dogs to vomit. Yuck.

When are God's people ever going to learn their lesson?! And how was it that Sisera was even there to begin with? Check Judges 1:19 (in the margin or your Bible) for the answer.

The Israelites had escaped the clutches of the Egyptian Pharaoh, only to fall prey to new oppressors.

God's people had failed to drive out the people living in the plains who had—you guessed it—iron chariots. Old Sisera.

These guys were supposed to be history years before—back in the days of Joshua. But it hadn't happened.

To be honest, Sisera and his army with their iron chariots would not have been easy for God's people to drive out. After all, the people of Israel were only foot soldiers—no iron chariots for them—in fact, no iron weapons at all. It's no wonder they adopted the scaredy-cat "live and let live" mentality.

The Canaanites were even known to strap knives to their chariot wheels, ready to slice and dice any unfortunate enemy foot soldier they might meet. How could God's people stand a chance?! (Hint hint: I'll let you in on a not-so-secret: they had God on their side. The Lord of heaven and earth, the Creator and Sustainer of the Universe—that's how!)

But they didn't drive Sisera out when God was poised and ready to help them. They had missed their chance. Now here the villain was, still lurking around, tormenting them, being the thorn-in-their-side that God had warned he'd be (Numbers 33:55)!

Again the Israelites did evil in the eyes of the LORD, now that Ehud was dead.

JUDGES 4:1

The Lord was with the people of Judah, and they took possession of the hill country. But they failed to drive out the people living in the plains, who had iron chariots.

JUDGES 1:19 NLT

Told You So

Sisera came from within the Israelites' own land. He was antagonizing Israel because they failed to defeat the enemy when God told them to. Now the fierce Canaanites were rallying once again and threatening to overthrow Israel on their own turf—how humiliating.

Surely the wayward people of God would hurry to call on Him now!

How long did they wait, according to Judges 4:3?

Because he had nine hundred chariots fitted with iron and had cruelly oppressed the Israelites for twenty years, they cried to the LORD for help Judges 4:3

Twenty years!! Twenty years!!! Can you believe it? That's time enough to go from Pampers to Princeton, time enough to go from toddler to blushing bride.

After twenty long years of oppression by big bully Sisera, the people of Israel were finally willing to humble themselves and call on God—the God whom they should have called on immediately. If they'd only listened to God, they never would have fallen into this mess to begin with.

But of course, the God of new-every-morning mercies (Lamentations 3:23) came quickly to their aid.

The steadfast love of the LORD never ceases; his mercies never come to an end; they are new every morning; great is your faithfulness. Lamentations 3:22-23 (ESV)

Enter the unlikely answer to the people's prayers: Deborah.

Who would God use to lead His people out of the mess they'd gotten themselves into, but the prophetess and judge Deborah?

She really is a remarkable character when you consider her rule during some of Israel's darkest days. In a time when the culture was patriarchal, with men holding nearly all the property and the power—God raised up Deborah to rule.

As a prophetess, Deborah had the task of discerning the voice and will of God, then telling it to her people—surely an unenviable job in her day when the people had a track record of not following God's voice to begin with.

Deborah had a choice to make: the people of God were squirming under the thumb of mighty Sisera, crying out in misery for help. What would she do? How would she lead?

From an earthly perspective, the odds were stacked against the puny people of Israel, as always.

But Deborah wasn't deterred.

What did she do, according to Judges 4:6-7?

> She sent for Barak son of Abinoam from Kedesh in Naphtali and said to him, "The LORD, the God of Israel, commands you: 'Go, take with you ten thousand men of Naphtali and Zebulun and lead them up to Mount Tabor. I will lead Sisera, the commander of Jabin's army, with his chariots and his troops to the Kishon River and give him into your hands.'"
>
> JUDGES 4:6-7

Deborah listened to God, heard His plan, and enacted it. She had heard from the Lord, and wasn't shy about doing His will. Her ear was enough attuned to God to know His will for her people, and despite the fact that they had a track record for doing anything but obey, she called them to follow God's plan—to see His kingdom come.

Anyone else impressed?

I know full well God's plan for my life (a.k.a. scripture) but some days it feels like following it is about as easy as brushing my teeth while eating Oreos.

Not Deborah, she was a woman of action. And so sure was she of God's plan, she told it like it was to Barak—the man God chose to be victorious over Sisera. What was Barak's response (verse 8)?

> Barak said to her, "If you go with me, I will go; but if you don't go with me, I won't go."
>
> JUDGES 4:8

Deborah, with full confidence in God, told Barak of the victory God would give. True to form for a man of his day, Barak trusted in prophetess Deborah more than the very God she heard.

And so, Deborah conceded to help Barak, despite his floundering faith, and trek with him to battle. What was the consequence for Barak's lack of confidence (verse 9)?

Barak wouldn't get the glory for finally defeating long-time enemy Sisera—that honor would be reserved for a woman. And Deborah's resume would include not only prophetess and judge, but warrior.

Being Quick to Listen

Deborah illustrates in these verses the importance of listening in our prayer lives. Despite her own people's abysmal lack of listening to the Lord, Deborah positions herself to hear His voice.

Friend, part of praying kingdom prayers is listening. Ask God to reveal His kingdom plans to you, then take the time to tune your ears to His voice: this can mean spending time in God's word, allowing Him to speak through scripture.

It could also mean being still before Him, quieting your soul, turning off and tuning out the other noise, readying yourself to hear the God who sometimes speaks in a still, small voice.

It means carving out the time to listen, and being intentional to hear God's kingdom plans. Part of praying God's kingdom come, is listening to hear what God's will is.

Our Own Modern-Day Sisera

A battle for the ages was about to unfold: mighty Sisera (according to historian Josephus) with access to 300,000 footmen, 10,000 riders, and 3,000 chariots versus the seeming underdogs of Israel and their piddly 10,000 foot soldiers—outnumbered and outweaponed by a landslide.

But before we dive into the details of this big-time battle, let's hit the pause button and think about what's happening here.

BOLD: Six Praying Women, One Faithful God

Deborah is an unlikely leader to a group of misfit people—a people not trusting or following the God who was supposed to be theirs—who just so happen to be oppressed through a fault completely of their own. She's surrounded by those who don't honor God or prioritize His kingdom. Sound familiar?

Before we comb through Deborah's story bit by bit and see her outcome, let's think about where we find ourselves.

Could it be our situation is not so different?

Could it be that we are surrounded by a people who've forgotten the God who's supposed to be theirs? Could it be that we live among a people oppressed by a cruel master—the very sin they've failed to drive out of their lives? Could it be that the greatest tragedy is that they don't honor God or prioritize His kingdom?

Could it be that those people are actually us?

The running prophet Jonah had an aha moment while he called out to God from the belly of the whale. Life-and-death situations have a way of helping us think clearly.

When faced with three days of soul searching among the whale's digestive juices, Jonah found himself confessing to God his discovery. Read it in Jonah 2:8.

> Those who cling to worthless idols turn away from God's love for them.
>
> JONAH 2:8

Could it be that the very things we're clinging to, those seemingly innocent little foxes, those pet sins of worry and pride, of selfishness and laziness, of unforgiveness and self-pity, are the very things keeping us from seeing victory?

Take a moment to reflect. What worthless idols might you be harboring? What is the source of your oppressive defeat that's turning you away from God's love, keeping you from His will?

Take heart! While we are weak on our own, like the people of Israel long ago, when we cry out to God we battle with strength enough to defeat any enemy! The key to becoming a conqueror?

31 What, then, shall we say in response to these things? If God is for us, who can be against us? 32 He who did not spare his own Son, but gave him up for us all—how will he not also, along with him, graciously give us all things? 35 Who shall separate us from the love of Christ? Shall trouble or hardship or persecution or famine or nakedness or danger or sword? 36 As it is written: "For your sake we face death all day long; we are considered as sheep to be slaughtered." 37 No, in all these things we are more than conquerors through him who loved us. 38 For I am convinced that neither death nor life, neither angels nor demons, neither the present nor the future, nor any powers, 39 neither height nor depth, nor anything else in all creation, will be able to separate us from the love of God that is in Christ Jesus our Lord.
ROMANS 8:31-32,35-39

Kingdom-mindedness, like Deborah.

We can let go of our worthless idols and cling instead to Christ. Then nothing can separate us from His love.

Read the following passage, our own victory cry from Romans 8:31-32, 35-39, circling the words of victory, our identity in Christ, and striking out the things that will not defeat us in Christ.

What are you up against? Trouble? Hardship? Need? Danger?

Friend, rest assured. In Jesus we can conquer it all. Nothing can separate us from His love.

Deborah knew that there would be victory with the Lord.

She knew that instead of going their own way, failing to listen to God and follow His commands, her people must follow God's plans and focus on His kingdom if they were ever going to be victorious.

Come back tomorrow and we'll see how it all plays out. You're going to love it.

> To truly live kingdom-minded, we must drive out anything that would pull us away from Christ, quiet our hearts to listen to His voice, and courageously follow His ways, even if no one else does.

Spend a few moments with the Lord in prayer:

- Ask the Lord to reveal to you any idols or bad habits you may be harboring in your life so that you can drive them out.
- Pray that God would speak His kingdom purposes, His will to you through His word and with His Spirit (then spend some moments quieting your soul to listen).
- Beg God for the courage to walk confidently in His ways, no matter what choices those around you are making.

Takeaway Truth – So, as the Holy Spirit says: 'Today, if you hear his voice, do not harden your hearts." Hebrews 3:7-8a

DAY 3: MIGHTY TO SAVE

MAIN TEXT
Judges 4:14-24

The LORD your God is with you, the Mighty Warrior who saves.
He will take great delight in you; in his love he will no longer
rebuke you, but will rejoice over you with singing.
Zephaniah 3:17

The purpose of prayer is to get God's will done. – Samuel Gordon

God is My Shield, My Victory

Over the years I've studied scripture, I shrank back from digging too deep into this story of the bold judge Deborah.

I had this underlying fear that if I learned too much about her, maybe the "be like Deborah!" call would hit too uncomfortably close to home. Content-to-be-a-wallflower personality that I am, I was not interested in this leading lady whose life might make me squirm.

But as we camp out in Judges 4-5, what we find is oh-so-good!

Take a look at verse 14 of chapter 4. Barak and Deborah have rallied the Israelites at Mt. Tabor. Sisera had caught wind of the Israelites' actions and was gathering his own formidable army with 900 of their chariots.

What was the outcome going to be, according to Deborah? Why? (Look at verse 14.)

> As we camp out in Judges 4-5, what we find is oh-so-good!

The Israelites would finally taste victory over Sisera once and for all—because God Himself would march ahead of them! Elohim Shomri—God my protector—went ahead of His people.

We already know what a sad state of affairs God's people found themselves in when Deborah stepped onto the scene, but just so

> "Then Deborah said to Barak, 'Go! This is the day the LORD has given Sisera into your hands. Has not the LORD gone ahead of you?' So Barak went down Mount Tabor, with ten thousand men following him."
>
> JUDGES 4:14

JUST HOW STRONG
WAS SISERA?

As we already learned, according to historians Sisera had access to thousands more soldiers and riders than the Israelites. But just how strong were his chariots? The style of chariots in Sisera's day each included a driver, warrior, and shield bearer. Three soldiers for the price of one. In addition to being made from iron—a resource the Israelites didn't yet have access to—the tank-like weaponry of Sisera would easily have overpowered any foot soldier. That is, unless they had the mighty hand of God on their side.

we remember how incredible the Lord's victory over Sisera's army was, let's take another look.

We get more insight into just how bad things had become if we jump ahead one chapter to Deborah's song, her prayer in Judges 5. When Israel had failed to drive out the foreigners, what had happened, according to Judges 5:8?

Israel chose new gods, then there was war in the city gates. Judges 5:8 (CSB)

Israel had done the unthinkable. They had broken God's first command (Exodus 20:3). They had other gods.

Matthew Henry's Commentary says, "It was their idolatry that provoked God to give them up thus into the hands of their enemies." So often, it's our own decisions that contribute to our demise.

And just like that, they were left vulnerable—without protection. No shield. Why? It was their own choice.

After all, God had made it clear that God was to be their shield. When choosing other gods, the Israelites found themselves not only without God's protection, but actually fighting against Him (Judges 2:15).

Deborah's people had removed themselves from God's protection. Because of their idolatry, He had ceased to fight for them—just like He'd warned.

Does it make you think differently about God's protection to realize that God allowed Israel to remove themselves from it? Why?

But though they'd been without a shield, fighting against God so long, now they were ready to turn back to the God of Abraham, the God of Moses, the God of their descendant David—the One who is a shield to His own.

They had cried out to God for help, and He'd sent kingdom-minded Deborah to lead His people faithfully. She had heard God's will and was not afraid to enter the battle—no matter how daunting the enemy.

Understanding how far Israel had fallen sets the stage for an even more miraculous victory. The Lord was ready to move heaven and earth to help His people. Why? Because they called on Him. Like the special signal summons the superhero, the desperate cries of God's children brought Him swiftly to their aid.

SISERA FEELS THE EARTH MOVE UNDER HIS FEET

Armed with the knowledge and assurance that God would give them victory (and little else) the once-bashful Barak marched Israel's army down Mt. Tabor to meet Sisera's warriors and chariots in the Kishon River valley. And this is where it gets good.

The underdog Israelites suddenly had the mighty hand of God on their side, who was about to impose His will in the battle against Sisera.

Be like a journalist, recording all of the important details of the battle you can find in Judges 4:14-16. Look for the Who, What, Where, When, Why, and How.

Who — Sisera and his army

What —

When —

Where —

Why —

How —

I can read the headline now: "Panic Strikes Canaanites in Sisera's Embarrassing Defeat."

> ## Understanding how far Israel had fallen sets the stage for an even more miraculous victory!
>
> Then Deborah said to Barak, "Go! This is the day the Lord has given Sisera into your hands. Has not the Lord gone ahead of you?" So Barak went down Mount Tabor, with ten thousand men following him. 15 At Barak's advance, the Lord routed Sisera and all his chariots and army by the sword, and Sisera got down from his chariot and fled on foot.
> 16 Barak pursued the chariots and army as far as Harosheth Haggoyim, and all Sisera's troops fell by the sword; not a man was left.
> JUDGES 4:14-16

Week 3 – Deborah: Your Kingdom Come   119

> "The earth trembled, and the cloudy skies poured down rain. The mountains quaked in the presence of the LORD … The kings of Canaan came and fought … but they carried off no silver treasures. The stars fought from heaven. The stars in their orbits fought against Sisera. The Kishon River swept them away … March on with courage, my soul! Then the horses' hooves hammered the ground, the galloping, galloping of Sisera's mighty steeds."
>
> JUDGES 5:4-5, 19-22 (NLT)

In what should have been an easy, squash-those-little-Israelites type of defeat, mighty Sisera saw a major upset. God Himself "threw Sisera and all his chariots and warriors into a panic" (v. 15, NLT). We find even more juicy details about this scene by looking ahead to Deborah's song in Judges 5.

Check out the following verses from Judges 5:4-5, 19-22, paying special attention to the natural phenomena—the sights and sounds of the battle. Mark anything that stands out to you (in the margin, or your own Bible).

My Hero
The God whom the Israelites had once forsaken was now moving heaven and earth on their behalf!

Sisera and his iron chariots were no match for the earthquakes and torrential rains the Lord sent their way. Just as God had jammed the Egyptians' chariot wheels in the muddy bottom of the Red Sea and thrown Pharaoh's army into panicky confusion, so did God use the rains to throw the Canaanite army into a muddy terror.

Horses' hooves pounded the ground, but to no avail as Barak and the Israelites drove Sisera's army back in retreat—killing every last warrior except the mighty Sisera himself, who was forced to make a humiliating escape on foot.

God had once again miraculously saved his people. *Elohim Shomri*—God my protector—went ahead of His people and brought them the against-all-odds victory.

And with this battle one thing becomes clear—the main character of Deborah's story isn't the strong warrior woman after all. The lead role is played by a God who shakes the mountains (Judges 5:5), who fights for us from the heavenly heights (5:20), who sweeps away our enemies with his torrential power (5:21), with whom we rise like the shining sun (5:31), who makes a way for us out of our own folly, if only we will cry out to Him.

The true hero of Deborah's story—and of our story—is God.

KINGDOM COME
In the story of Deborah leading God's people to victory over the Canaanites, we see a clear picture of the beauty of God's

kingdom purposes and plans. Deborah, being a prophetess who heard God's voice, knew what God's will for her people was. And that's just the direction she led her people.

Although Israel's army faced tall odds, wise Deborah knew that with their God moving heaven and earth her people couldn't fail. She could move forward with confidence, the cry of her heart for God's kingdom to come, for His will to be done.

It was clear that God's will for His people was to live in victory in their Promised Land. He had made it painfully clear. And yet, they had fallen to temptation. They had sought a future for themselves outside of God's will—and paid the consequences.

But with their desperate cry to God and Deborah leading them to step forward in obedient faith, God's people again embraced His will. And when they did, the victory was oh-so-sweet!

We know that Deborah wanted God's plans, His kingdom, His will to prevail. She prayed it at the end of her famous song in Judges 5:31 when she said, "So may all your enemies perish, LORD! But may all who love you be like the sun when it rises in its strength."

And in her words ring a strong resemblance to the words of our Savior, Jesus, when He said, "Your kingdom come, your will be done, on earth as it is in heaven" (Matthew 6:10).

Deborah knew her people's victory wasn't about them—it was about God. It was about showing His powerful hand and bringing about His purposes. He wasn't just prospering His people no matter their behavior—we already know He fought against them when they were in rebellion—it was about having His people walk out His kingdom purposes on earth. That's when His glory shone true.

And I wonder what lesson is there for us in this. Because, after all, it's not really about us either, is it?

Are we seeking out God's purposes? Are we walking in obedient kingdom-mindedness? Are we praying Deborah's—or even better—Jesus's type of prayers?

As I look over my prayer list, I can't help but notice the need for a kingdom-minded tune-up. While God wants us to share every concern, every need with Him, He also clearly wants us to cry

Deborah knew her people's victory wasn't about them... it was about His kingdom purposes on earth. That's when His glory shone true.

> We need to tune our ears to hear God's voice… so that our heart's cry in our times of prayer would be, "Oh Lord, your kingdom come! Your will be done."

out to Him in a way that calls for His will to be done. Can I honestly say I've carved out much time for those types of prayers?

I can think of many prayers I've prayed asking for specific outcomes that would be easy or comfortable for me. I can think of many prayers I've prayed that were preoccupied with my little family and what's going on right under my nose. Am I seeking God's kingdom? Or really just my own?

Looking back on my life, I can see moments when I struggled to serve God, to bring His kingdom by my own strength, in my own way, on my own terms. And I failed. I ended up exhausted and defeated.

I remember the end of a season of ministry that felt like a gut punch. A moms' ministry I had initiated was in desperate need of new leadership. I had loved leading the ministry, but I needed a maternity leave as I was ready to give birth. Surely God would help give me success in finding a successor.

But it just wouldn't work. The plans I had put in place when I started the ministry fell through. Scrambling for a plan B, I prayed, and asked (and asked, and asked!) other women to share my vision, and take on leadership of the group temporarily. To no avail.

How could this be? I had been so certain of God's hand in this group. It was a vibrant ministry. It didn't make sense that it had run its course in such a short time—that no one would help carry it forward. But finally, I realized, that's just what God had in mind. If only I had listened sooner.

We need to tune our ears to hear God's voice. To quiet our souls so they are soft to His leading, so that our heart's cry in our times of prayer would be, "Oh Lord, your kingdom come! Your will be done."

> But seek first his kingdom and his righteousness, and all these things will be given to you as well.
>
> MATTHEW 6:33

God is calling us to choose His ways. He's calling us to pray His path—may our Lord grow in my heart those Deborah prayers! I pray He will make my heart beat more and more steadily for His kingdom. That's all I'll ever need anyway. Because if I seek His kingdom first, He's assured me I'll have everything else as well (Matthew 6:33).

Just think of the Israelites we've been studying. In their short-sightedness they walked in their own ways, surrounding themselves with temptations they found irresistible.

They replaced the One True God, their real hope, with counterfeit gods—leaving themselves vulnerable and helpless. They ended up miserably oppressed, and couldn't have ever found their own way out.

The path that made the most sense to them led to destruction (sound familiar? Matthew 7:13). Oops.

If they'd only lived according to God's clear plan—His perfect will. So much trouble and heartache could have been avoided.

And the same is true for us.

God's no kill-joy—His kingdom brings true joy. He's laid out in scripture a clear path for us—one of love, of hope, of obedient surrender to Him. That's our part in His unfolding kingdom. Will we take it? Or walk in our own way? Struggling in our own strength?

We know where true life, true freedom can be found. John 10:10 says, "The thief comes only to steal and kill and destroy; I have come that they may have life, and have it to the full." Let's walk in it.

> Enter through the narrow gate. For wide is the gate and broad is the road that leads to destruction, and many enter through it.
>
> MATTHEW 7:13

> God, our shield, is the real hero of Deborah's story, and He longs to bring kingdom victory in our battles as well.

Spend a few minutes in prayer:

- Ask God to reveal to you any ways you might be walking in rebellion and removing yourself from His protection.
- Praise God for being the shield who shakes heaven and earth to bring His Kingdom Come and to bring His people the underdog victory.
- Spend a few moments in silence, asking the Holy Spirit to show you God's will for the battles you face.

> Takeaway Truth –
> "As for God, His way is perfect; The word of the LORD is proven; He is a shield to all who trust in Him." 2 Samuel 22:31 (NKJV)

GOD-THE-SHIELD COMES THROUGH

See for yourself how God wanted to protect His people: how he'd shield those who sheltered in Him. Copy onto this shield the words that describe God's protection from these verses:

Genesis 15:1 (God's promise to Abraham) "Do not be afraid, Abram. I am your shield, your very great reward."
Deuteronomy 33:29 (Moses blessing Israel before his death) "Blessed are you, Israel! Who is like you, a people saved by the LORD? He is your shield and helper and your glorious sword. Your enemies will cower before you, and you will tread on their heights."
2 Samuel 22:31 (David's song when God delivered him from Saul—this would have been after Deborah's battle) "As for God, his way is perfect: The LORD's word is flawless; he shields all who take refuge in him."
What amazing protection we have in God!

Just this week my family experienced God's protection on our way to my daughter's tumbling program.

We were driving our big, 12-passenger Ford Transit 55 miles-per-hour in the black dark of a late-fall evening. My usually-alert husband was driving us, but somehow didn't see the huge, 12-point buck casually strolling across the road as we made our way down the two-lane country road. Right into our lane.

We plowed into the massive deer.

And even though our van was mangled to the point of being not-drivable, those of us inside had really felt only a small bump.

Had my husband noticed the deer sooner—wildlife enthusiast that he is—he might have slammed on the brakes or swerved our top-heavy van dangerously and unintentionally put us more at risk.

I am so thankful that my husband didn't see the deer the way the rest of us did. It could have been so much worse.

And while it's an inconvenience to have a vehicle in the shop for who-knows how long, and to deal with the paperwork and insurance (not to mention hubby missing my daughter's recital as he waited bone-cold in the vehicle for a tow). I praise God-the-shield for His protection of our lives that cold, dark night.

DAY 4: A SONG OF KINGDOM VICTORY

MAIN TEXT
Judges 5

Hear this, you kings! Listen, you rulers! I, even I, will sing to the LORD; I will praise the LORD, the God of Israel, in song.
Judges 5:3

All true prayer must be offered in full submission to God.
– D.L. Moody

Choosing the True God and King

The Israelites had chosen other gods over the One True God of their ancestors. And as we found, they had paid the price.

Which gods specifically had they chosen, according to Judges 2:13?

1.

2.

They forsook him and served Baal and the Ashtoreths.

Judges 2:13

Israel's struggle had, ironically, come at their own hands. They themselves had chosen foreign gods—and paid the price. Their hardships had originated in their own choice to worship the Canaanite gods (Judges 2:14-15).

False gods are characterized by false promises. And the Canaanite gods were no different.

The Israelites bought into worshipping Baal and Ashtoreth for their promises of power and prosperity. And why wouldn't they? After all, everyone else was doing it.

But the battle of Barak versus Sisera would be an eye-opener for the Israelites and Canaanites alike.

It's especially telling if we note what, in particular, Baal and Ashtoreth's powers were supposed to be. Baal was worshipped by the Canaanites as the god of the cosmos—controlling the moon and stars. He was also their god of storms and severe weather. (Copy this information next to your answer above). Closely related to Baal was Ashtoreth, who was a female god of fertility, war, and storms.

Baal and Ashtoreth were no match for the True God of the Heavens.

But as we learn from Deborah's song in Judges 5, Baal and Ashtoreth were no match for the *True* God of the Heavens—who rules not only the stars in the sky, but the mountains and the waters on earth.

Take a closer look at Deborah's song of prayer and praise, noticing how God showed up in power during the battle of Barak and Sisera—putting Baal and Ashtoreth to shame.

What do you see in the following verses of Judges 5 about God's powerful hand in battle?

Verse 4 –

Verse 5 –

Verse 20 –

Verse 21 –

It became oh-so clear just how powerless were the empty promises of the false gods.

Eye-opening, isn't it? Though the Canaanite gods were supposed to rule over the stars, the weather, and wars, it was the One True God who shook the earth (verse 4), poured down rain (verse 4), rattled the mountains (verse 5), rallied the stars against Sisera (verse 20), and swept away His enemies with torrential floods (verse 21) to win the victory.

And with the powerful intervention of God on behalf of His people, it became oh-so clear just how powerless were the empty promises of the false gods Baal and Ashtoreth.

How foolish of the Israelites to believe the empty promises of such weak, counterfeit gods! How could they have possibly thought that the way to power and prosperity would be through worshipping the small gods of those around them.

And yet, are we not also lured by the gods of our day? Do we not also fall into false beliefs about the path to power and prosperity? The well-trodden path so many of us follow?

   BOLD: Six Praying Women, One Faithful God

I know that I have too many times fallen into silly thinking about my own position of power and prosperity—trusting that my bank account, my husband's job, my property, my education, my earthly citizenship, my relationships will all provide me with the security and prosperity I need.

What foolishness!

Just as silly as trusting in Baal or Ashtoreth is my tendency to trust my money, position, or earthly relationships. Because those things can all be swept away in the blink of an eye.

Just like Sisera and his powerful army were brought to their knees by the mighty hand of the One True God, all the things we falsely trust don't actually offer the security we crave.

But you know the good news? We've got access to the true source of power and prosperity—the kingdom that never ends, and the King of Kings Himself is on our side.

If we only cry out to Him.

We have to understand that all of these things that the world sees as glittering treasures actually pale in comparison to the true treasure of knowing Christ and participating in His kingdom.

Don't get sucked into the temptations and distractions. Don't focus on the temporal and forget the eternal. If you do, you're missing the whole point.

Deborah's prayer illustrates this for us beautifully. Instead of singing her own praises, she praised God, recognizing He was the one she should lift up—rather than taking the credit herself (Judges 5:3).

She prayed God's kingdom come, His will be done on earth and in heaven. She was not lured

THE IDOLS WILL FALL

Those false gods we foolishly look to for our power and prosperity are really paper dolls when compared to the matchless name of Christ. In Him we find the real story about (look up at least two):

Our assets – (Psalm 50:10, 2 Corinthians 9:8)

Our position – (John 1:12-13, Romans 8:17)

Our education – (1 Corinthians 1:19-21, 1 Corinthians 3:18-20)

Our citizenship – (Philippians 3:20)

Our relationships – (Luke 14:25-27)

It's not that we shouldn't have finances, or position, or degrees, or earthly citizenship, or families—that's not the point. The point is that we have to see all of those things—the things we're tempted to worship and depend on for our security and power—for what they really are: temporary, and worthless in comparison to God's kingdom (Philippians 3:7-9).

7 But whatever were gains to me I now consider loss for the sake of Christ. 8 What is more, I consider everything a loss because of the surpassing worth of knowing Christ Jesus my Lord, for whose sake I have lost all things. I consider them garbage, that I may gain Christ 9 and be found in him, not having a righteousness of my own that comes from the law, but that which is through faith in Christ—the righteousness that comes from God on the basis of faith.

PHILIPPIANS 3:7-9

in by the glittering illusion of power and prosperity that Baal and Ashtoreth offered. Let's take a closer look, because there are valuable lessons in this powerful prayer:

To whom does Deborah give credit throughout her song in Judges 5? (Pay special attention to verse 3, 9, 11, 31.)

Deborah is quick to acknowledge God's part in the victory—going so far as to acknowledge His part in the victory time and again.

Israel's leaders were only along for the ride—it was really God who brought the victory!

In fact, Deborah recounts how dysfunctional and disastrous life had become in the days of Israel's disobedience. What do you notice in verses 6-8?

Without God, the Israelites' lives were filled with struggle and defeat. The same can be true in ours. Deborah was reminding her people of the sweet victory of walking with the Lord, in contrast to the turmoil of worshipping other gods.

Who all should remember God's faithfulness, according to Deborah in verses 10-11?

Deborah was saying, "Look, whether you drive a Mercedes, or ride the metro, listen up! God is victorious! And when we walk in His ways, we're victorious too!" Deborah was calling out to all

 BOLD: Six Praying Women, One Faithful God

those in Israel, rich and poor, to remind them of God's kingdom and purposes prevailing.

Those Sheepish Reubenites

Was all Israel united in their defeat of Sisera? Look at Judges 5:13-23 and see what Deborah pointed out. Who came, and who didn't? How did victory come?

Barak and Deborah led only some of God's people in battle. Sadly, many refused to come. While Zebulun and Naphtali and the princes of Issachar came to battle with Barak—Reuben, Gilead, Dan, and Asher were left out. What was holding them back? We don't know if it was fear, lack of faith, complacency, or their immersion in the culture that surrounded them that kept them from joining the battle.

But what we do know is that they missed out, big time.

God didn't need them—after all He shook the earth, moved the mountains, and swept away the enemies in torrents—but can you imagine the experience they could have shared firsthand? God desired to bless them by allowing them to take part in the miraculous battle where He would show up in mighty ways.

But instead of witnessing a battle of cosmic magnitude, one where the God who comes like fire and who moves mountains showed up (Isaiah 64:1-3), where did the tribe of Reuben decide to stay (Judges 5:16)? Why might they have done this (hint: see Numbers 32:1; Matthew 6:21)?

> Oh, that you would rend the heavens and come down, that the mountains would tremble before you! … come down to make your name known to your enemies and cause the nations to quake before you! [3] For when you did awesome things that we did not expect, you came down, and the mountains trembled before you.
>
> ISAIAH 64:1-3

With their sheep! Instead of being part of a historic battle (on the winning team, no less!) some of God's people decided to stay with their sheep. After all, they had lots of them.

And maybe, just maybe those sheep were their only treasure—because Jesus cautioned that if our earthly treasure is too great

> The Reubenites and Gadites, who **had very large herds and flocks,** saw that the lands of Jazer and Gilead were suitable for livestock.
>
> NUMBERS 32:1 (emphasis mine)

> What a tragedy! To miss out on real victory because of the distraction of our earthly treasures.

our hearts will be bent toward the temporal treasure we have here.

What a tragedy! To miss out on real victory—the treasure of heaven—because of the distraction of our earthly treasures and responsibilities.

With hindsight we see this clearly. How foolish of the Reubenites to miss out on their chance to play a part in the battle against Sisera! But do we realize we may be in the very same boat?

Let's take our cues from Deborah's prayer and learn from the mistakes of the Reubenites. Let's take our eyes and our minds and our hearts off of those things that are earthly and temporal and instead fix our eyes on God's kingdom, on the spiritual battles we face, and the spiritual purposes and paths God is calling us to follow.

Take a moment to reflect: how might your earthly responsibilities and treasures be distracting you from God's kingdom purposes in your life? How can you remedy your misplaced priorities?

The most important way that we can pray and live like Deborah is to pray kingdom-minded prayers and live kingdom-minded lives.

No, it's not about rising up to lead (unless God is calling you to that specifically), no, it's not about being outspoken and brazen (though there may be a time for that in serving the Lord and furthering His kingdom)—it's about a sensitivity to God's plans and purposes, and a willingness to follow Him in faith above all else.

Follow Christ, even when it goes against the culture around you.

Follow Christ, even when you feel like the underdog.

Keep Him first, even when it seems foolish from an earthly point of view. God is all about doing audacious things when it serves His purposes. So, get on board. Because, after all, you don't want to miss out on your chance to be a part of His Kingdom Come.

You don't want to be back at the sheepfold when He's calling you to the frontlines.

So what happened to the Reubenites, who pledged they'd join the fight, only to go back on their promises to God? Surely it wasn't that big of a deal, right? Wrong. Look up Numbers 32:23, and copy the second half of the cut-to-the-quick verse here:

> But if you fail to do this, you will be sinning against the Lord; and you may be sure that your sin will find you out.
>
> NUMBERS 32:23

For the Reubenites, keeping their word to God wasn't optional—slacking off meant serious business: sin. And not sin they'd get away from, but sin they'd be called out for in Deborah's famous song of victory.

Battling on Our Knees

What can we learn about bold prayers through Deborah and her song and story? Plenty!

When we listen to God's voice, hearing His kingdom purposes and His will, making them a priority in our lives, we see action!

We see mountains shake. We see our enemies flee. We have a God who goes before us as a shield. We get to be part of something bigger and better than anything we could ever accomplish on our own—why?

Because our King is that good. Because His will and His kingdom and His ways are life!

And I don't know about you, but I don't want to plod through my whole life without really living!

So make your heart's cry, "Your kingdom come, Lord, your will be done."

Cry it out today. Cry it out always.

> When we listen to God's voice, hearing His kingdom purposes and His will, making them a priority in our lives, we see action!

Then listen for His voice, follow Him into the battles He calls you to face—He'll be your shield, and He'll bring His kingdom victory, no matter how impossible it may seem.

Anything else is just a distraction—an empty idol, a false god, a paper doll in comparison to the King of Kings, the God of the cosmos whose holiness and might are unmatched, and who longs to have you draw near.

Come to Him in surrender today.

> We'd be fools to preserve our own paper-doll kingdoms when God is poised to empower us for victorious living as we cry, "Your kingdom come!"

Spend a few moments in prayer:

- Thank God for ruling the heavens, the skies, and the mountains.
- Ask God to give you a heart willing to leave anything behind in seeking His kingdom—no matter how costly the sacrifice.
- Quiet your heart and listen for God's clear call to battle, praying He guides you to face courageously whatever enemies you meet, for His glory.

Takeaway Truth—""*Some trust in chariots and some in horses, but we trust in the name of the LORD our God.*" *Psalm 20:7*

MAIN TEXTS
John 18:33-40
Isaiah 61

DAY 5: KINGDOM VICTORY TODAY

The LORD is with me; I will not be afraid ...The LORD is with me; he is my helper. I look in triumph on my enemies. It is better to take refuge in the LORD than to trust in humans. Psalm 118:6-8

So great is the kingdom of Heaven that the things of this world pale into insignificance. – Matthew Kelly

This week we've learned that Deborah's legendary leadership was characterized by her kingdom-mindedness. Instead of focusing on her own purposes, plans, and glory we see from her interactions with others and her prayer of praise to God that she was preoccupied with His glory and His kingdom.

As a prophetess she had ears to hear the direction God had for her and for His people, and even when it didn't make sense to others, she followed His lead alone.

We saw firsthand in our journey through Judges 4 and 5 how her obedience to God's leading allowed her to witness firsthand God's miraculous, earth-shaking victory and deliverance from Israel's strong-handed oppressors.

Likewise, as a believer in Christ, you've followed God's plans and purposes for your life, turning them over to Him and following His lead. You've seen firsthand how He's gone the distance, giving His very Son to drive out the enemies of sin and death from your own life.

Since you've experienced such a sweet victory in salvation from your spiritual enemies, will you not also continue to follow God's lead, walking in Deborah's same kingdom-mindedness—living for God's purposes, plans, and directions?

Our Reigning King

It's no mystery who should rule the throne of our hearts—God alone. There's a reason we call Him "Lord." Because He is. Our every thought (2 Corinthians 10:5), our every move (1 Corinthians 10:31), our very being should be lived unto God (Ephesians 5:8).

And yet how often do we take back the steering wheel? How often do we draw up our own plans and act as though we know what is best for our lives?

But God has so much more in store for us than we can see or imagine. Just think of Deborah: she could have looked out at the powerful Sisera and sunk into despair. She could have responded with fear when God called her to battle, and refused to rally the troops. She could have taken the power and glory and accolades all for herself.

But instead, she listened to the Lord (Judges 4:6), she followed His lead (Judges 5:14), and she gave Him the rightful glory for His feats (Judges 5).

> But God has so much more in store for us than we can see or imagine.

We ought to be careful to discern God's lead and then boldly charge in!

We ought to do the same, being careful to discern God's leading and then boldly charge in!

But this does not come naturally to us.

Why? Because we expect an earthly king. Much like the Israelites of 1 Samuel 8 or the Jews of Jesus's day we want in-the-flesh, here-and-now leaders. We want visible results.

We are quick to see ourselves as citizens of our respective countries, or to identify ourselves with our denomination. But God's kingdom doesn't work that way.

Let's listen in on a perplexing conversation from John 18 between Jesus and Pilate, just before the crucifixion, to gain some insight into the kingdom to which we belong:

> 33 Pilate then went back inside the palace, summoned Jesus and asked him, "Are you the king of the Jews?"
>
> 34 "Is that your own idea," Jesus asked, "or did others talk to you about me?"
>
> 35 "Am I a Jew?" Pilate replied. "Your own people and chief priests handed you over to me. What is it you have done?"
>
> 36 Jesus said, "My kingdom is not of this world. If it were, my servants would fight to prevent my arrest by the Jewish leaders. But now my kingdom is from another place."
>
> 37 "You are a king, then!" said Pilate.
>
> Jesus answered, "You say that I am a king. In fact, the reason I was born and came into the world is to testify to the truth. Everyone on the side of truth listens to me."
>
> 38 "What is truth?" retorted Pilate. With this he went out again to the Jews gathered there and said, "I find no basis for a charge against him. 39 But it is your custom for me to release to you one prisoner at the time of the Passover. Do you want me to release 'the king of the Jews'?"
>
> 40 They shouted back, "No, not him! Give us Barabbas!"

In this conversation we see a completely befuddled Pilate trying to figure out what in the world is going on with Jesus's relationship to the Jews. He was supposedly their king, but they were the ones crying out in rage for His death.

Jesus was a king, but not the kind of king the Jews wanted. And he ruled a kingdom that didn't look like what they expected.

They wanted power and might and prosperity and success (who doesn't?!). But Jesus told them to expect humility (Mark 9:35), to value meekness (Matthew 6:5), to expect persecution (Matthew 10:22), and even death (Philippians 2:5-8).

It's head-scratching, but true. It's only in losing our lives, in dying to our own pride and power and plans, that we truly live (Matthew 10:39). Everything else is, after all, only an empty pursuit (Ecclesiastes 1:14).

But the kingdom, the victory, the battle doesn't look like what we expect. That is why we must bow to our king; we must give our Lord the power and pray prayers seeking His kingdom and His righteousness first (Matthew 6:33).

Left to our own desires, we will end up striving for prosperity, or power, or comfort, or happiness, or any number of meaningless pursuits—only to find that, in the end, we have only been chasing the wind and have lost the greatest treasure of all (Matthew 6:19-21; Philippians 3:19), our only true treasure, Christ Himself (Romans 8:38-39).

May we never, like the Jews of Jesus's day, foolishly cry out for Barabbas when we could have Jesus.

May we stop grabbing for the prosperity and power and prestige of the world and instead cling to Christ (Philippians 3:7-21). So that in dying to our flesh, we can truly live.

The Playbook is in Our Hands

The task at hand may be daunting. Praying kingdom-minded prayers like Deborah can seem like a strange and foreign pursuit. Especially after learning how backward and upside-down our priorities can be when compared to God's priorities and His kingdom. How can we know His mind, His heart for us? How can we hear from God, like Deborah?

The good news is, we're not alone. God hasn't left us without a guide and without direction. He has given us Himself, in the Holy Spirit (John 14:26). What a relief! But not just that—we've got

> Jesus was a king, but not the kind of king the Jews wanted. And he ruled a kingdom that didn't look like what they expected.

> Every word of God is flawless;
> he is a shield to those who take refuge in him.
>
> PROVERBS 30:5

> The more you feast on the word of God as your daily bread, the more it will nourish and grow kingdom-mindedness in you.

> What we have received is not the spirit of the world, but the Spirit who is from God, so that we may understand what God has freely given us … for, "Who has known the mind of the Lord so as to instruct him?" But we have the mind of Christ.
>
> 1 CORINTHIANS 2:12, 16

the words of our King—the King of Kings. To know Him is to know His heartbeat and His passions, and a great way to do this is to take in His words—regularly. Feed on them (Matthew 4:4). After all, they're perfect (Proverbs 30:5).

The words of our King are so important, your Bible may have even printed them in red so you can find them quickly and easily. Start with any of the Gospels, or fast-track your kingdom-mindedness by heading straight to Jesus's most lengthy, comprehensive sermon that begins in Matthew 5.

At first glance His words seem disorienting and perplexing because they are so incredibly different from our nature, but don't give up. Camp out there and feed on His words regularly for the rest of your life—you won't be sorry.

The more you feast on the word of God as your daily bread, the more it will nourish and grow you in kingdom-mindedness.

After all, you wouldn't want to stray from the only King worth following. There are many loud voices clamoring for your attention—don't forget to quiet your heart and listen for the Voice that is sometimes still and small (1 Kings 19:11-12).

The key to praying Deborah-like prayers—the kingdom-minded prayers that Christ commanded us to pray (Matthew 6:10) is studying the Bible with the aid of the Holy Spirit. Because it is only through the Spirit that we can know the mysterious mind of Christ (Isaiah 40:13).

An Army of Pray-ers

Can you imagine what it might look like if we put this into practice? If, in our prayer lives, we pray God's kingdom come? How incredible would that be?!

I believe that if we, as women of God, would feed on God's word, and be guided by His Spirit to hear His voice, and pray bold, kingdom prayers that we would—just like Deborah—see mountains move and enemies flee before us.

We would see a victory that would be possible no other way but by the power of our God's mighty hand.

I believe that we would see Isaiah 61 come true before our eyes.

According to Isaiah 61 what does God's kingdom come look like?

 BOLD: Six Praying Women, One Faithful God

Verse 1:

Verse 2:

Verse 3:

Verse 4:

Verse 7:

Verse 10:

Verse 11:

Oh, this is good! We don't want to miss this—when we pray God's kingdom come, we see the power of the gospel transform lives. We see **prodigals return home**, those who are **enslaved find freedom**, the **brokenhearted are healed**, those blinded to the truth **see the light**, the **mourning find comfort**—even joy, **ashes transform to beauty**, **despair turns to praise**, spiritual **babies grow into maturity**, **relationships restored**, **shame gives way to joy**, **we'll wear salvation** like clothing, and the all **the earth will bring praise and glory to God**. Anyone else want to see that? I do!

Go to your above list, and ask God to lay on your heart a specific person or situation for each verse. For example, for verse 1 perhaps you can think of someone who needs the gospel, someone who is brokenhearted, or someone who needs freedom from a bondage of sin or addiction. See if you can fill in a specific kingdom request as you pray through the passage. Use your ideas in your prayer times over the next few days and weeks.

Join the battle on your knees.

So may we follow the call of Deborah—of our sweet Savior—to pray God's kingdom come. And may we see it ushered in before our very eyes. Not a kingdom of earthly power and prestige. Not a kingdom of earthly wealth and wisdom—no. A kingdom greater and much better.

A kingdom of transformation, of restoration, of freedom, of healing, of new vision, of joy, of beauty, of praise, of growth, of reconciliation, of salvation—all for the glory of the One who created it all, and who gives us the privilege of witnessing Him usher it in firsthand. Join us in the battle on our knees. I have a feeling heaven and earth are ready to move. It's about to get good.

> Feasting on God's word and letting go of our earthly way of thinking are keys to bold, kingdom-minded prayers.

Share a simple prayer time with the Lord:

- Ask the Lord to increase your appetite for His word, creating a longing in your soul that only feasting on His word will satisfy.
- Pray that as you feast on God's word, He would turn your heart to His kingdom and His will.
- Cry out for God's kingdom to come in your life: in your relationships, your home, your community, your job, your church, your family, your heart—after all, nothing could be better! (Use the above Isaiah 61 exercise to get you started on ideas).

Takeaway Truth—*"This, then, is how you should pray ... your kingdom come, your will be done, on earth as it is in heaven.'" Matthew 6:9a, 10*

Friend, hold fast to the main truth we learn from the life of Deborah, and don't let go:

To pray bold prayers of victory, our hearts' cry must be, "Your Kingdom Come, Your Will Be Done."

Pause for Praise— By plumbing the depths of Deborah's life— her ears to hear God, her unwavering courage, her victory, and her song—we've learned that bold prayers pour forth from a heart that beats for God's kingdom—for His purposes and His will alone. Tuning our ears to hear God's voice instead of the false promises of the world or the evil desires of our hearts puts our priorities right where they belong—on God's kingdom, and on His plans. We saw that the plans of our unshakable God are to shake heaven and earth to bring victory, if only we would join in the kingdom fight! Before you go on with your day, pause for some special time with the King who reigns in majesty. Allow your spirit to praise Him for being the King of your heart. I suggest you watch the lyric video for Chris McClarney's "Speak to the Mountains" on YouTube. If you prefer a more traditional style, try Martin Luther's "A Mighty Fortress is Our God." Allow yourself to be lost in the majesty of the King of Heaven who reigns above all. Think on the perfect plans for His kingdom victory! He is the King of Kings—there is none like Him!

Our Father in heaven
hallowed be Your name,
Your kingdom come,
Your will be done,
on earth as it is in heaven.

GIVE US TODAY
OUR DAILY BREAD

And forgive us our debts,
as we also have forgiven our debtors.
And lead us not into temptation,
but deliver us from the evil one.

DAY 1	UGLY CRY OUT TO GOD
DAY 2	HANNAH HOLDS LOOSELY
DAY 3	CAN'T OUTGIVE GOD
DAY 4	SILENT NO MORE
DAY 5	DAILY BREAD FROM HEAVEN

WEEK FOUR
HANNAH
LOOK ON MY SORROW
& REMEMBER ME

DAY 1: UGLY CRY OUT TO GOD

The LORD is close to the brokenhearted and saves those who are crushed in spirit. Psalm 34:18

God never denies us our hearts' desire except to give us something better. – Elisabeth Elliot

One of the things I love the most about studying the women in scripture is the authentic, unfiltered view we have of their lives. We don't read a Photoshopped, Instagram-worthy, fairy-tale version of their stories—not even close.

We get the nitty-gritty, ugly details: the bad attitudes, the wrong thinking, the unhappy circumstances, the unfortunate relationships, the suffering—we see it all. No pretending or hiding. One hundred percent transparency.

But we also see the hope.

We have a front-row seat to God's work in the lives of the women in scripture; we get the privilege of seeing His purposes, His timing, His redemption, His fingerprints all over their lives—transforming their ugly into beautiful right before us—all for His glory.

What a blessing and an encouragement for us, who may very well be in the midst of our own ugly—whether in our relationships, our circumstances, or even our own heart.

That's why I'm here right now on this sunny Saturday morning, clacking away on this keyboard instead of pushing my babies on the swings (don't worry, there'll be time for that later).

I want to see the hope in it all. I want to see the redemption and the beauty and the growth that come from the pain and the suffering and the hard. I want you and I to know and to remember how He is working it all out, and our part is just to love Him for it, and to follow His lead.

Three's A Crowd

At this point in our study we shift from studying the kingdom-minded prayers of Deborah and Jesus to studying the prayer life

> I want to see the **hope** in it all. I want to see the redemption and the beauty and the growth that come from the pain and the suffering and the hard.

of Hannah. Like Deborah, Hannah also lived in the dark, sad time when the Judges ruled Israel.

Though God's people had reached the Promised Land and had tasted some sweet victories, they still failed to walk in God's ways. As a nation, Israel still struggled.

In the opening lines of 1 Samuel, we learn the family situation of our main character for the week, Hannah. Using the information found in 1 Samuel 1:1-2, what do we know about the following people:

Elkanah-

Hannah-

Peninnah-

Hannah was married to a man named Elkanah, who was also married to a woman named Peninnah—probably because Hannah was childless. It was common practice for a man to take a second wife or to divorce and remarry if he didn't have children with his first wife.

Infertility was thought to be the fault of the wife, and having heirs was extremely important. Children meant helpful labor, furthering the family line, passing down property, being cared for in your old age, a sign of God's divine favor, and—the most desired blessing of all—the chance to be foremother to the Messiah.

So, not only was childless Hannah thought to be defective among the women of her culture, but her future didn't look so bright either.

But one thing Hannah did have was the love of her husband (v. 5). Elkanah loved Hannah and stuck by her. The only problem was that Peninnah decided to pull out all the stops to turn the relationship into a full-on sister-wives rivalry.

Is there an echo in here? This storyline seems oddly familiar...

> There was a certain man from Ramathaim, a Zuphite from the hill country of Ephraim, whose name was Elkanah son of Jeroham, the son of Elihu, the son of Tohu, the son of Zuph, an Ephraimite. [2] He had two wives; one was called Hannah and the other Peninnah. Peninnah had children, but Hannah had none.
>
> 1 SAMUEL 1:1-2

> But to Hannah he gave a double portion because he loved her, and the Lord had closed her womb.
>
> 1 SAMUEL 1:5

We've heard this plot twist time and time again in the Old Testament. History is repeating itself.

A polygamous marriage with too many wives in the household meant problems abounded. We saw it in the case of Sarah and Hagar, Rachel and Leah, and now we see it between Hannah and Peninnah.

One wife has kids (Peninnah), the other doesn't (Hannah). One is loved (Hannah), the other isn't (Peninnah).

And to top it all off, one of them can't resist being nasty to the other, because the grass is always greener on the other side of the fence.

It turns out that not following God's perfect design of one man and one woman for marriage (Genesis 2:24) has some pretty bad consequences (Deuteronomy 17:17) — especially when there's selfishness and sin involved. Go figure!

Kicked When She's Down

In verses 6-7 we see just how bad things got.

Look at the situation, as told in verses 6-7, marking it accordingly:

- circle how Peninnah treated Hannah.
- underline why Peninnah treated Hannah that way.
- put a box around how often this happened.
- underline twice the effect Peninnah's treatment had on Hannah.

Hannah is battered and bruised. Not only is she childless, but she's got a rival for a sister wife that won't let her forget it—ever.

Year after year Hannah's devout family travels to Shiloh to worship at the Tabernacle, and year after year Peninnah's taunting leaves Hannah so sick she can't even bear to eat the rich feast her beloved husband provided for her.

Though they lived in one of Israel's darkest times, Hannah and Elkanah show a rare, dogged devotion to the Lord. Notice how often Hannah and Elkanah traveled to the Tabernacle at Shiloh to worship.

How often did they go, according to verse 3?

> So Peninnah would taunt Hannah and make fun of her because the LORD had kept her from having children. Year after year it was the same—Peninnah would taunt Hannah as they went to the Tabernacle. Each time, Hannah would be reduced to tears and would not even eat."
>
> 1 Samuel 1:6-7 NLT

   BOLD: Six Praying Women, One Faithful God

What did this show about them?

A yearly trek to the Tabernacle to worship shows Elkanah's dedication to God. Hannah was not required to accompany Elkanah on his journey, but we see that she also came year after year—a testament to her own devotion to the Lord.

But Peninnah was not making things easy. Peninnah's harsh treatment made Hannah's suffering acute.

Challenges often reveal our true character, and we'll see this proved true in Hannah's life.

I remember how quickly the blissful, carefree lifestyle of early marriage took a sharp turn when our firstborn child arrived on the scene.

Even though I had dreamed all my life of snuggling my own precious babe in my arms (it was a dream come true!) the sleepless nights and endless needs of our helpless newborn put stress on our honeymoon-esque marriage that hadn't been there before.

Suddenly, I found myself worn out and grumpy with my wonderful husband whom I had waited six long years of dating to marry. What gives?!

The responsibility of raising our children had a way of bringing out my own selfishness in ways I didn't see coming. Our trials lay us bare in a way nothing else can.

From the Depth of Anguish

Elkanah, seeing Hannah's despair, tried to comfort his distraught wife in vain. What comfort did he offer her in verse 8?

Elkanah's plea of, "Don't cry, honey, at least you have me!" fell on deaf ears. Perhaps Hannah knew, deep down, that God had

> Year after year this man went up from his town to worship and sacrifice to the Lord Almighty at Shiloh, where Hophni and Phinehas, the two sons of Eli, were priests of the Lord.
>
> 1 SAMUEL 1:3

> Her husband Elkanah would say to her, "Hannah, why are you weeping? Why don't you eat? Why are you downhearted? Don't I mean more to you than ten sons?"
>
> 1 SAMUEL 1:8

something bigger in store for her than a happy marriage—something of more eternal impact.

Could it be that part of the anguish in Hannah's heart was longing for a child not only for her sake, but for the sake of her people?

Hannah knew their need for an upright leader—a godly man who would hear from the Lord and lead His people wisely. Although she was barren, Hannah trusted that God would provide. She longed to be part of God's redemptive plan to raise up a leader who would see His people through unprecedented times.

And her soul was sick of waiting.

So, what's a girl to do?

Pray bold.

Here's where it starts to get good.

In Hannah's prayers we'll hear an echo of Jesus's words, "Give us today our daily bread"—a gut-wrenchingly honest pleading for provision. We'll go into the details of her exact vows tomorrow, but today we'll look at her heart.

Hannah's prayer was heartfelt. She was soul-sick and the words used to describe her feelings as she prayed at the Tabernacle are emotion-filled.

> Hannah felt bone-deep sorrow, and she didn't hold back her feelings from God.

See what some of the different English versions have to say, or take a few minutes on your Bible app to do some of your own digging:

NIV: deep anguish, weeping bitterly, misery, deeply troubled, great anguish and grief

NKJV: bitterness of soul, wept in anguish, affliction, sorrowful spirit, abundance of complaint and grief

HCSB: deeply hurt, wept with many tears, affliction, depth of anguish and resentment, despondent

These different adjectives paint a picture of the bone-deep sorrow Hannah felt. And she didn't hold back her feelings from God.

My husband is a pastor, and often counsels people to be real with God.

"Tell Him—He can handle it," he says. And it's true. God can handle our ugly feelings—our hurt, our disappointment, our anger, our despair, our resentment, our guilt, our accusations—He wants us to bring it all to Him.

And if we can learn one thing from our time studying Hannah today, may we learn to cry out to the Lord in our hour of need. He hears. And He can handle it.

God invites us to bring all our cares to Him (1 Peter 5:7). We don't need to carry them ourselves. There's freedom in surrendering our burdens to the Lord. We see that in Hannah's life (1 Samuel 1:18) and in our own.

A Striking Family Resemblance

One of my favorite places to go in scripture when I'm feeling all the ugly feelings is to the book of Psalms—because they remind me, I'm normal after all.

So often in the Psalms we see the writers crying out to God with surprising audacity, laying their own hearts bare before the Lord. And in doing so, finding relief, and ultimately a much-needed perspective shift.

As we read the following verses from the Psalms and from the life of Hannah, we can't help but see the striking similarities. Notice the parallels:

> Cry out to the Lord in your hour of need.
> He hears.
> And He can handle it.

Cast all your anxiety on him because he cares for you.

1 PETER 5:7

Hannah	Psalmist
"LORD Almighty, if you will only look on your servant's misery." 1 Samuel 1:11	"May my prayer come before you; turn your ear to my cry." Psalm 88:2
"Remember me, and [don't] forget your servant." 1 Samuel 1:11	"Why do you hide your face and forget our misery?" Psalm 44:24
"Her rival also provoked her severely, to make her miserable, because the LORD had closed her womb." 1 Samuel 1:6 NKJV	"You make us a joke … a laughingstock … my disgrace is before me all day long, and shame has covered my face." Psalm 44:14-15 HCSB
"Therefore she wept and did not eat … she was in bitterness of soul, and prayed to the Lord and wept in anguish." 1 Samuel 1:7, 10 NKJV	"My tears have been my food day and night, while people say to me all day long, 'Where is your God?' These things I remember as I pour out my soul …" Psalm 42:3-4

Eli thought she was drunk [14] and said to her, "How long are you going to stay drunk? Put away your wine."

1 SAMUEL 1:13b-14

These are the men David put in charge of the music in the house of the LORD after the ark came to rest there ... here are the men who served, together with their sons: ... Heman, the musician, the son of Joel, the son of Samuel, the son of Elkanah, ... the son of Korah ..."
1 CHRONICLES 6:31, 33-34, 37
(emphasis mine)

Both the psalmist and Hannah cried out for God to be attentive to their suffering. They both called on God to remember them. They both suffered humiliation, and wept bitterly, to the point of not being able to eat. What a powerful example of bringing it to all God.

People may not understand your pain—just look at Hannah. When she cried out to God in her misery, the priest Eli thought she was drunk (1 Samuel 1:14). But God understands. He sees you. He knows you. He wants you to bring Him your pain, because He will provide.

There is more than just honest, strong emotion that connects Hannah to the psalmists whose words we read above—there are genes. This is so cool.

I'll show you.

Read the verses from 1 Chronicles 6, in the margin. Look for important names—the last two especially:

Now look in your Bible at the headings of the psalms that paralleled Hannah's heart cry, paying special attention to their authors (Psalm 42, 44, 88). Do you see it?

The very psalms that echoed Hannah's cries of misery, her pleas for God's attentiveness, are penned by her descendants.

Hannah and Elkanah's future son Samuel, God's great provision to a land in need of godly leadership, would also be the grandfather to some of the temple worship leaders. How cool is that?!

These worship leaders prayed some of the very same types of brutally honest prayers, crying out to God just like their foremother Hannah. Prayers that are preserved in scripture today. Scriptures that help us to remember God is our refuge (Psalm 46:1), that we can be still and know He's God (Psalm 46:10), and that as the deer pants for water, our souls thirst for Him (Psalm 42:1). Pretty amazing, isn't it?

And just like Hannah (and her great-grandson) prayed in anguish, so did our Lord. Jesus, too, knows what it's like to hurt.

Read about Jesus's intense prayer in Luke 22:39-46. What do you notice from this passage?

Anguish drove Jesus to pray more fervently. And God sent an angel from heaven to strengthen Him. God didn't take Jesus out of the trial—it wasn't the Father's plan to remove Jesus from His difficult situation. But God heard Jesus's intense prayers and sustained Him.

My own anguish has likewise driven me to pray. I remember discovering something upsetting a child had hidden from me. It shook my world. To the undiscerning child's judgement, it had seemed innocent enough, but I could already see the spiritual war being waged against my child. I saw the enemy gaining a foothold. How could this be?!

This mama bear wasn't going to have it. This situation was a new one for me, something I never anticipated, but I blared the praise music that proclaims victory in battle while my soul cried out in anguish. Suddenly nothing else seemed nearly as important. I prayed bold like never before.

Anguish drives us to fervent prayer.

We can be like Hannah. We can be like Jesus. When our outlook seems grim, when we are in the depths of despair, when there doesn't seem to be hope, we can pour out our hearts to God. And when we do, we will likely end up just like Hannah. Verse 18 of 1 Samuel 1 says that after she "poured out her soul before the Lord," (v. 15) her "face was no longer sad" (v. 18, NKJV).

When we give it to God, suddenly things look different.

Then we too, like Hannah's descendants, the sons of Korah, can have a perspective shift. We can proclaim with new strength,

> *"Why am I discouraged? Why is my heart so sad? I will put my hope in God! I will praise him again—my Savior and my God!" (Psalm 42:11 NLT)*

> And being in anguish, he prayed more earnestly, and his sweat was like drops of blood falling to the ground.
>
> Luke 22:44

Let your anguish drive you to fervent prayer.

Let your anguish and despair drive you to the Lord in earnest prayer because He wants to hear it all from you–the good, the bad, the ugly.

Spend a few moments with the Lord in prayer:

- Thank God for always being ready to listen, attentive to what you have to say.
- Bring to God anything ugly, uncomfortable, or difficult, without hesitation—knowing that He can handle it.
- Ask God to graciously give you a perspective shift where needed in your life, heart, or attitude—like we so often see in the Psalms—so that you can have a face that is "no longer sad" like Hannah.

Takeaway Truth—" *The eyes of the LORD are on the righteous, and his ears are attentive to their cry.*" *Psalm 34:15*

MAIN TEXT
1 Samuel 1:9-28

DAY 2: HANNAH HOLDS ON LOOSELY

My God will meet all your needs. He will meet them in keeping with his wonderful riches. These riches come to you because you belong to Christ Jesus. Philippians 4:19 NIrV

I must pour out my heart ... and more than that, I must trust in the Spirit to speak the unutterable groanings of my spirit, when my lips cannot actually express all the emotions of my heart.
- Charles Spurgeon

As a devout follower of God, how could Hannah help but notice her people's depravity?

A Broken Heart and a Contrite Spirit

Yesterday we talked about how grieved Hannah was over her childlessness. Both her situation and the situation of her people were not good. She was barren—and her rival Peninnah wouldn't let her live it down.

On top of her own personal heartache, she had a burden for her people. As a devout follower of God, how could she help but notice her people's depravity? They were experiencing spiritual barrenness.

They were living in the long-awaited Promised Land, and yet still struggling with idolatry and defeat. Plagued by corruption and nefarious leadership, they were in desperate need of godly men to pave the way for their people to live the victorious lives God had intended for them.

But Hannah was wise. She did not wallow in her self-pity. She did not carry these burdens on her own—she carried them to God, and left them at His feet.

We learned that Hannah's deep anguish motivated her prayer life and—much like Christ—fueled her intense, heartfelt prayers. Sometimes God uses our periods of waiting and suffering to mold our hearts into ones that are ready to pray earnestly and rightly to Him.

Today we'll pick apart Hannah's prayer and put it under the microscope to see just what her earnest prayers contained.

After the taunting of Peninnah over her childlessness, after the pleas of her husband to find fulfillment in his love, after lacking an appetite to feast at the sacrificial meal, Hannah took her own sacrifice—a broken and contrite spirit (Psalm 51:17) to the Lord.

> The greatest sacrifice you want is a broken spirit. God, you will gladly accept a heart that is broken because of sadness over sin.
>
> Psalm 51:17 NIrV

Hannah's time of suffering had formed in her heart godly attitudes and purposes we'd be wise to emulate. The first of which is her posture of running desperately to a providing God.

When we go to God in our hour of need, pleading with Him brokenheartedly, He meets us there.

How did Hannah address God? Look at 1 Samuel 1:11 in the margin, underlining how she described God.

What does Hannah's way of describing God have to do with His ability to provide for her (and your) needs?

> And she made a vow, saying, "Lord Almighty, if you will only look on your servant's misery and remember me, and not forget your servant but give her a son, then I will give him to the Lord for all the days of his life, and no razor will ever be used on his head."
>
> 1 SAMUEL 1:11

Look at another once-childless person in Genesis 17:1. How does God describe Himself to Abraham in this verse?

Hannah had reached the end of herself. She knew God was omnipotent—that He was strong enough to command even heaven's armies. And she also knew her own place. Look at 1 Samuel 1:11 in the margin, circling how Hannah speaks of herself.

> When Abram was ninety-nine years old, the LORD appeared to him and said, "I am God Almighty."
>
> GENESIS 17:1

Not only did Hannah recognize God's almighty power—but she also recognized her own humble relationship to Him.

In the same way, the Spirit helps us in our weakness. We do not know what we ought to pray for, but the Spirit himself intercedes for us through wordless groans. [27] And he who searches our hearts knows the mind of the Spirit, because the Spirit intercedes for God's people in accordance with the will of God.

Romans 8:26-27

Not only did Hannah recognize God's almighty power—but she also recognized her own humble relationship to Him. In the original Hebrew, Hannah refers to herself three times as God's "amah," His maidservant.

In case you think this might be an honorable position, it is not. It's the same label Sarah spat out with disdain as she spoke of Hagar to Abraham in Genesis 21. To be a maidservant is to be lowly.

When you cry out to God in your despair and desperation, it's good to recognize that God is mighty—and you are not. When you realize that God's arm is strong and powerful and sufficient, it puts your perspective in the right place. You can bring your heartbroken pleas before the Lord, resting in His power and sufficiency to provide. You might be in need, but He is enough, so you can boldly go to Him.

Sometimes your brokenness runs so deep, you don't even have words. But God the Good Provider knows this, and has gone before you to make provision even for the times you are so beside yourself you don't know what to say.

How comforting that our weak, broken souls can be laid bare before God, and He has given us a beautiful gift in helping us when we feel we can hardly even pray. What a good God!

And just as David knew in Psalm 51:17 that God desires a sacrifice of a broken and contrite spirit, Hannah knew He wouldn't despise her request. She pled to almighty God.

When we come to the end of ourselves, when we know our own brokenness and insufficiency, we can cry out to the sufficient provider, the almighty God for help. And the good news is—He's the same Father God who sees, the same Holy God who parts waters, the same King who rules in majesty—our God provides.

His Lavishness Fills Our Lack

Hannah's time spent waiting on the Lord hadn't diminished her faith in His provision—if anything, it seemed to make her that much surer He'd provide. It bolstered her faith.

So sure was Hannah of God's answer to her begging, that she told God her plan of what would happen with the son He'd provide. She'd give him back to God.

These are Hannah's words: "I will give him to the Lord for all the days of his life, and no razor will ever be used on his head."

In a way, this seems counterintuitive to me. Hannah was so desperate for a son, so heartbroken over her inability to conceive that she couldn't even bear to go through the motions of her daily life—she couldn't even eat.

And yet, I believe her heartbrokenness over her people's spiritual health was just as deep. She knew her people needed a godly leader, and she knew that her future son could be God's provision for His spiritually needy children.

Hannah knew that the son she'd bear was not only God's provision for her—removing her shameful childlessness, but an even greater provision for His people—removing their spiritual barrenness.

The bottom line was—Hannah knew her son was never hers to begin with—he belonged to God.

Turn to Psalm 50:10. What does it say about our property?

But if we hope for what we do not yet have, we wait for it patiently.

Romans 8:25

> Hannah knew her son was never hers to begin with—he belonged to God.

Much in the same way that the wild beasts are God's, so are the cattle of a thousand farms. Though we may think of property as belonging to us, the whole earth is the Lord's (Psalm 24:1). Hannah knew this truth, and lived it.

Does realizing that God has anything and everything at His disposal affect your prayer life? Why or why not?

"For every animal of the forest is mine, and the cattle on a thousand hills."
Psalm 50:10

The earth is the LORD's, and everything in it, the world, and all who live in it.
Psalm 24:1

For me, knowing that God owns it all helps me to pray bold. Why? Because if all things are at God's disposal, then why not ask for what I need?

My children are much (much!) more likely to ask for chocolate if they see it in my hand or catch a scent of it on my breath. (This is why so many moms resort to eating it in the closet on the sly!)

But I think there's something telling about that—when we remind ourselves that the earth is the Lord's and everything in it, our boldness in prayer is increased. We can ask Him for anything because we know He is able to give us anything!

In the same way, we pray more rightly when we realize that even after God has granted our request, what He's given us is still rightly His—and that we can and should live generously. We'll cover the benefits and joys of a generous lifestyle more in tomorrow's lesson.

Hold on Loose

> [Jacob] struggled with the angel and overcame him; he wept and begged for his favor. He found him at Bethel and talked with him there.
>
> Hosea 12:4

Though Hannah tearfully petitioned God for a child, much like Jacob wept and begged for God's blessing (Hosea 12:4), the blessing was not for her to keep for herself. She'd give her beloved son Samuel back to God, and His people would benefit, for eternity.

And in Hannah's sweet spirit, we see an example of what our own attitudes should be in response to God's miraculous provision in our lives. Though we are only God's lowly servants, we receive from our mighty God lavish provision for our needs. And all we have is His!

You can hold loosely to that which God has entrusted to you.

You can hold loosely to that which God has entrusted to you, knowing it came from Him, and ultimately it belongs to Him. Jesus taught in Matthew 10:8, "Freely you have received; freely give." If God has provided what you've got already, then certainly He has the power to supply all your needs (Philippians 4:19).

Hannah's prayer is a beautiful, paradoxical picture of a woman who is feeling desperation and heartbreak, crying out to the God she knows will provide—while at the same time proclaiming confidently that she'll offer right back to Him what's rightfully His. What a beautiful dance of faith!

Hannah's dedication of her child to the Lord reflected her understanding that children are from God to begin with (Psalm 127:3). She displayed the same attitude of holding them loosely that we see from Job who, when told his own children had died, proclaimed remarkably: "The LORD gave and the LORD has taken away; may the name of the LORD be praised." (Job 1:21).

She also understood the privilege a life of service to the Lord really is. As her great-grandson would one day pen in the Psalms, "Better is one day in your courts than a thousand elsewhere; I would rather be a doorkeeper in the house of my God than dwell in the tents of the wicked" Psalm 84:10.

And because of Hannah's devotion to the Lord and her desire to dedicate Samuel's life to serving Him, Samuel would grow up to serve the Lord as the godly leader His people so desperately needed.

Eternal Benefits

The pastor life gets a pretty bad rap. As a pastor's wife, I've heard it firsthand. People tend to focus so much on the challenges—the criticisms, the sometimes-paltry pay, the difficult personalities, the church politics—that they lose sight of the privileged life that it is. Of course, there are difficulties and discouragements. Any job comes with those. But a lifestyle of serving the Lord also comes with blessings beyond compare.

Life in ministry is often accompanied by timely displays of support - "I'm praying for you," "Thank you," an encouraging note, a thoughtful gift; not to mention myriad chances to pour out your life serving others, crying out in prayer, and studying God's word.

A pastor's family likely won't store up the treasures a highly successful businessman would—but the heavenly treasures are longer-lasting. As my husband explained to a potential employee in an interview, the job benefits are eternal!

And so it would be with Hannah's much-awaited son Samuel— the benefit of offering him back to God carried significance far beyond his lifespan. So she gave her baby back to God.

Trust the Lord for your needs. And as you freely receive, freely give. Offer it all right back to Him and watch as He pours out even more than you ever imagined. In tomorrow's reading we'll

NO SHAVE, NO HAIRCUT, NO PROBLEM

You may be wondering why Hannah told the Lord in her prayer that, "no razor will ever be used on [her son's] head," 1 Samuel 1:11.

The vow that Hannah was making to the Lord was called a Nazirite vow. This meant that her son would be dedicated to the Lord. As an outward symbol of his or her devotion to the Lord, these individuals would not cut their hair. Additionally, during their time of dedication to the Lord the Nazirite would not drink wine and would not touch a dead body (Numbers 6).

Some were Nazirites for a limited amount of time. Samuel was dedicated by Hannah to be a Nazirite for his entire life. Other notable Nazirites were Samson and John the Baptist.

Children are a gift from the LORD; they are a reward from him.

Psalm 127:3 NLT

see this very concept playing out in Hannah's life. And it's going to be good.

> Part of praying bold and trusting in God the Provider is realizing that everything is His—both before and after He graciously gives it to us.

Spend a few moments in prayer:

- Thank the Lord for gladly accepting your heart—even when all you can give Him is a broken one—asking the Spirit to help you in your weakness, groaning on your behalf when you don't have words.
- Ask God to help you live and pray bold, standing on the truth that everything is His, and holding to it loosely, like Hannah.
- Pray that God would allow you to live a life with eternity in mind, beefing up your heavenly bank account for His glory.

Takeaway Truth – *"In the same way, the Spirit helps us in our weakness. We do not know what we ought to pray for, but the Spirit himself intercedes for us through wordless groans."* Romans 8:26

MAIN TEXT
1 Samuel 2:12-36

DAY 3: YOU CAN'T OUTGIVE GOD

Give generously to [the poor] and do so without a grudging heart; then because of this the LORD your God will bless you in all your work and in everything you put your hand to.
Deuteronomy 15:10

[Prayer is] the breath of our spiritual life
– John Wesley

All Shook Up

Have you ever met a person that you just couldn't outgive? Every time you host them for dinner, you receive two return invitations. Every time you bake them a treat, your pan comes back filled with a reciprocal baked good. Every gift brings about something more in return. They even write a "Thank you" note for a "Thank you" note! These people are outlandishly generous and impossible to outgive.

God's like that.

No matter how much we give to God, we can't possibly outgive Him. It's one of the reasons we can hold so loosely to what He gives. It's the principle Jesus taught in Luke 6:38. Read it here.

I heard a missionary teach this verse with a powerful illustration. He was talking about how God's blessing pressed down and shaken together would be miraculously more than we can picture. He used the illustration of the tribal people he worked with and how they stored rice.

He said they would fill containers with rice all the way up to the brim. The container would seem to be completely full and overflowing—not able to hold even one grain more.

Then, they shook it.

As the wise tribal people shook and tapped their rice storage containers, something happened. The rice settled into every nook and cranny of space within the container, and suddenly there was room for more.

The same is true of God's blessing in our lives. He presses down and shakes it together so that He can fill every nook and cranny of our lives with His blessing—until it's overflowing.

This can be hard to see because God's timing doesn't always line up with ours. For example, we may tithe, expecting that God will instantly replenish our bank account—but God's generosity doesn't work that way. It doesn't happen how and when we expect.

Sometimes He waits until our hour of need to show up. I remember tight times financially, when somehow, in miraculous, unexplained ways our bank account never hit rock bottom. Like the widow of Zarephath's oil that never ran dry (1 Kings 17:16), every time we checked, there was money there.

But other times we may not see His spilling-over blessing earthside.

> Give, and it will be given to you. A good measure, pressed down, shaken together and running over, will be poured into your lap. For with the measure you use, it will be measured to you.
>
> Luke 6:38

He presses down and shakes it together so that He can fill every nook and cranny of our lives with His blessing—until it's overflowing.

In God's sovereignty He sees the whole picture. He's got a better plan than ours. Our investment in God's kingdom often reaps rewards for eternity (Matthew 6:20) that we only see a shadow of today.

Good things come to those who wait.

HIGH PRIESTS REACH A NEW LOW

So far this week as we've studied Hannah's life and prayer, we've observed a woman who was both heartbroken and hopeful—a woman of desperation and confidence.

Following her lead in bold prayer, we see firsthand the benefits of bringing our brokenness to God: that He wants us to bring our ugly thoughts, feelings, and circumstances to Him—and when we do, we leave changed.

The gift Hannah's people desperately needed was a godly leader. The time of the judges had been a tumultuous one filled with idolatry and rebellion, darkness and corruption. The outlook didn't look much better for the future either.

> Year after year this man went up from his town to worship and sacrifice to the LORD Almighty at Shiloh, where Hophni and Phinehas, the two sons of Eli, were priests of the LORD.
>
> 1 SAMUEL 1:3

Look at 1 Samuel 1:3. Who were the leaders of God's people during Hannah's day? Circle their names.

Let's dig into scripture further to see exactly what Hophni and Phinehas, the sons of Eli, were like. Look up the following verses and note what they were up to:

1 Samuel 2:12—

1 Samuel 2:13-17—

1 Samuel 2:22—

The English translations of the verse 12 description of Hophni and Phinehas would almost be funny if their sins weren't so grievous. They're described in different translations as, "scoundrels," "dishonest," "sons of Belial," "evil men," "worthless," "wicked," "good-for-nothing," "nothing but trouble," "corrupt," "useless," "sons of worthlessness."

BOLD: Six Praying Women, One Faithful God

These guys were losers.

So what's the bottom line? What really was their sin?

Selfishness.

Verses 13-17 of 1 Samuel 2 describe in detail just how selfish these high priests of Israel were. While the sacrifice of meat was being offered to the Lord, these corrupt priests would have the meat removed from the pot—fat still on it—and have a nice pot-roast for themselves.

Maybe you'd think this isn't a very big deal, to partake of the sacrificial meat as a roast instead of boiled. After all, God provided the meat for the priests' sustenance, right?

Wrong. It's a *very* big deal. This was deliberate disobedience. Why? Because God clearly outlined the process for the priests to cook and eat the meat. There was a very specific way it was to be done.

Leviticus 7 gives the details. See the recipe for a successful sacrifice in the margin.

What is to happen to the fat? The thigh and breast?

Feel the Burn

Who knew fat burning was biblical?! Ha! Your Jazzercise instructor will be happy to know.

But all joking aside, why would God want the fat to be burned, and the priest to eat only the thigh and breast (without the fat)? Backtrack a few verses in Leviticus 7 to verse 25: "Anyone who eats the fat of an animal from which a food offering may be presented to the LORD must be cut off from their people."

So Hophni and Phineas are doing waaaaaay more than just clogging their arteries by eating the fat of the temple sacrifices. They—Israel's high priests by birth—are directly disobeying the specific instructions God had given

The LORD said to Moses, [29] "Say to the Israelites: 'Anyone who brings a fellowship offering to the LORD is to bring part of it as their sacrifice to the LORD. [30] With their own hands they are to present the food offering to the LORD; they are to bring the fat, together with the breast, and wave the breast before the LORD as a wave offering. [31] **The priest shall burn the fat** on the altar, but the breast belongs to Aaron and his sons. [32] You are to give the right thigh of your fellowship offerings to the priest as a contribution. [33] The son of Aaron who offers the blood and the fat of the fellowship offering shall have the right thigh as his share. [34] From the fellowship offerings of the Israelites, **I have taken the breast that is waved and the thigh that is presented and have given them to Aaron the priest and his sons** as their perpetual share from the Israelites'" (emphasis added).

LEVITICUS 7:28b-34

If the person said to him, "Let the fat be burned first, and then take whatever you want," the servant [of the priest] would answer, "No, hand it over now; if you don't, I'll take it by force." [17] This sin of the young men was very great in the Lord's sight, for they were treating the Lord's offering with contempt.

1 SAMUEL 2:16-17

Moses. What an abysmal example of leadership! They even go so far as to demand the fat when those bringing the offerings try to protest (1 Samuel 2:16).

Like the leaders described in Isaiah 56:11: "They are dogs with mighty appetites; they never have enough. They are shepherds who lack understanding; they all turn to their own way, they seek their own gain."

Unlike Hannah, who was willing to give the good gifts that God had given her right back to Him, the sons of Eli were caught up in serving their own appetites rather than God (Romans 16:18). Their self-centered actions reveal their selfish attitudes of ungratefulness at God's provision. Instead of being thankful for the way that God provided for them as priests (Leviticus 7:34), they greedily snatched for more. No wonder Hannah was sick over her people's situation!

This would be bad enough behavior coming from any follower of God, but the high priests?! Yikes!

The high priests had reached a new low. And it wasn't just their bellies' lust for roast. They wanted even more.

Dirty Rotten Scoundrels in the Temple

Now Eli, who was very old, heard about everything his sons were doing to all Israel and how they slept with the women who served at the entrance to the tent of meeting.

2 SAMUEL 2:22

Remember the troubling news we read in 2 Samuel 2:22? Hophni and Phineas were also sleeping around. But not with just anyone—with the women who served at the temple.

Modern-day versions of this same sad story are frequent—big-time pastor falls from grace with a woman serving in his own congregation—and the name of God and His church both get a black eye.

It is tragic enough when any man breaks his marriage vows and commits adultery. But when a man whose life is dedicated to serving God preys on a woman who is also supposed to be serving the Lord, it is an especially hard, especially far fall.

These men are like the leaders described in Jeremiah 5:7-9: "[They] have forsaken me ... I supplied all their needs, yet they committed adultery ... They are well-fed, lusty stallions, each neighing for another man's wife. Should I not punish them for this?' declares the LORD."

Hebrews 10:26-27 says, "If we deliberately keep on sinning after we have received the knowledge of the truth, no sacrifice for sins is left, but only a fearful expectation of judgment and of raging fire that will consume the enemies of God." How ironic that no sacrifice would be left for Hophni and Phinehas, who sinned by desecrating sacrifices to God.

But maybe these stories of eating fat-marbled roasts and lusting after temple workers just don't seem to hit home. After all, we're living after Christ's once-for-all, amazing-grace sacrifice. Our scarlet sins have become white as snow. It's not like we make yearly temple trips, like Hannah. Or have instructions to burn the fat like Hophni.

But before we turn the page and move on to the next passage of scripture, let's look again.

Because I have an inkling that there's something here for us, in the middle of this story of corruption and lust—though at first it may not seem so.

Let's take it back to our topic for this week: bold prayers for God's provision. How can two incredibly selfish high priests teach us about God's provision?

Well, we know that Eli's wicked sons Hophni and Phinehas were greedily taking from the offerings. God had provided plenty for them, but it wasn't good enough.

Boiled meat? Bleh. They wanted roast.

They wouldn't do things God's way. So instead of following the Lord, they followed their fleshly cravings and tried to satisfy themselves in the ways they thought were best—first with fatty foods, and when that wasn't enough, with sensual indulgence.

They didn't have regard for God's ways, but gratified their wayward hungers instead of acting out God's plan.

Is it so far-fetched to think we might sometimes do the same? Have there been times in your life when God's clear instructions didn't seem good enough? Or when satisfying one sinful desire led to another? What does this reveal about our view of God as good provider? Write some thoughts in the margin.

No sacrifice would be left for Hophni and Phinehas, who sinned by desecrating sacrifices to God.

Or perhaps a lack of faith in God's provision caused you to grab at what He's given and keep it for yourself? What might God have called you to offer to Him that you've instead kept back, white-knuckling it for yourself? How does this reflect your view of Him as provider?

This scarcity mindset can come out in all different ways—big and small.

It can rear its ugly head when we see the panhandler on the corner with his hand-scrawled cardboard sign, and we puff up with pride, thinking, "How lazy! Why doesn't he just get a job?!" Instead of compassionately asking God if He wants us to help.

Or when we're asked to give our time and we think to ourselves, "I've had such a hard week! I need time to rest and recharge with some self-care. God wouldn't possibly want me to help with that. I'd burn out." Instead of asking the Lord if He'd have us serve.

Or when we feel God tugging on our heartstrings to provide a home for a needy soul, and think, "I don't have room, food, or even enough mental energy to spare. I couldn't possibly (host that person/take in that foster kid/have that baby); I have a hard enough time with my family and household already! We don't have room for them." What if the Lord is asking you to open your heart and home to one more of His image bearers?

Could it be that the scarcity mindset is holding *you* back?

Could it be that the scarcity mindset is holding *you* back?

Let's allow the story of Hophni and Phinehas to be a wake-up call for the very real consequences of our own selfish, scarcity mindset. (Spoiler alert: they died because of their sin. Yikes! See 1 Samuel 2:34.)

Instead, let's emulate Hannah.

Let's be women who—despite not yet having all the desires God places on our hearts fulfilled—cry out to Him in earnest faith anyway.

Let's be women who call out to the great Provider, knowing that as He pours out His blessing—pressed down, shaken together, running over—we can't possibly outgive Him.

Because who would want some fatty meat and some temporary, fleshly temptation when you could instead have the One who provides real satisfaction? Why preserve our own failing flesh and follow our own wicked hearts?

No thanks! I want to echo the psalmist's cry when he says, "My flesh and my heart may fail, but God is the strength of my heart and my portion forever" (Psalm 73:26).

God provides.

We find all we need—all we could ever really want—in Him.

> When our view of God's provision is small, our actions are ugly and selfish—but when we see clearly God's good, more-than-enough provision, it prompts in our hearts a generosity that fills our lives to overflowing with God's blessings.

Spend a few moments in prayer:

- Ask God to root out any distorted, small view of God's provision lurking in your heart and replace it with appreciation for God's spilling-over blessing.
- Pray that God would cultivate in you a heart of generosity, ready to turn back to Him any blessing you receive.
- Plead with the Lord to use whatever you offer back to Him like He used Hannah's precious Samuel, to be a light breaking through the darkness and bringing God's purposes in our generation.

Takeaway Truth – *"A generous person will prosper; whoever refreshes others will be refreshed." Proverbs 11:25*

DAY 4: SILENT NO MORE

MAIN TEXT:
1 Samuel 1:19-2:10

> We find all we need— all we could ever really want—in Him.

Open my lips, Lord, and my mouth will declare your praise.
Psalm 51:15

There's no question God will duck, no battle He can't win, no topic He doesn't know. You can't make Him uncomfortable. You can't push Him too hard. So go ahead, hit Him with your best shot. - Karon Phillips Goodman

When Salvation Looks Like a Baby with a Mom Who Prays Bold

We've been focusing on the wickedness of Eli's sons, and rightly so. But I don't want us to miss some important interruptions in the story of their sad, sordid affairs.

Take note of the following verses: glimmers of hope in 1 Samuel 2. What do they tell us about Hannah's son Samuel? Jot some notes after each set of verses below:

GLIMMERS OF HOPE IN 1 SAMUEL 2

[11] Then Elkanah went home to Ramah, but the boy ministered before the LORD under Eli the priest.

[18] But Samuel was ministering before the LORD—a boy wearing a linen ephod. [19] Each year his mother made him a little robe and took it to him when she went up with her husband to offer the annual sacrifice. [20] Eli would bless Elkanah and his wife, saying, "May the LORD give you children by this woman to take the place of the one she prayed for and gave to the LORD." Then they would go home. [21] And the LORD was gracious to Hannah; she gave birth to three sons and two daughters. Meanwhile, the boy Samuel grew up in the presence of the LORD.

[26] And the boy Samuel continued to grow in stature and in favor with the LORD and with people. (Notice a striking similarity in this verse to Luke 2:52, "And Jesus grew in wisdom and stature, and in favor with God and man.")

BOLD: Six Praying Women, One Faithful God

These important interruptions to the depressing story of Eli's wicked sons speak of God's great provision for His people—the prophet Samuel.

Hannah had dedicated Samuel's life to serving God, and that's just what he did. Samuel grew up at the temple and served under Eli.

And Hannah's beautiful gift to God—the answer to her desperate prayers—the long-awaited, much-loved boy—grew into a powerful, incredibly important man of God.

God's grace that should have fallen on the sons of the high priest, Eli, instead came upon the nobody, country-bumpkin Samuel who had—you guessed it—a mom who prayed.

He was **the only man to serve as prophet** (1 Samuel 3:19-20), **priest** (1 Samuel 2:18), **and judge** (1 Samuel 7:15). **He led Israel victoriously** against their enemies the Philistines (1 Samuel 7:13), **anointed Israel's first king**, Saul (1 Samuel 10:1) **as well as the beloved King David** (1 Samuel 16:13), and **likely wrote the very scriptures we're reading** today.

It all began with a woman who wasn't afraid to call out to God in her heartbroken time of need. A woman who was so confident in the One who would provide that before He could even bless her, she turned the blessing back to Him—and in doing so blessed her entire nation.

Not only that, but through the prophet Samuel would shine glimmers of the best prophet, priest, and king God's people would ever have—God's own "faithful priest," Jesus Christ (1 Samuel 2:35).

In the same way that God provided baby Samuel during a time when godly leadership was desperately needed, God would provide Jesus at the time when the light of salvation was desperately needed in our dark world. Hallelujah!

So cry out to God in your broken places of need. Cry out in desperation to the One who provides enough—the pressed-down, shaken-together, running-over, audacious blessing of enough!

He will respond as you boldly call out to Him: "Give me this day my daily bread!" Just be ready to offer it all right back to Him in

IN PRIESTLY FASHION
You may think that Samuel's clothing was of zero importance in this story.
You'd be wrong. Our God is, after all, a God of details.
Samuel wore the priestly ephod, a special piece of clothing. It was a garment that often contained the Urim and Thummim, used to discern God's will. So wearing the ephod was significant—it meant you were a priest who would receive important direction from God Himself.

It all began with a woman who wasn't afraid to call out to God in her heartbroken time of need.

your next breath. And watch as His blessings pour out, overflowing into the lives of others as well.

What a change we see in Hannah as we read her prayer of praise in 1 Samuel 2. The woman—once too heartbroken to eat, too upset to pray out loud (1 Samuel 1:15), seemingly drunk with sorrow—now had come full-circle, and cried out to God in a prayer proclaiming His praise!

Hannah had experienced the miraculous. Her once-barren womb brought forth new life—a life that meant spiritual renewal for her people. She'd birthed her son Samuel, weaned him, and dedicated him to God.

Hannah made good on her pledge, returning her young son to the Lord. But this time, she couldn't keep her prayers in—she had to sing God's praises.

Parallel Prayers

When it comes to praying, Mary, mother of Christ, was a student of Hannah. As you study their prayers, you can't help but notice the parallels and similarities between Hannah's prayer of praise in 1 Samuel 2 and Mary's Magnificat in Luke 1:46-55.

Hannah's confidence in God the good Provider shone through her beautiful, prophetic words of prayer and praise in 1 Samuel 2. And Hannah was right on.

Right off the bat in Hannah's prayer, we see that she absolutely had the proper perspective in her praise. Rather than sing the praises of the gift she'd been given—a beautiful son who'd grow to serve and to save God's people, bringing them back to Him—Hannah wisely praised the Giver of all good things.

Hannah knew deep down into her very bones that the greatest gift, the greatest provision she could ever receive, was God Himself. That's why she proclaimed, "My heart rejoices in the LORD … for I delight in your deliverance" (1 Samuel 2:1), a phrase that would be all-but-exactly repeated hundreds of years later, by a similarly humble, grateful mother Mary, who said, "My soul glorifies the Lord, and my spirit rejoices in God my Savior" (Luke 1:46-47).

Hannah and Mary both knew that rather than sing of the glory of the gift, they should praise the Giver, the Source of all good

> Rather than sing the praises of the gift she'd been given Hannah wisely praised the Giver of all good things.

BOLD: Six Praying Women, One Faithful God

things. Why did Hannah proclaim God worthy of praise? Copy down the evidence of the following in Hannah's prayer in 1 Samuel 2:1-10

-There is no one like Him. None can compare to our God.

"Who is God except the Lord?"
2 SAMUEL 22:32 (NLT)

-He is powerful. Mighty and solid as a rock (Deuteronomy 32:31).

For their rock is not like our Rock, as even our enemies concede.
DEUTERONOMY 32:31

-He is wise. God "understands all hearts" (Proverbs 24:12 NLT).

Does not he who weighs the heart perceive it?
Does not he who guards your life know it?
PROVERBS 24:12

-He is just. Hannah recounts all the ways God brings about justice, by exalting the humble and humbling those who exalt themselves.

All those who exalt themselves will be humbled, and those who humble themselves will be exalted"
LUKE 18:14

And though Hannah's Samuel was only a small boy, only just starting his service to the Lord, Hannah's words smacked of her supreme confidence in the God who laid the very foundations of the earth (v. 8), wisely understanding that the One who founded it all could certainly be counted on (Job 38:4).

In her words we see not only the prophecies that would come about in her own day, but echoes of the best Gift to come, many years later.

> *"He will guard the feet of his faithful servants, but the wicked will be silenced in the place of darkness … The Most High will thunder from heaven; the LORD will judge the ends of the earth. 'He will give strength to his king and exalt the horn of his anointed'" 1 Samuel 2:9-10.*

Messiah means "anointed one." This one is hard to miss—Hannah's talking about Jesus.

Like Hannah's prophetic words about God's anointed Messiah, Psalm 2 also tells of this anointed one, (Psalm 2:2). In this psalm we learn that God will raise up Christ, His Son, giving Him power over all the earth. Psalm 2:7-8, "I will proclaim the LORD's decree: He said to me, 'You are my son; today I have become your father. Ask me, and I will make the nations your inheritance, the ends of the earth your possession.'"

Jesus has a way of showing up all through scripture—whether we expect Him there or not.

Jesus has a way of showing up all through scripture—whether we expect Him there or not. And I hope we see Him with fresh eyes each time, never taking Him for granted.

I love how my children help me see things in new ways—I remember watching a Christmas play my children put together for our family. The older ones donned bathrobes and one playing Mary put the beachball under her shirt. As they made their way to the inn, the characters replayed the familiar conversation.

"There's no room for you at the inn!" the innkeeper said.

But my two-year-old was moved by the situation. He left his place in the audience to intervene. Brows knit in perplexion, he approached the innkeeper, hands on his hips, and inquired, "Why not?!"

Oh, the wonder of seeing Jesus with fresh eyes.

Praising God for the Already, Not Yet

In Hannah's prayers we see this amazing example of a woman who both at once prayed in desperation and confidence. We see a woman who, having dipped her toes in the beginning of a blessing for herself, foresaw the coming tidal wave of overwhelming blessing for all humanity.

The woman who couldn't hold back her tears, became the woman who couldn't hold back her praise. Not just for what God had done, but for what she was certain He was yet to do.

She knew that God her Great Provider was like no other—powerful, wise, just, and the creator who was sovereign over the whole earth.

If only I had the eyes of Hannah.

So often, I am nearsighted.

Yes, I wear eyeglasses (well, contact lenses really), but if only that were the extent of my nearsightedness. No, unfortunately I am spiritually nearsighted as well.

I seem to have eyes only for the "here and now" all too often. I can't always see beyond the end of my nose.

Like Paul, I complain of the thorn in my flesh, mercifully placed there by a God who wants to see me grow in grace. Sometimes my ears are too full of my own complaints to hear His gentle, "my grace is sufficient for you, for my power is made perfect in weakness" (2 Corinthians 12:9).

Or like Jonah, I am bitter about what I have or don't have—throwing a hissy fit about what I've lost, as if it were ever mine to begin with (Jonah 4:1-10). Acting as if I were entitled to comfortable circumstances of my own design, instead of remembering, as I once knew, "But you, LORD my God, brought my life up from the pit" (Jonah 2:6). And that's, after all, all that matters anyway.

Or I read about the rich young man who fell on his knees before Jesus, eager to know how to gain eternal life—and I hear Jesus's answer, "Go, sell everything you have and give to the poor, and you will have treasure in heaven. Then come, follow me" (Mark 10:21). And my fingers tighten their grip on my treasures. Sheesh.

"Certainly God can't want all of me?! That seems like too much!" I think. Too quickly I forget Jesus's promise that "everyone who has left houses or brothers or sisters or father or mother or wife or children or fields for my sake will receive a hundred times as much and will inherit eternal life" (Matthew 19:29). And that if I want to truly live, I must release my grip.

Friends, I pray that we would stop being so nearsighted and instead see clearly!

Like the first time my nearsighted eyes wore glasses and saw the beautiful intricacy of each distant leaf of a tree dancing in the breeze—that we may have the vision to see clearly every far-off detail of God's eternal work, like Hannah. Let's trade in our nearsighted prayers for ones that see far, praising God for the

Let's trade in our nearsighted prayers for ones that see far.

Hannah so rightly proclaimed, "there is no Rock like our God."

goodness He's yet to give and for the goodness of the Giver Himself.

Truly we only see a dim shadow of what is to come. We only see traces of the eternal work God is doing, but like Hannah, we should cry out in praise to the God who sees fit to do so much more than we can ever see or comprehend.

Thinking about your need, and God as Provider, in what ways might you be shortsighted? How could having a vision for God's eternal work help you to trust more deeply and pray more boldly for God's provision?

We must boldly cry out to Him in our time of need, counting on the Good Provider, turning back to Him the gifts He gives, and praising Him for who He is and the great He is going to do—the things too wonderful for us to imagine.

After all, as Hannah so rightly proclaimed, "there is no Rock like our God" (1 Samuel 2:2).

> Because of God's sovereignty as our Provider, we can praise Him confidently for who He is and for what He has yet to do.

Spend some time with the Lord in prayer:

- Revisit God's character qualities that Hannah pointed out in her prayer in 1 Samuel 2, thanking God for who He is—Provider of all good things.
- Praise God boldly for the good He's going to do, that He hasn't done yet.
- Ask the Lord to reveal to you any areas you may be nearsighted in, and beg Him to correct your vision

Takeaway Truth – *"I will be fully satisfied as with the richest of foods; with singing lips my mouth will praise you." Psalm 63:5*

DAY 5: THE DAILY BREAD OF LIFE

MAIN TEXTS:
1 Samuel 2:1-11
Matthew 7:7-11
Luke 18:1-7

So don't you think God will surely give justice to his chosen people who cry out to him day and night? Will he keep putting them off? Luke 18:7 (NLT)

Brokenness causes us to persevere in prayer" -Tim Walter

The Big Ask

We've all known that kid that Just. Keeps. Asking.

They ask for a movie at bedtime. They ask for sweets at the check-out register. They ask for special outings and the latest toys and technology. We've all witnessed the power of a kid endlessly asking for something. Even the steadiest of parents can get worn thin with enough asking. Kids know—sometimes persistence pays.

There's something about asking.

In Jesus's prayer in Matthew 6:11, He teaches us to say, "Give us today our daily bread." He wants us to ask—to cry out daily for the Great Provider to meet our needs.

Just as Hannah cried out to God in her heartbroken despair, we should daily cry to God in our own desperation. After all, are we not desperate without Him?

Let's press further into this idea of asking.

Later in that very same sermon, Jesus expands this idea of the "big ask." Read His words in the margin, marking the words and ideas you see as significant.

What do you notice? First of all, we are called to be diligent askers. Keep on asking. Keep on searching. Keep on knocking. Jesus tells a story in Luke 18 about a persistent widow who repeatedly went to a judge and pleaded her case. Even though he initially refused, the woman Just. Kept. Asking.

And guess what? He caved.

"Keep on asking, and you will receive what you ask for. Keep on seeking, and you will find. Keep on knocking, and the door will be opened to you. For everyone who asks, receives. Everyone who seeks, finds. And to everyone who knocks, the door will be opened.
"You parents–if your children ask for a loaf of bread, do you give them a stone instead? Or if they ask for a fish, do you give them a snake? Of course not! So if you sinful people know how to give good gifts to your children, how much more will your heavenly Father give good gifts to those who ask him."

MATTHEW 7:7-11, NLT

The judge said, "Even though I don't fear God or care what people think, yet because this widow keeps bothering me, I will see that she gets justice" (vv. 4-5).

He gave in. She was nearly driving him bonkers, and even though he could care less about doing the right thing or impressing others, he gave in to her request. Pretty crazy, huh?

But those of you who have a raised a preschooler know just what that feels like ... am I right? One can only endure the request for candy, TV, or whatever the desired treat is, for so long. With the right amount of persistence on our children's part, we are bound to have moments of weakness where even the most strong-willed of us cave to their persistent request.

But why did Jesus tell His disciples this story? Check out verse 1 of Luke 18. What's the explanation?

> Then Jesus told his disciples a parable to show them that they should always pray and not give up.
> LUKE 18:1

The "give us our daily bread" that Jesus is calling us to is not some halfhearted, namby-pamby asking. It's a full-on, determined, gut-wrenching, asking-with-the-persistence-of-a-toddler-who-wants-a-lollipop kind of asking.

And why keep on asking? Because our Good God gives!

God our Father is a way better giver than we are. We cave to our sweet-toothed kids when they ask us the 37th time for our Kit Kat candy bar, but the good gifts God gives are so much sweeter!

If imperfect people like us can give good things, how much more can our Provider.

But so many times the good gifts God gives are not the ones we had in mind:

We might want the latest, greatest minivan with all the bells and whistles (I'm a mom, folks!), but get a used one with rust and an automatic door that doesn't work. But the van runs.

We might want flawless, tanned skin, but get skin with pimples, moles, freckles, and wrinkles instead. But the skin protects our bodies.

 BOLD: Six Praying Women, One Faithful God

We might want our kid to be the valedictorian and the MVP on the championship-winning team, but get a kid that struggles with algebra and can't throw a strike to save her life. But she is a blessing.

We might want a dream job we love, with great pay, tons of vacation, and awesome co-workers, but get a steady job with modest benefits and co-workers we can occasionally tolerate. But it pays the bills.

Just because we want something, doesn't mean we need it.

A few years ago, I wanted a bigger house.

We had seven children at the time, and our modest starter home was just about bursting at the seams—at least I thought so.

I scanned the online listings for the perfect house, but it just never seemed to work out. The locations weren't right, or they were out of our price range, or someone else got an offer in before we did.

We were stuck.

And though I was thankful for our home, every time I was getting ready for church in our teeny half bath, running an extension cord from the kitchen for the hairdryer, and dropping my mascara in the toilet for the third time while stowing my makeup in the cupboard above, I just couldn't help but feel a bit sorry for myself (First World problems, right?). Didn't God know that we needed more space?

But we serve a God who knows our needs better than we know them ourselves!

Because my need to learn contentment despite our small home was greater than my need for a luxurious master bath with a jacuzzi tub. And my children's need to befriend the neighborhood kids was greater than their need for a big backyard.

And right there, despite the laughably small bedrooms and the postage-stamp front yard, our family learned to giggle and play and grow and thrive and trust in God the Provider. We saw Him meet our every need, time and again.

And I wouldn't trade it for anything.

> But we serve a God who knows our needs better than we know them ourselves!

Thankfully our good Provider—the One who set this earth in motion—both loves us better and knows us better than we know ourselves. He's so good.

Bread From Heaven

We've spent the week picking apart Hannah's diligent prayers to her faithful God. We've seen in her life His miraculous provision: **bold prayers heard,** an **empty womb filled,** a **godly leader given** for a wayward people, a **way made for the Messiah.** God came through big-time when Hannah cried out to Him in her need. He provided.

Let's take a moment to reflect on God's provision through the gift of Samuel to his praying mama. Flip back to 1 Samuel 2 and take a moment to absorb all of the beautiful ways Hannah highlighted what God had done.

In the space provided, pick some of the phrases from the passage that speak to you the most. Write them with fancy calligraphy, or if you're a doodler, sketch the scenes—whatever is most meaningful to you. Just take some time to reflect on God's gifts, according to Hannah.

Some of the phrases and imagery I love are: God rescuing us (v. 1), the weak made strong (v. 4), the hungry filled (v. 5), the barren are fruitful (v. 5), God raising us up (v. 6), God exalting and caring for the needy (vv. 7-8), sending Christ (v. 10).

The ways God provided in Hannah's life were astounding. But this wasn't the Provider's first rodeo. Not by a longshot! God had a track record of giving His people just what they needed at just the right time.

In Exodus 16—just a few short verses after Miriam had led her people in praising the powerful God who miraculously delivered His people from their enemies through the Red Sea—we find His people complaining about their need.

God had led them out of their miserable slavery by His mighty arm, but now all they could see was the wilderness they found themselves in. And they were hangry.

God took care of His ungrateful people, raining down bread from heaven—sending manna to fill bellies that once grumbled in more ways than one. And Aaron stored up a jar of God's miraculous, heaven-sent bread, so future generations could see and remember the God who gave even to grumblers (Exodus 16:32).

> Moses said, "This is what the Lord has commanded: 'Take an omer of manna and keep it for the generations to come, so they can see the bread I gave you to eat in the wilderness when I brought you out of Egypt.'"
>
> EXODUS 16:32

When God gave His people manna, His purpose was bigger than proving He was a Heavenly Baker. What was it, according to Deuteronomy 8:3 (bonus points if you know where this verse is quoted in the New Testament)?

> He humbled you, causing you to hunger and then feeding you with manna, which neither you nor your ancestors had known, to teach you that man does not live on bread alone but on every word that comes from the mouth of the Lord.
>
> DEUTERONOMY 8:3

When God provided manna to His people, the lesson He really wanted to teach was that their groaning bellies weren't their deepest hunger. Their empty stomachs weren't their most pressing need—what they really needed was Him.

> Their empty stomachs weren't their most pressing need—what they really needed was Him.

Because even though they ate their fill each day with the sweet bread from heaven, sure enough, the pangs of hunger would return the next day.

And the next.

And the next.

But one day, God would send a much better bread from heaven—the One who would meet our every need—One to fill every nook and cranny of our empty souls. And we'd never be hungry again.

Fast forward a few thousand years and hungry crowds pressed in on Jesus (John 6). After all, He'd been known to take a boy's modest lunch and feed a whole mob, with leftovers to boot.

So again, God's followers came to Him with grumbling bellies and grumbling mouths.

They thought they needed bread, but Jesus pointed out their real need.

> *"Jesus said to them, 'Very truly I tell you, it is not Moses who has given you the bread from heaven, but it is my Father who gives you the true bread from heaven. For the bread of God is the bread that comes down from heaven and gives life to the world ... I am the bread of life. Whoever comes to me will never go hungry, and whoever believes in me will never be thirsty ... This is the bread that came down from heaven. Your ancestors ate manna and died, but whoever feeds on this bread will live forever."*
> *John 6:32-33, 35, 58*

The Giver is the Gift

The most beautiful provision that our good God gives isn't bread to satisfy our hunger. It's not a once-empty womb now filled. It's not a godly leader, or a full bank account, or a beautiful home, or a clean bill of health.

The best gift of God is Jesus Christ Himself.

Because it's only through Him that our true hunger is satisfied. It's only through Him that we are truly fruitful and led and prosperous and sheltered and whole and healed. Earthly gifts are temporary. They fade away, but God's best gift is eternal (Romans 6:23); everything else fades in comparison.

So, let's ask for Him today! And just like once-barren, desperately needy Hannah ended up bearing six children (1 Samuel 2:21) and receiving in her son Samuel the godly leader her people needed, may we beg God to meet our own true need.

Because He'll fill every hunger, every ache, every lonely longing with a pressed-down, shaken-together, overflowing abundance of life, meeting our every need through His Son.

When we boldly bring our broken hearts to Him, begging persistently for His good gifts, willing to give all back to Him, He will give us the best gift of all—Jesus.

Give us today our daily bread, Lord. Give us our bread from heaven. We're hungry, Lord. We're asking you boldly to give us what we need.

Give us You.

> Because God the Provider knows our needs, He has given the best gift—Jesus Christ Himself.

Spend a few moments in prayer:

- Ask God to help you persist in prayer—not giving up, no matter how you feel.
- Pray that God would open your eyes to His provision in your life, so you, like Hannah, can lift up a heart of praise to the Provider.
- Thank God for the Bread of Heaven, Christ Himself, asking God to increase your hunger for the only Bread that satisfies.

Takeaway Truth – *"For there is one God and one mediator between God and mankind, the man Christ Jesus."* 1 Timothy 2:5

He'll fill every hunger, every ache, every lonely longing.

Sisters, hold tight to our main takeaway from the life and prayers of Hannah:

To pray bold, we must pour out our heartbreak to God, and watch in amazement as He provides our every need.

Pause for Praise — In hearing the woes and wails of heartbroken Hannah and following her tale from despair to delight, we've learned that God can handle our heartbreak—so we might as well boldly bring it all to Him.

In fact, we learned that we can come to God with persistent desperation, pleading with Him to provide, while at the same time confident He will. And when we do, we change—like Hannah, our faces are no longer sad. When we allow God to correct our nearsightedness, we receive His provision with joy and contentment—offering His blessing right back to Him.

We learned that our prayers can be emboldened with the knowledge that He owns it all, and that He calls us to persistently ask of Him. We also learned that the best provision the Giver has given is Himself, the hunger-satisfying Bread of Heaven, Jesus—all we could ever want or truly need.

Before you go on with your day, pause for some special time with God the Provider who owns it all and pours out His blessings upon us. I suggest you watch the lyric video for "Jireh" by Elevation Worship. If you prefer a more traditional style, try "Come Thou Fount" instead.

Get caught up in God's goodness, bringing any gnawing need, any aching hunger, any heartbreak you have to the God who longs to provide from His abundance.

He is everything we need!

This, then, is how you should pray:

Our Father in heaven
hallowed be Your name,
Your kingdom come,
Your will be done,
on earth as it is in heaven.
Give us today our daily bread.

AND FORGIVE US OUR DEBTS

as we also have forgiven our debtors.
And lead us not into temptation,
but deliver us from the evil one.

DAY 1	I OWE IT ALL TO HIM
DAY 2	ACTIONS SPEAK
DAY 3	IT'S A DOG-EAT-DOG WORLD
DAY 4	THE SEAT IN THE TOMB
DAY 5	RUN AND TELL THAT

WEEK FIVE

MARY MAGDALENE

I HAVE SEEN THE LORD

DAY 1: I OWE IT ALL TO HIM

Listen to my cry, for I am in desperate need; rescue me from those who pursue me, for they are too strong for me.
Psalm 142:6

[Prayer] is the grand means of drawing near to God.
- John Wesley

Credit cards, student debt, mortgages, car loans, HELOCs—our options to indebt ourselves are plenty. Creditors are clamoring to get us on the hook.

And yet, our greatest liability of all, no matter how many thousands we owe—is our debt of sin, paid by Christ alone.

"And forgive us our debts, as we also have forgiven our debtors"

MATTHEW 6:12

In Jesus's words, the Lord's Prayer of Matthew 6, He taught us to pray, "And forgive us our debts, as we also have forgiven our debtors" Matthew 6:12. Following His example means asking for forgiveness.

Desperate for Deliverance

We ended our study of Hannah by acknowledging that even more important than our day-to-day sustenance, God's greatest provision is Himself—Father, Son, and Spirit. Our Bread of Heaven is what we desperately need more than anything. And we should ask daily for God to provide our every need: both the physical and spiritual.

This week we wade into thus-far uncharted waters for this study by looking in-depth at a woman who walked with God in the flesh daily.

She literally talked with Jesus. Mary Magdalene.

Mary Magdalene knew Jesus in a very special way—she holds a privileged spot of closeness to Christ that only a handful of women were able to experience on earth. And today, we'll start by focusing on her condition when Jesus met her.

Mary Magdalene wasn't a woman who had it all together when she met Jesus—far from it!

What was she like when Jesus met her? Examine Luke 8:1-3, marking any words or ideas you find significant:

Soon afterward Jesus began a tour of the nearby towns and villages, preaching and announcing the Good News about the Kingdom of God. He took his twelve disciples with him, along with some women who had been cured of evil spirits and diseases. Among them were Mary Magdalene, from whom he had cast out seven demons; Joanna, the wife of Chuza, Herod's business manager; Susanna; and many others who were contributing from their own resources to support Jesus and his disciples. (NLT)

Mary Magdalene was a woman who suffered affliction at the hands of evil spirits. Whether it was mental anguish, physical ailment, spiritual suffering, or all of the above, we don't know the specifics—but what we do know is that her situation was desperate.

In fact, she had not one, but **seven**—a number that shows how completely awful her situation was without Jesus (Matthew 12:45). But we also know that Christ delivered her! And because of that deliverance, Jesus became Mary Magdalene's ride or die, His most devout roadie—travelling with Him to the very end, as we'll see throughout this week of study.

Oppressed By Darkness

Let's do our homework to see what demon possession was like, according to scripture. Look at the following verses and note what you find. Mark the verses or jot down your thoughts in the margins:

Matthew 15:22
A Canaanite woman from that vicinity came to him, crying out, "Lord, Son of David, have mercy on me! My daughter is demon-possessed and suffering terribly."

Mark 5:5
Night and day among the tombs and in the hills he would cry out and cut himself with stones.

Matthew 9:32-33
32 While they were going out, a man who was demon-possessed and could not talk was brought to Jesus. 33 And when the demon was driven out, the man who had been mute spoke. The crowd was amazed and said, "Nothing like this has ever been seen in Israel."

When an impure spirit comes out of a person, it goes through arid places seeking rest and does not find it. 44 Then it says, 'I will return to the house I left.' When it arrives, it finds the house unoccupied, swept clean and put in order. 45 Then it goes and takes with it seven other spirits more wicked than itself, and they go in and live there. And the final condition of that person is worse than the first.

Matthew 12:43-45

Matthew 8:28

28 When he arrived at the other side in the region of the Gadarenes, two demon-possessed men coming from the tombs met him. They were so violent that no one could pass that way.

The demon-possessed "suffered terribly" (Matthew 15:22). Demons were known to cause people to harm themselves (Mark 5:5), sometimes keeping them from being able to speak (Matthew 9:32-33) and causing them to be violent toward others (Matthew 8:28).

Demon possession was a miserable condition that rendered its victims helpless and drove them to become outcasts. Prior to meeting Jesus, Mary Magdalene was utterly hopeless—she was in a bad way.

Encountering Jesus and experiencing the deliverance only God could provide was a game-changer for Mary Magdalene. No longer oppressed and distressed by evil powers, Mary Magdalene was given a new lease on life—and we can see from our readings this week that she jumped at the chance to join Jesus's crew, getting a front row seat to all Jesus was doing in Galilee.

And through our study this week, we will see in the life of Mary Magdalene one who—because of her precious deliverance from peril—loved and clung to her sweet Savior.

Clearing the Confusion and Loving Much

Mary Magdalene is often thought of in pop culture as one or more of the nameless adulterous, sinful women who encountered Jesus in scripture. It doesn't help that ministries who rescue such women are sometimes called "Magdala Houses."

But scholars now agree that these women weren't likely Mary Magdalene. In the scriptures, Mary Magdalene's defining condition is her former possession by evil spirits—not adulterous, sexual sin. To be true, Mary Magdalene felt her connection to Jesus keenly, and owed Him a debt of gratitude. But this gratitude sprung from her deliverance from evil spirits, according to Bible scholars.

> Encountering Jesus and experiencing the deliverance only God could provide was a game-changer for Mary Magdalene.

And yet, let's take a moment to pause and press into the story of one of these sinful women—not because she's Mary Magdalene, but because—in a sense—she is all of us.

We have all missed the mark (Romans 3:23). We have all been adulterous in the sense that we've loved something else more than God—whether our own selves or our comfort, our security, our relationships, our plans—whatever we've chosen over Him.

If you haven't already, review the story of the sinful woman who anointed Jesus. It's found in Luke 7:36-50.

Notice what you can about each character, taking notes below:

The Pharisee (Simon):

Jesus:

The immoral woman:

The woman loved Jesus deeply—and brought Him a costly gift. Her profound experience with God is reflected in her actions—her anointing of Christ, her weeping, her bowing, the wiping with her hair—her expression of humility and faith is beautiful.

Women weren't invited to banquets in Jesus's day—they weren't permitted to eat with, or even to speak with, Jewish rabbis in public. And yet, this woman loved Jesus so boldly that she went against the customs of her day; she took Jesus up on the invitation He had just made for

MARY THE MOST MENTIONED

Mary Magdalene rose to a position like no other on Jesus's ministry team. She is the single most mentioned among His female followers, and is referred to more often than most of Jesus's twelve male disciples. In fact, **she is found 14 times in scripture**, the majority of which list her first among the women who travelled with Christ.

In our bra-burning, post-women's-lib culture, we can't begin to grasp how significant it was that Mary Magdalene is Jesus's principal female follower. We're used to women serving as elected officials and CEOs for major companies. The ancient world was completely different. For any woman it was a long shot to get the chance to learn directly from a rabbi–it just wasn't done.

And yet, it is clear from the early verses of Luke 8 that women made up a substantial group of Jesus's first followers–not only leaving high positions for Him, but spending their wealth in support of Him.

weary people to come to Him. She knew she'd been forgiven much, and she showed much love in return.

Jesus revealed in this passage that He is both a Prophet and God—shocking and upsetting the Pharisees there. Knowing Simon's heart revealed that Jesus was a prophet. Forgiving the woman based on her faith revealed Christ's deity. The words of Jesus in this encounter reveal that we owe a debt of sin, and God's forgiveness frees us from that debt. And when we realize just how much a debt we've been forgiven, we respond with much love.

The Pharisee Simon was a religious man—he knew all the rules and was too big for his britches. Though he thought he saw the situation clearly, Simon was spiritually blind. Simon thought he had things figured out. He thought Jesus wouldn't have time for a woman like her. *Ain't nobody got time for that!* was Simon's sourpuss attitude. Holier-than-thou Simon couldn't help but be grumpy about the sinful woman approaching Jesus—how dare she?!

Know-it-alls!! We've all met someone who, by some crazy notion, thinks they know our situation better than we do and has expert advice, right? Like the lady in the grocery store checkout who, seeing that you're purchasing bacon, tells you, "You know, bacon clogs your arteries; that's a heart attack waiting to happen!"

Or the man, seeing your pregnant belly and your three other small children, offers, "There's no sense in bringing more kids into this awful world! You should just stop already! Don't you know how babies are made?!"

Or the angry driver you accidentally pulled out in front of, who calls out expletives, honking his horn, and hollering out his open window, "You should go back to driver's ed and learn how to drive!"

Or maybe the know-it-all is too often you, or me. Are we so busy looking around at the behavior, decisions, and lifestyles of others—making a running commentary on their every little move—that we're too busy to see our own shortcomings?

Jesus read Simon's mind, knew his bad attitude, and addressed it head-on. Don't you just love how Jesus knew him so well? Even

We owe a debt of sin, and God's forgiveness frees us from that debt.

though Simon the Pharisee was really just thinking to himself how sinful the woman was, Jesus answered his thoughts with an eye-opening story—of debts big and small, and love big and small.

Then comes the real zinger, Luke 7:47: "I tell you, her sins—and they are many—have been forgiven, so she has shown me much love. But a person who is forgiven little shows only little love" (NLT).

The irony of the situation, of course, is that Simon saw himself as wise. He saw himself as devout—but really, it was the sinful woman who showed true wisdom in accepting Jesus's forgiveness in faith. From our vantage point it seems so simple, right?

But not everyone accepts the grace freely given them—no matter how simple it may seem.

In 1830 a man named George Wilson was arrested and sentenced to be hanged for mail theft. In a happy turn of events for George, President Andrew Jackson pardoned him. You'd think Wilson would respond with a happy dance, right? Wrong!

For reasons no one knows (but maybe Simon the Pharisee understands), George Wilson would not accept his pardon. He'd been offered forgiveness for his debt to society—and he didn't take hold of it (!). Supreme Court Chief Justice John Marshall ruled that, if not accepted by the prisoner, the pardon was invalid, declaring, "George Wilson must be hanged!" And according to some sources, that's just what happened.

Don't make the same mistake of foolish Mr. Wilson! Be pardoned. Take hold of the forgiveness found in Christ.

Let's pause for some reflection on our own lives. Which character can you relate to the most? The woman, knowing she'd been forgiven much, who lavished her love on Christ? Or the prideful Pharisee, too busy looking down his nose at others to see his own faults?

Unfortunately, these interactions with Christ hit all too close to home for me. Too often I forget just how much I've been forgiven. Too often I get hung up on comparing myself to others and puffing up in pride when I feel I've come out on top. Too often I fall prey to the lie that I can be good on my own. Too often

> I tell you, her sins—and they are many—have been forgiven, so she has shown me much love. But a person who is forgiven little shows only little love.
>
> LUKE 7:47 (NLT)

> Too often I'm spiritually blind, unable to see my flaws, and to grasp just how deeply Christ has forgiven me.

I'm spiritually blind, unable to see my flaws, and to grasp just how deeply Christ has forgiven me. Cringe.

Perhaps I haven't committed adultery like the woman the crowds were ready to stone in John 8, but neither can I cast a stone. For I am not without sin—I've committed spiritual adultery, loving other things more than God.

I've been guilty of loving the wrong things too much—myself, my family, my health, my comfort, my financial security. But all who come to God in repentance have been forgiven this spiritual adultery.

> We all owe Christ a debt of gratitude, because He is the one who has forgiven us all, delivered us from our bondage. Now we are free to love much.

Thankfully you and I have been forgiven much. Lord, help us to love much!

While the sinful woman who anointed Christ likely wasn't Mary Magdalene, these two women show a strong resemblance to one another. How?

They loved much! They loved the One who had delivered them from their evil oppressors—whether their evil spirits, or their evil slave masters of sin. As we walk through Mary Magdalene's story this week we'll see for ourselves just how much her love for Christ was.

We'll see how she, just like the sinful woman of Luke 7, is a beautiful example of a woman living forgiven, a life poured out at the feet of Christ. A life lived with the heart cry of "Forgive us our debts!" then reflecting the freedom of forgiveness in steadfast love.

We all owe Christ a debt of gratitude, because He is the one who has forgiven us all, delivered us from our bondage. Now we are free to love much.

And that's exactly what we'll see in the life of Mary Magdalene this week—a life lived in love with Christ, poured out as a prayer before Him.

> We must cry out to God for forgiveness, and living forgiven means loving much.

Share a simple prayer time with the Lord:

- Ask God to forgive you—to cancel your debt and remember your sins no more. Pray for eyes that are always open to see your desperate need for His forgiveness.
- Thank God that He has forgiven you completely, and that your sins are removed as far as the east is from the west!
- Ask God to cultivate in your heart a deep love for Him as His forgiveness washes over you—like the sinful woman. Since we have been forgiven much, we must love much!

Takeaway Truth — *"Blessed is the one whose transgressions are forgiven, whose sins are covered." Psalm 32:1*

DAY 2: ACTIONS SPEAK

MAIN TEXTS:
Luke 8:1-3
Luke 10:38-42

But you, dear friends, by building yourselves up in your most holy faith and praying in the Holy Spirit, keep yourselves in God's love as you wait for the mercy of our Lord Jesus Christ to bring you to eternal life. Jude 20-21

The successful prayer must be one without condition ... Then we must throw ourselves before Him and pray with boldness for whatever we know our good and His glory require, and the cost is no object! - A.W. Tozer

Much Love, Bold Prayer

In yesterday's passages we witnessed women sold out for Christ—their lives poured out for Him, living out the prayer, "Forgive us!"

Mary Magdalene, having been delivered from oppression by seven demons, left any other ambition behind—following Jesus to His very end on earth—present even when His male disciples fell away. She had been forgiven much, and her life was proof that she loved much.

The sinful woman who anointed Jesus also poured out her life before Him, offering up costly perfume, overcome by her need of His forgiveness, and bowing at His feet. Her actions were so bold, they garnered the disdain of the onlooking Pharisees, and were evidence of her faith in Christ.

After this, Jesus traveled about from one town and village to another, proclaiming the good news of the kingdom of God. The Twelve were with him, [2] and also some women who had been cured of evil spirits and diseases: Mary (called Magdalene) from whom seven demons had come out; [3] Joanna the wife of Chuza, the manager of Herod's household; Susanna; and many others. These women were helping to support them out of their own means.

LUKE 8:1-3

Mary Magdalene became eyewitness to the turning point of history.

So too can our heart's bold prayer be, "Forgive us," knowing that we do not deserve it, and yet reaching out to take hold of God's precious forgiveness with all the faith we can muster. And as we realize our need to be forgiven much, a deep love grows in our hearts as a result.

We grow to boldly live forgiven.

The Bitter End

We know that Mary Magdalene travelled extensively with Jesus, witnessing miracles, hearing Him teach, supporting His ministry—surely her life was spent in devotion to Him! But one of the greatest testaments to her devotion was her staying power. What do we learn about Mary Magdalene from the following passages. Dig in for yourself to Matthew 27:50-61 and Luke 24:1-10 in your Bible.

Where was Mary Magdalene in these passages, and what did she witness?

We see in these passages that Mary Magdalene became an eyewitness to the turning point of history—Jesus's death, burial, and resurrection (!). The whole world had been waiting millennia for this—nothing more important had ever happened or would ever happen—and Mary Magdalene (formerly demon-possessed woman that she was—forgiven much, loving much) was right there, seeing it all firsthand!

She watched Jesus, in excruciating pain, breathe His last on the cross. She saw dead bodies raised up out of the ground, the earth shake, the curtain torn, rocks split—she saw it all firsthand. But her devotion didn't die there.

BOLD: Six Praying Women, One Faithful God

She followed to the tomb where she saw Jesus's body laid to rest, and the stone rolled in front to seal His body in. But she didn't desert Him then.

She rose up early and saw the empty tomb. She spoke with angels; she wasted no time in being the first to testify of Jesus's resurrection—the best news in all of history, and Mary Magdalene got to bear it!

Friends, I don't think our puny brains can comprehend the significance of the staying power Mary Magdalene displayed. Her steadfastness can be an example in our lives of how being forgiven much—having our debt paid—can lead to a life of love for Christ: one that doesn't give up when the going gets tough. One that doesn't fall away when things don't make sense.

Being Part of Jesus's Crew – Good News, Bad News

Yes, Jesus delivered Mary Magdalene from demonic oppressors—she surely had reason to follow Him because of that. Her response was to love Him. But we can't forget that He didn't look like the conquering king whom Mary's people anticipated in their thousands of years of waiting. He wasn't what everyone was expecting.

You've heard it before, but it's worth mentioning again that as a woman—particularly a demon-possessed woman—Mary would have been an outcast. Among the lowest of the low.

To be a woman was bad enough, but a demon-possessed one was even worse. Why mention this again? Because it's such a big hairy deal!

Mary Magdalene was in Jesus's inner circle despite the fact that most of her people wouldn't have given her the time of day. What an amazing opportunity.

In Luke 4:18-19, Jesus kicked off His ministry with a public reading of a scripture from Isaiah. The good news for Mary Magdalene (for us all) was that Jesus came to set the oppressed free (v. 18). This meant that even women like Mary could be part of Jesus's kingdom. Whoopee!!

But there's good news/bad news when it comes to Jesus's inbreaking kingdom reign—at least looking at it from the perspective of Mary's contemporaries.

The Spirit of the Lord is on me, because he has anointed me to proclaim good news to the poor. He has sent me to proclaim freedom for the prisoners and recovery of sight for the blind, to set the oppressed free,[19] to proclaim the year of the Lord's favor.

LUKE 4:18-19

38 As Jesus and his disciples were on their way, he came to a village where a woman named Martha opened her home to him. **39** She had a sister called Mary, who sat at the Lord's feet listening to what he said. **40** But Martha was distracted by all the preparations that had to be made. She came to him and asked, "Lord, don't you care that my sister has left me to do the work by myself? Tell her to help me!" **41** "Martha, Martha," the Lord answered, "you are worried and upset about many things, **42** but few things are needed—or indeed only one. Mary has chosen what is better, and it will not be taken away from her."

LUKE 10:38-42

Without the benefit of hindsight, the ministry of Jesus is a bit of a head-scratcher. After all, the new king was supposed to rid God's people of their oppressors and usher in the victory.

So how was that going to happen if he was busy hanging out with lepers and women?! What about that posh, successful life everyone had been looking forward to? What about overturning the oppressive Roman rule?

Well, it was precisely because Jesus's reign included the very least that Mary Magdalene was invited into His inner circle—and yet the fact that His ministry was not what everyone expected certainly made following Him challenging.

We can't forget that Jesus made enemies—people were out to get Him. He wasn't winning any popularity contests. Leaving behind any life she'd had and following Jesus wasn't without risk—but boy was it worth it. And Mary Magdalene found that out firsthand.

But today I want to contrast Mary Magdalene's quiet devotion, her steadfastness in sticking with Christ, to another female friend of Jesus—Martha.

"Jesus, Don't You Care?!"
In Mary Magdalene's life we see a woman who seizes the golden opportunity of falling into step with Christ, no matter what the cost, no matter the danger. But not everyone responded this way to Jesus. Let's look at the story of a woman whose first reaction to Christ was not exactly one of extreme devotion: Martha.

Now at first glance, Martha might seem totally devoted. Luke 10:38-42 recounts the day she hosted Jesus in her home. And in her own eyes, she was devoted. Actions speak louder than words, right?

But that's just the problem.

Martha was busying herself doing exactly what women were expected to do—being the hostess with the mostest. Move over Martha Stewart, this Martha was ready to go above and beyond the call of duty. Martha was striving to host Jesus, and she was trying to do it well.

BOLD: Six Praying Women, One Faithful God

The problem was that even though her culture expected good hosting of her, and even though she expected it of herself, good hosting wasn't what Jesus expected of her.

Jesus wanted Martha to sit at His feet and learn. Jesus wanted Martha to follow Him. And how in the world would Martha be able to follow Christ if she was pan-searing the tilapia?

Jesus wanted Martha to follow Him.

But before we're too hard on Martha, I'd like to let you in on a secret: We are a lot like Martha. Ouch.

Think of it this way: how often do you have something you're trying to do and you have punched your ticket on the struggle bus. You feel like it's the right thing to do—it might even be something you're doing for Jesus—a ministry endeavor, serving a friend or neighbor, helping someone in need, or caring for your family. And it's at the top of your "to do" list. You expect yourself to do it. Everyone else expects you to do it. And yet, it's like you're running on a hamster wheel—getting nowhere fast.

Maybe you're overwhelmed just thinking about it. Maybe you are rushing through your Bible study reading in order to get to it.

And you're Just. Plain. Tired.

Can I encourage you to take a minute to breathe? Let's learn together from Martha.

Before we rail at Jesus and pull a Martha, saying, "Lord, don't you care?!" (v. 40) let's have a moment of soul-searching and step back. Is that overwhelming thing we're trying to do actually what Jesus wants us to do? Or is it something we've put on ourselves? Or maybe we allowed others to put pressure and expectations on us.

Why is it important to discern how these things got on our "to do" list to begin with? Because it's likely Jesus wasn't the one who put them there.

How do I know this? Scripture, and my own life.

It's not that Jesus doesn't call us to hard things—in fact, He calls us to very (VERY!) hard things. Probably the hardest things we'll ever do.

The paradoxical, amazing, merciful, knock-your-socks-off, almost-too-good-to-be truth is that He also gives us everything we need to accomplish the super-hard things He calls us to do (Matthew 11:30).

If you're currently in that Martha funk of, "Seriously, Jesus, can I get a little help here?!" can I propose that maybe you're trying to do something for Jesus that He doesn't even necessarily want you to do, or you're trying to serve Him in your own strength and in your own way?

I'm preaching to myself here, sister. Believe you me.

This lesson hit me so hard a few years back. I was struggling to push a ministry endeavor forward. Ever have the rolling-a-boulder-up-a-hill-and-getting-nowhere feeling? Yeah, that pretty much summed it up.

And I remember crying (literally) out to God, "Lord, serving you is exhausting! No one is helping me, and this is going nowhere. Why aren't you helping me? Why is this so hard?!"

Then it hit me.

"Rachel, Rachel," Jesus gave me the same gentle rebuke He gave Martha. "You're worried and upset about many things, but only one thing is needed. Choose better! Choose Me."

Let me tell you: it makes all the difference.

Martha's story isn't about rest versus work—it's about priorities. Are we busying ourselves with what God wants us to do—serving Him according to His way and His plan? Or have we created our own agenda and begun to serve Him according to how we think best?

We have to sit at Jesus's feet and listen. We have to abide in Him, to follow His footsteps closely enough to know what it is He wants us to do.

Otherwise, we'll struggle. We'll be card-carrying members of the "Martyrs Like Martha" club. Otherwise, we'll be overwhelmed and weighed down by our own burdens—because we can't do it on our own.

And, friend, you can't expect God to give you the strength to serve Him according to your own plans. That's not how it works!

Martha's story isn't about rest versus work— it's about priorities.

You have to submit your schedule to Him. Surrender your agenda. Turn over your day planner to Him and ask Him to fill it with His appointments. Lay your calendar at His feet.

I'm guessing you'll be pleasantly surprised.

Why? Not because your calendar will be cleared of all duties and all your time will be spent in personal devotions. Ha! Far from it. You'll still have the laundry to do and the dishes to clean and the bills to pay.

But Jesus will help you live abundantly—with more boldness in your life and your prayers.

He'll fill your calendar with beauty and purpose and refreshment and life.

So if you're experiencing overwhelm and discouragement, sister, give it to Him! Take a moment of quiet at Jesus's feet right now. Think especially of the burdens you are carrying. What could it be that you're shouldering right now that Jesus wants to take from you? Friend, His yoke is easy. Jot some thoughts below. Give them to Him. Let Him renew your strength.

> He'll fill your calendar with beauty and purpose and refreshment and life.

Living Your Best Life

Maybe you're scratching your head right now thinking, "Well, Martha and Mary Magdalene had the opportunity to sit at Jesus's feet and learn, but I don't have that luxury. It's not like He's sitting in my living room right now."

I get it.

But I think you know just what to do.

Breathe in His word—make it your life breath. Listen to audio Bible apps. Decorate your home with scripture. Fill it with worship music. Spend time reading your Bible (leave it sitting open on the kitchen counter if you have to!). Memorize verses and say them to yourself anywhere and everywhere. Sing scripture songs. Talk about God's word to those around you.

Live your life as a pray-er—no matter what you're doing.

Sitting at Jesus's feet for me isn't usually done while literally sitting.

I treasure the moments I can sit in the still and drink in God's word—often this happens when I rock my baby to sleep. These are special, life-giving moments.

> Often my soul is sitting at His feet while my body is moving.

But often my soul is sitting at His feet while my body is moving. I'm chopping the vegetables for supper or taking a walk with my husband or learning the dance motions to teach the kids at VBS or cleaning the toilets or weeding the flower beds or changing yet another diaper.

It may not be obvious to a casual observer. The daily duties and motions of my life probably seem very ordinary. But on the inside, when I'm abiding in Christ, sitting at His feet and listening, surrendering my own agenda to His—I'm living my best life. Nothing else even comes close in comparison.

That's living life as a bold pray-er—living forgiven—life as Mary Magdalene knew it. She spent her days side-by-side with Jesus, in His inner circle, on Jesus's crew.

And boy, do I want to too.

> Living our best life—instead of an overwhelmed life—means laying our plans at the Lord's feet and learning from Him.

Spend some time with the Lord in prayer:

- Ask God to help you live forgiven, instead of taking a ride on the struggle bus.
- Pray that the Lord would write your "To-do" list; that God would fill your calendar with His plans, and cross off anything that you've put there yourself.
- Praise God for the strength He gives to serve Him, and the easy yoke of a life lived boldly forgiven.

Takeaway Truth – *"Open their eyes and turn them from darkness to light, and from the power of Satan to God, so that they may receive forgiveness of sins and a place among those who are sanctified by faith in me." Acts 26:18*

DAY 3: IT'S A DOG-EAT-DOG WORLD

MAIN TEXTS:
Mark 14
Matthew 15:21-28

And without faith it is impossible to please God, because anyone who comes to him must believe that he exists and that he rewards those who earnestly seek him. Hebrews 11:6

Nothing in your daily life is so insignificant and so inconsequential that the Lord will not help you by answering your prayer. -O. Hallesby

Never Say Never

There's something special about being the first—the first grandchild, the first to finish the race, the first to break a record—the first can never be replaced because, well, they're the only ones who can be first.

Who were Jesus's first disciples, according to Matthew 4:18? Why might it be significant that they were first? (Note also who is listed first in Matthew 10:2).

As Jesus was walking beside the Sea of Galilee, he saw two brothers, Simon called Peter and his brother Andrew. They were casting a net into the lake, for they were fishermen.

MATTHEW 4:18

Simon Peter and his brother Andrew were the first disciples that Jesus called. I want you to see for yourself some of the amazing experiences Peter was able to have as one of Jesus's closest disciples. What did Peter witness, according to the following passages (fill in at least four):

Luke 5:1-10

Matthew 8:14-16

THE ROCK WHO FALTERS

Listen to these startling rebukes Jesus had for His "rock" Peter:

"Are you still so dull?" Matthew 15:16 Jesus to Peter after Peter asked the meaning of a parable.

"Get behind me, Satan! You are a stumbling block to me; you do not have in mind the concerns of God, but merely human concerns." Matthew 16:23 Jesus to Peter when Jesus said He must die and be raised.

"Put your sword away! Shall I not drink the cup the Father has given me?" John 18:11 Jesus to Peter after Peter had cut off the ear of Malchus (a servant of high priest).

"Couldn't you men keep watch with me for one hour?" Matthew 26:40 Jesus to Peter at Gethsemane when the disciples slept instead of watching and praying.

"Simon, Simon, Satan has asked to sift all of you as wheat. But I have prayed for you, Simon, that your faith may not fail. And when you have turned back, strengthen your brothers." Luke 22:31 Jesus to Peter at the Last Supper.

Suddenly the Rock doesn't quite seem so solid ...

Matthew 14:22-34

Matthew 16:15-19

Matthew 17:1-6

Matthew 17:24-27

Matthew 19:28

Mark 11:21

John 13:12

Fishing nets pulled full from an empty sea, sick women healed, demons driven out, walking on waves, Jesus shining like the sun, appearances of Moses and Elijah, a coin appearing in the mouth of a fish, a withered cursed tree—these are just some of the firsthand experiences Peter had face to face with Christ. God had promised Peter the keys to the kingdom, and Jesus had washed Peter's feet.

It's hard to imagine any human being closer to Christ than Peter. And perhaps Peter was the closest person to Christ. But that doesn't mean he was steadfast.

Denial Isn't Just a River in Egypt

If you read Mark 14 at the beginning of today's lesson, you saw clearly how quickly Peter, one of Jesus's closest disciples, went from proclaiming, "Even though they all fall away I will not" (v. 29, ESV) to swearing he doesn't know Christ (v. 71).

Bible scholars estimate only three to four hours elapsed between these two polar-opposite proclamations.

The man who once walked on water, who looked forward to judging on a throne, who'd hold the very keys to God's kingdom—assured Jesus he'd never fall away, only to claim a few hours later he didn't know Christ when an inconsequential servant girl asked him (vv. 67-68).

The one who said he wouldn't fall away had fallen far, and hard.

Peter was afraid, very afraid. In fact, we don't know if he came out of hiding any time soon after his denial—he may have missed the whole crucifixion. The next we hear of him is after the crucifixion and death of Jesus—even after the tomb was found empty by others. This prominent character in the narrative of Jesus's story all but disappeared for the climax.

I point this out not because I expect perfection of Peter—all have sinned and fallen short (Romans 3:23). I point this out so that you and I understand how significant it was for the ones who stood by Jesus through His death, His burial, and His resurrection. These were uncertain, terrifying times.

Who stood close to Jesus's cross, according to John 19:25?

> Mary Magdalene's grit and determined loyalty remind me of another steadfast woman from scripture.

Read again the account of Jesus's death from Matthew, noting Mary Magdalene's presence and part:

According to Matthew 27:45-61, who was present at both Jesus's death (v. 56) and burial (v. 61)?

> Near the cross of Jesus stood his mother, his mother's sister, Mary the wife of Clopas, and Mary Magdalene.
>
> JOHN 19:25

We see in Mary Magdalene a rare steadfastness. Where was Peter? James? Andrew? We do not know. But Mary Magdalene was there.

Her grit and determined loyalty remind me of another steadfast woman from scripture—an unlikely recipient of Jesus's praise.

It's A Dog-Eat-Dog World

In Matthew 15:21-28 we find a story about Jesus that feels a little uncomfortable to read. If you didn't start off today's study by reviewing the main text passages, take a moment to look this one over now. Jesus is doing ministry in a region that's primarily non-Jewish when this episode takes place.

Going into Gentile territory would have been a head-scratcher for His disciples, devout Jews who had waited ages for Him to appear. Wasn't Jesus coming to save God's people? That's what the disciples were likely wondering and, ironically, what this passage is all about—Jesus came for all people.

The funny thing is, the Jesus we see in this passage is just the opposite—no warm, fuzzy, Jesus-loves-me Messiah here—this Jesus seemed about as prickly as a sea urchin.

What was the nationality of the woman in this passage, according to verse 22?

> A Canaanite woman from that vicinity came to him, crying out, "Lord, Son of David, have mercy on me! My daughter is demon-possessed and suffering terribly."
>
> MATTHEW 15:22

Not surprisingly, a woman whose daughter was in need of healing sought out Jesus. But what was surprising? Her origin.

Canaanites worshipped false gods. They were not God's people and had been cursed thousands of years earlier by Noah (Genesis 9:25). They repeatedly led God's people astray and were enemies of His chosen ones.

> "Cursed be Canaan! **The lowest** of slaves will he be."
>
> GENESIS 9:25
> (emphasis mine)

So why would Jesus be doing ministry here? Because Jesus broke the mold. Jesus broke curses. Jesus came for all. Let's press into this scene and see just how it played out.

The woman cried to Jesus from a distance. How did she address Him, according to verse 22? And for what did she initially ask?

The woman rightfully called Jesus the son of David. This revealed her faith—she was acknowledging Him as the King of Kings, the Anointed One, the Lord. She was putting herself under His authority and recognizing Him as the Messiah.

Her request was, "Have mercy on me!" Again, she was proclaiming her faith and her humble position before Jesus. She knew of her need and asked for forgiveness. In contrast to the prideful, self-righteous religious leaders of Jesus's day, this woman was sure of her desperate need for Jesus, and she didn't try to hide it. Surely Jesus would be quick to come to the rescue!

But Jesus gave her the cold shoulder.

What was her reaction to this? Look in verse 23. Even though it's not spelled out, the disciples give it away.

Jesus did not answer a word. So his disciples came to him and urged him, "Send her away, for she keeps crying out after us."

MATTHEW 15:23

She persisted. Jesus did not acknowledge her desperate pleas, and yet, she kept crying out.

The "rock" Peter may have given up and lied about knowing Jesus when questioned by a servant girl, but this nameless faith-filled Canaanite woman Kept. Crying. Out.

When the disciples' patience had worn completely thin, they asked Jesus to send her away. Though He did not, He gave a puzzling reply, "I was sent only to the lost sheep of Israel" (v. 24).

But she didn't give up. She knelt before him, a position of desperate humility, and begged for help (v. 25).

Still Jesus put her off with, "It is not right to take the children's bread and toss it to the dogs" (v. 26).

"You are to be my holy people. So do not eat the meat of an animal torn by wild beasts; throw it to the dogs."

EXODUS 22:31

Let me assure you that our modern construct of "grand-dogs," fur babies, and pampered poodles are not what Jesus is referring to. Calling someone a dog in the ancient world was always an insult. That which was rejected by people would be fit for dogs (Exodus 22:31).

With dogged determination (ha! Too corny? I liked it), the woman still persisted. She embraced the low dog-like position of a non-Israelite and persisted in faith. Read her declaration in verse 27 in the margin.

"Yes it is, Lord," she said. "Even the dogs eat the crumbs that fall from their master's table."

MATTHEW 15:27

Can you believe the persistence of this woman? I like her already. She said that even though she was a dog, she just wanted the crumbs from the table. I think she knew it was better to be the lowest of the low at God's table than anywhere else.

Her sheer determination proved her deep faith. And the disciples saw it firsthand. Jesus did nothing to egg this lady on. If anything, you'd think His cold shoulder would dissuade her. It didn't.

The fact that Jesus initially paid her no attention gave the Canaanite woman a chance to show just how much she believed — how far she'd go because of her faith. We know Jesus wanted to do ministry to her people—why else would He have travelled miles to come to her hometown?!

Jesus loves to raise up the humble and to shame the wise. He does it, time and again. The disciples, so sure she should be sent away, got schooled in Jesus's desire to reward true faith in all people.

The woman wouldn't be dissuaded. Like Job, who proclaimed, "Though he slay me, yet will I hope in him" (Job 13:15), she continued and wouldn't be spurned.

Could it be God wants the same diligence from me?

Could it be those times when it seems He's cold-shouldering me, He's really giving me the opportunity to show diligence?

> Don't give up. Show up boldly and diligently, in prayer, even when it seems God is distant.

Maybe God wants to see just how far you or I will go—for our own good.

Anyone else inspired to be doggedly determined right now?

Is there an area of your life right now where God seems to be giving you the cold shoulder? What is it? How might you show determination in this area? Put your thoughts in the margin.

Maybe God doesn't seem to be listening to your prayers, and that's why you've picked up this study in the first place.

Maybe you've been begging for that wayward child to come home, or that cancer to be in remission, that broken marriage restored, that wound to be healed, that need to be met—but the answer seems far off.

Keep on. Don't give up. Show up boldly and diligently, in faith-filled prayer, even when it seems God is distant. Take the opportunity to show the enemy just how determined you are to hold on to Jesus.

Copy Jesus's words to the Canaanite woman from verse 28, and let them sink in deep.

Then Jesus said to her, "Woman, you have great faith! Your request is granted." And her daughter was healed at that moment.

MATTHEW 15:28

Great faith.

Jesus had a way of finding the most precious of things in the most unlikely of places. Great faith, in a woman who didn't flinch at being treated like a dog.

And just like that, the tables were turned.

Jesus knew that those who had great faith weren't dogs at all. He gave His life as a ransom for many—many precious souls. And it was the ones who tried so hard to live by the law and rejected the faith who were the real dogs after all (Matthew 7:6, Philippians 3:2).

I want to circle back and re-emphasize something important: the Canaanite woman asked for mercy.

Sound familiar?

Remember how Jesus taught us to pray, "Forgive us our sins"? This Canaanite woman, humble as a dog, faithful in her humility, begged first for mercy. Not help, not healing, not money or food or wisdom—but mercy.

We do well to emulate her.

Because in her relentlessly determined faith, chasing after God's mercy—she found it. God responds to our diligence in seeking Him (Matthew 7:7-8), though not always how we want or expect.

Do not give dogs what is sacred; do not throw your pearls to pigs.

MATTHEW 7:6

Watch out for those dogs, those evildoers, those mutilators of the flesh.

PHILIPPIANS 3:2

"Ask and it will be given to you; seek and you will find; knock and the door will be opened to you. [8] For everyone who asks receives; the one who seeks finds; and to the one who knocks, the door will be opened."

MATTHEW 7:7-8

YOU TOO, MARY MAGDALENE

I am so encouraged by the testimony of my friend who owns a local Christian bookstore. She tells of her customers' faith, evident in their buying behavior during shaky times.

During 2020, when the throes of economic shutdown and the threats of disease threw our nation into a panic, the customers of her small business showed an interesting pattern.

Her store is filled with beautiful products: mugs, art, jewelry, music, cards, Christian books and Bible studies—many wonderful faith-building products. But do you know what sold the most during the season of uncertainty? Bibles. By a landslide.

When the store opened back up after shutdown, sales of Christian products were slow, but Bible sales shot up by 24%. That's nothing to sneeze at! During a time of instability, people turned to the only thing that is truly stable —faith in God alone. What a wonderful thing!

In chasing after God's mercy—she found it.

Mary Magdalene loved much, and lived faithful.

Just like the Canaanite woman didn't give up, neither did Mary Magdalene. Her soul cried, "Forgive me! Have mercy on me!" She knew that clinging to Jesus was the way to find life. Mary Magdalene followed Jesus, and stayed by His side—to the cross, to the grave, and as we'll see in the action-packed next few days of our study: the resurrection.

> Living forgiven means having faith that doesn't give up — even when it seems like you're getting God's cold shoulder, because you know He responds to your bold, determined prayers.

Spend some time with the Lord in prayer:
- Beg God for a faith that won't back down—even in discouraging circumstances—but instead stands the test of time.
- Give God (again) that area of your life that He seems to be cold-shouldering. And give it again tomorrow. And the next day. And the next.

- Praise God that living forgiven means loving much and praying bold in diligence, "Have mercy! Forgive me!" and seeing God respond to your faith.

Takeaway Truth – *"We want each of you to show this same diligence to the very end, so that what you hope for may be fully realized." Hebrews 6:11*

DAY 4: THE SEAT IN THE TOMB

MAIN TEXTS:
John 20:1-16
Mark 16:1-13

Love is as strong as death, its jealousy unyielding as the grave. It burns like blazing fire, like a mighty flame. Song of Songs 8:6

Faith starts prayer to work—clears the way to the mercy seat.
-E.M. Bounds

Mary's Love Endures to the Grave

This week we're zooming in on the line of the Lord's Prayer where we are to cry out for God's mercy. "Forgive us our debts" is to be our heart's cry as we approach the Lord in prayer.

On day one, we reviewed the story of the sinful woman who anointed Jesus at the home of a Pharisee named Simon, found in Luke 7. We especially keyed in on the concept Jesus taught in verse 47, that whoever has been forgiven little, loves little, and whoever has been forgiven much, loves much.

Jesus encouraged us to cry out for this forgiveness when we pray to God.

As we've examined the life of Mary Magdalene this week, we've seen a woman whose life was a prayer—her devotion to the Lord a testimony of the deep love she felt for Him. She lived her life forgiven. Today we see her finest moments of devotion to God as one who knew she'd been forgiven much. Mary Magdalene loved much.

Peter chickened out as the rooster crowed, but Mary Magdalene stuck with Christ to the bitter end of His earthly life. She followed Him all the way to the cross, and stayed by His side until His death.

In the gospel accounts, which detail the individuals who were present at the cross, Mary Magdalene is specifically mentioned more than any other person (Matthew 27:56; Mark 15:40; Luke

> Peter chickened out as the rooster crowed, but Mary Magdalene stuck with Christ.

8:2, 23:49; John 19:25). She was the last to be with Jesus at the cross, and the first to be at the empty tomb.

Song of Songs says that "love is strong as death." Mary Magdalene's love for Christ carried well beyond His death. Yes, her love was "enduring as the grave" (Song of Songs 8:6 NLT).

We know this, because as soon as Mary Magdalene could, that's just where she went—Jesus's grave.

The Bold, Beautiful Early Bird

Both Mark 16:2 and John 20:1 say that Mary Magdalene was up bright and early after the Sabbath was over and, spices in hand, headed to Jesus's tomb to honor Him by anointing His body.

She wanted to anoint God's Anointed One (Acts 4:26-27, Psalm 2:2).

But this wasn't the first time she cared for Christ. What does Matthew 27:55-56a tell us about Mary Magdalene's care for Jesus?

> Many women were there, watching from a distance. They had followed Jesus from Galilee to care for his needs. [56] Among them were Mary Magdalene
>
> MATTHEW 27:55-56a

From the time of Jesus's early ministry in Galilee, Mary Magdalene had been caring for His needs. In other words, Mary cared for Jesus all along—even to the grave.

Maybe this seems like a weak, feminine thing to do—to tend to the body of the Savior. But as we take a closer look at John 20 and Mark 16, we see that it is just the opposite. Mary Magdalene leading the women to anoint Jesus's body was anything but weak—it was bold; it was beautiful.

You may remember that in the story of the sinful woman who anointed Jesus in Matthew 26, Christ made clear the beauty of what she had done, saying "She has done a beautiful thing to me" (Matthew 26:10) and "wherever this gospel is preached throughout the world, what she has done will also be told, in memory of her" (Matthew 26:13). Anointing was an act of beauty. Of deep love.

But it was also bold.

Let me explain: Mary Magdalene and the other women had plenty of large, fearful obstacles standing in their way.

For one: **the stone**. Mary Magdalene couldn't have been sure that she would have access to Jesus's body. After all, the body was laid behind a huge tombstone and (for all she knew) sealed too tightly for her to reach.

We know from Matthew 27 that she had been there when the tomb was sealed.

She was well aware of this challenge (Mark 16:3) but approached the tomb anyway—demonstrating her deep love and devotion for Christ. We don't know exactly how heavy the stone was—some guess more than a ton. But Mary Magdalene didn't hesitate. She wasn't going to let anything come between her and her Lord, not even a massive, unwieldy tombstone.

Can I honestly say I've got the same boldness? Hardly!

When I come up against what seems like a boulder-of-an-obstacle in my life, I tend to be a pessimist. I see all the problems and reasons why I can't do it and it just won't work. My tendency is to shrink back from a challenge. Oof.

Lord, give me to boldness to face any challenges you have for me ahead!

But the bulky and burdensome stone wasn't the only problem Mary Magdalene faced with boldness—it was only the first. Secondly, **Jewish law** forbade the touching of corpses or graves. To do such would make one "unclean" (Numbers 19:16).

We may not keep the Jewish ceremonial cleanliness laws anymore, but I think we've got our own ideas of clean and unclean today. Am I ready to minister to those on the fringes, even if that means they're different from me in a way that's uncomfortable?

What if they're homeless, or sick, or mentally ill, or disabled, or living a lifestyle I don't agree with? Am I willing to sacrifice my own reputation for the sake of Christ if that's what it comes to? Even if my friends misunderstand, and I don't fit in anymore?

Thirdly, going to visit the grave of Christ was **dangerous**. We already learned how "the rock" Peter was so afraid to be associated with Jesus he wouldn't even admit to a servant girl

Mary Magdalene and the other women had plenty of large, fearful obstacles standing in their way.

Joseph ... rolled a big stone in front of the entrance to the tomb and went away. [61] Mary Magdalene and the other Mary were sitting there opposite the tomb.

MATTHEW 27:59-61

And they asked each other, "Who will roll the stone away from the entrance of the tomb?"

MARK 16:3

Anyone who touches a human bone or a grave, will be unclean for seven days.

NUMBERS 19:16

that he was a follower; how much riskier it would have been for Mary Magdalene to visit the grave of the treasonous blasphemer from Nazareth!

Having just witnessed the crucifixion of Jesus, the danger of punishment would have been all-too-real. Not only that, visiting the grave put herself in danger of being misunderstood and a grave robber, a realistic fear (see Matthew 28:11-15). She was risking her own life to show her love for Jesus (John 15:13), showing the greatest love of all.

Can I honestly say I show this same "no fear" attitude? I hope so, but my life doesn't always show it—like when the finances are tight or I find a suspicious lump or the economy is uncertain or when my kid is rebellious.

And if I can't even live without fear in the little things, how on earth can I have the kind of faith it takes to lay down my life! Lord, help my unbelief.

Neither giant rocks, nor uncleanness, nor danger would dissuade determined Mary Magdalene. She knew firsthand the perfect love that drove out her fears (1 John 4:18), even though she walked through the darkest valley of Jesus's death, she feared no evil (Psalm 23:4).

Mary Magdalene was bold. Her passion for Christ spoke louder than any prayer she uttered. Hers was a life that radiated the love of God. It wasn't Peter the rock who was first to the empty tomb. It wasn't John, the one Jesus loved. It was Mary Magdalene, the forgiven one who loved much.

What is the connection between being forgiven much, loving much, and being unafraid of any obstacle that might stand in our way? How can studying these traits in Mary Magdalene's life change our lives and increase the boldness of our prayers? Record any thoughts the Lord brings to mind.

> Greater love has no one than this: to lay down one's life for one's friends.
>
> JOHN 15:13

> There is no fear in love. But perfect love drives out fear, because fear has to do with punishment.
>
> 1 JOHN 4:18

> Even though I walk through the darkest valley, I will fear no evil.
>
> PSALM 23:4

Mary Magdalene's deep love and devotion were rewarded with an indescribably great gift—Mary Magdalene (spoiler alert!) was the first to see the risen Savior.

But we are getting ahead of ourselves ... before we talk about Jesus's post-resurrection encounter with Mary Magdalene, we need to take a closer look at the tomb to see what we find about forgiveness there.

The Seat in the Tomb

In John 20, we learn that Mary Magdalene ran to tell Peter and John about the empty tomb (v. 2). Peter and John came, found Jesus's graveclothes neatly there, and went home (v. 3-10). But Mary stayed.

Still not perceiving what had happened, Mary continued to grieve (v. 11)—her Lord was not only dead, but now missing. She would not even be able to honor Him by anointing His body.

As she wept, she bent over to look into the tomb [12] and saw two angels in white, seated where Jesus' body had been, one at the head and the other at the foot.

JOHN 20:11b-12

What did Mary Magdalene see when she looked into the grave (v. 12)?

When she peered into Jesus's grave, Mary Magdalene saw two angels, one at either end of the place Jesus's body had been laid.

This is significant—and you're about to see why.

Read the following instructions God gave to Moses on constructing the ark of the covenant in Exodus 25 (CSB). Notice what was between the two angels (cherubim). Underline the name of this special, between-angels place:

The top cover of the ark of the covenant was called the "mercy seat," between two angels, one at either end. It was where Moses would hear from God. It was the place where God was enthroned (1 Samuel 4:4). It was the place where God's people would find forgiveness on the Day of Atonement.

Here's what would happen: "[The priest] will sprinkle some of the blood with his finger before the mercy seat seven times … He is to sprinkle it against the mercy seat … He will make atonement for the most holy place in this way for all their sins" Leviticus 16:14-16 (CSB).

God's people would find freedom from their sins; they'd meet His very presence there—between two angels on the mercy seat.

And you know what Mary Magdalene found that early morning?

The Mercy Seat in-the-flesh.

She'd no longer need the mercy seat on the ark of the covenant. She'd no longer need a sprinkling of blood seven times over to be forgiven. She'd met the mercy seat Himself, Jesus Christ, who'd delivered her from her own slave masters of sin and evil, seven times over, once-and-for-all.

The writer of Hebrews knew this well. He said, "The cherubim of glory were above the ark overshadowing the mercy seat"

Hebrews 9:5 (CSB). But he knew that no more would the blood of bulls and goats be needed for cleansing. He wrote in chapter 9: "How much more, then, will the blood of Christ, who through the eternal Spirit offered himself unblemished to God, cleanse our consciences from acts that lead to death, so that we may serve the living God!" Hebrews 9:14.

Likewise in Romans we read, "God presented him as the mercy seat by his blood, through faith, to demonstrate his righteousness, because in his restraint God passed over the sins previously committed" Romans 3:25 (CSB).

Friends, Jesus is our mercy seat. He is our forgiveness. His body broken means our sins forgiven—praise the Lord! You and I can be sure that when we cry out, "Forgive us our sins," God hears and forgives our sins.

Why? Because Jesus, our mercy seat, has risen! His blood covers us, and in Him we are washed clean. No need for striving, no need for sacrifices—it is finished! You and I can be confident of Jesus's finished work. Amen!

Mary Magdalene found the Mercy Seat and left her own sin and death in the grave, and so can we! Because Jesus is risen, because He has become our Mercy Seat, our own sin and death can stay in the graveyard, buried forever so that we can be raised to new life in Christ.

MY SINS AND STRUGGLES

Take a moment to bring your sins and struggles to the Mercy Seat. These could be sins you thankfully left behind in the past, and you want to praise God for freedom, or they could be sins you still struggle with. Write some on the tombstone, leaving them behind you, in the grave:

You may have written fear, jealousy, anger, rebellion, bitterness, addiction, perfectionism, gossip, or any number of sins you've faced. Take a moment in prayer to thank God that because of the Mercy Seat, you can leave these sins behind, at the grave.

Mary Magdalene, weeping, seeing the angels, was on the cusp of the biggest moment of her life. She'd seen evidence that the risen Jesus was the mercy seat, though she hadn't understood it quite yet. She was still looking for the living among the dead, but she was about to find Him for herself.

> Living forgiven is characterized by love for God that's fearless—strong as death, leaving our own sin and death in the grave, and being raised to new life in Christ.

Spend some time with the Lord in prayer:

- Ask God to pour His love into your heart—a strong love that can't stop, that won't stop for anything—a love that's unafraid of any obstacle you may face.
- Thank God that Christ himself has become the Mercy Seat through His shed blood and resurrection—that He is the very reason we can cry, "Forgive us!"
  - Praise God for the death of sin in your life—that forgiveness means new life.

Takeaway Truth - *"The death he died, he died to sin once for all; but the life he lives, he lives to God. In the same way, count yourselves dead to sin but alive to God in Christ Jesus." Romans 6:10-11*

MAIN TEXTS:
John 20:11-18
Isaiah 43
Mark 12:41-43

DAY 5: RUN & TELL THAT

After Jesus rose from the dead early on Sunday morning, the first person who saw him was Mary Magdalene, the woman from whom he had cast out seven demons. Mark 16:9 (NLT)

Have you ever said, 'Well, all we can do now is pray'? ... When we come to the end of ourselves, we come to the beginning of God.
– Billy Graham

New-Morning Mercies
Mary Magdalene was still in shock—her precious Jesus who'd given her new life, free from the demons of her past—had died. Not only that, but His body was now missing. She was being

robbed of the chance to even mourn properly. She was devastated.

The irony of this situation is that if she only knew why Jesus's body was missing, her mourning would have turned to dancing!

She was so sad that Jesus's body was gone, but if only she had understood what God was doing—that Jesus was alive, raised back to life after having defeated death (Romans 6:9), her tears would have been tears of joy.

But she just can't see it yet.

Isn't that so often how it is with us? We are weak and shortsighted. We complain about the creature comforts we lack, the undesirable circumstances we find ourselves in, the trials we face—and yet if we only knew the treasure the Lord was using those difficulties to produce in us—the closeness to Him we would achieve through our troubles, we would thank Him for them!

Romans 5:3-5 (NLT) says, "3 We can rejoice, too, when we run into problems and trials, for we know that they help us develop endurance. 4 And endurance develops strength of character, and character strengthens our confident hope of salvation. 5 And this hope will not lead to disappointment."

But Mary Magdalene didn't realize what was going on. And so, she wept in despair. The angels in the tomb inquired why she was crying.

How did she refer to Jesus in verse 13 of John 20?

She calls Him *my* Lord.

Jesus was not just any lord to Mary—He was her Lord. Isn't it sweet? Of course, she was heartbroken. She was the one who loved much, and the rug had been pulled out from under her.

Everything seemed wrong, but things were about to be more right than ever before.

> If she only knew why Jesus's body was missing, her mourning would have turned to dancing.

For we know that since Christ was raised from the dead, he cannot die again; death no longer has mastery over him.

ROMANS 6:9

They asked her, "Woman, why are you crying?" "They have taken **my Lord** away," she said, "and I don't know where they have put him."

JOHN 20:13 (emphasis mine)

Everything seemed wrong, but things were about to be more right than ever before.

Just when all seemed lost, just when she was ready to finally give up and leave Jesus's empty tomb—there He was. But in her sorrow, she still didn't recognize Him. Until a tender moment in verse 16.

What happened in verse 16 that caused Mary to recognize Jesus?

Jesus said to her, "Mary." She turned toward him and cried out in Aramaic, "Rabboni!" (which means "Teacher").

JOHN 20:16
(emphasis mine)

He spoke her name. It was that simple—Mary heard the voice of Jesus. He called her name and she knew all at once it was Him. Just like the Good Shepherd of John 10:3-4, "The sheep listen to his voice. He calls his own sheep by name and leads them out ... he goes on ahead of them, and his sheep follow him because they know his voice."

Mary Magdalene knew His voice.

Much like Hagar's unlikely encounter with the Lord in the wilderness when He called her by name, so had Mary Magdalene now encountered a God who saw her, who knew her by name, who dried her tears and lifted her up.

Perhaps the words of Isaiah the prophet were ringing in her ears, "Do not fear, for I have redeemed you; I have summoned you by name; you are mine" Isaiah 43:1 (see the box on the following page).

And perhaps, upon hearing His voice call her name, her soul at once knew the deep truth of the precious promises of our faithful God.

She Can't Keep It in

All at once it all made sense—the empty graveclothes weren't needed anymore because Jesus wasn't dead—He was alive!

Not only that, but His life meant life for all. And the freedom found in Him was worth sharing.

And a woman who'd once been trapped by demons, and only moments before been overcome with grief, became the first to see the risen Christ, and the first to share the gospel message: "I have seen the Lord!"

Mark the truths that are the most precious to you from this passage spoken by **the God who calls you by name** (Isaiah 43) today:

[1] But now, this is what the LORD says – he who created you, Jacob, he who formed you, Israel: "Do not fear, for I have redeemed you; I have summoned you by name; you are mine.

[2] When you pass through the waters, I will be with you; and when you pass through the rivers, they will not sweep over you. When you walk through the fire, you will not be burned; the flames will not set you ablaze.

[4] Since you are precious and honored in my sight, and because I love you, I will give people in exchange for you, nations in exchange for your life.

[10] "You are my witnesses," declares the LORD, "and my servant whom I have chosen, so that you may know and believe me and understand that I am he. Before me no god was formed, nor will there be one after me.

[11] I, even I, am the LORD, and apart from me there is no savior.

[12] I have revealed and saved and proclaimed – I, and not some foreign god among you. You are my witnesses," declares the LORD, "that I am God.

[13]   Yes, and from ancient days I am he. No one can deliver out of my hand. When I act, who can reverse it?"

[16] This is what the LORD says—he who made a way through the sea, a path through the mighty waters,

[18] "Forget the former things; do not dwell on the past.

[19] See, I am doing a new thing! Now it springs up; do you not perceive it? I am making a way in the wilderness and streams in the wasteland.

[25] "I, even I, am he who blots out your transgressions, for my own sake, and remembers your sins no more.

Take a moment to praise God for being with you when you pass through the waters. For calling you precious. For doing a new thing. For blotting out your sins. For forgiveness.

She'd planned to wash Jesus's body with tears of mourning and anoint his limp frame with spices, but her mourning became dancing as she now knew the true new life and forgiveness offered by the One who knew her by name—who knew her and loved her even in her unbelief.

And it was this woman, the woman who loved much, that He chose to receive the beautiful gift of seeing His resurrected body first.

Offering it All

As Jesus looked up, he saw the rich putting their gifts into the temple treasury. [2] He also saw a poor widow put in two very small copper coins. [3] "Truly I tell you," he said, "this poor widow has put in more than all the others. [4] All these people gave their gifts out of their wealth; but she out of her poverty put in all she had to live on."

LUKE 21:1-4

There's something so powerful about the redemption Jesus offers—something so poignant about having the lostness and loneliness we feel without Christ replaced by His presence. It makes you ready to give it all back to Him.

In Luke 21:1-4, Jesus sees a poor widow offer a few pennies among the rich, who gave lavish amounts. But Christ said that even though she gave pennies, she gave more—because she gave it all.

This passage has always spoken volumes to me. I always wish I had more to give Jesus—more time, more talent, more devotion.

But because of this poor widow, I know I have enough to give, if only I give my all.

God wants us to follow Him with reckless abandon. Like Mary Magdalene, willing to run and tell about seeing Jesus—saying "I have seen the Lord!" We too can tell others about the God who called us by name. We can say, "We have seen the Lord!" because we've encountered the Mercy Seat himself, and found the forgiveness and healing we couldn't find anywhere else. We can share His goodness.

Not because we have the perfect words. Not because we are so talented. Not because of any gift or ability that we have—but because when we called out, "Forgive us our sins!" He listened. He forgave.

How about we run and tell that?

Mary Magdalene's Prayer?

Well, you've probably picked up on this fact, but I'll point it out in case you haven't. Mary Magdalene doesn't have words of a prayer recorded in scripture. We don't know what she prayed.

So why in the world study her life to deepen our understanding of Matthew 6, "And forgive us our debts, as we also have forgiven our debtors"? And how can this help us in our quest to pray bold?

Mary Magdalene deepens our understanding of our love for God as a result of our indebtedness because she lived it.

We don't have "on record" an instance of Mary Magdalene crying out to God for forgiveness—but her life was a prayer that resounded the gospel. She lived forgiven—the loving-much, forgiven-much, unafraid, doggedly-determined life of a close Jesus-follower. Maybe closer than anyone else.

Who wouldn't want to emulate that?

And how can Mary Magdalene's life inspire our own bold prayers and courageous faith?

I won't answer *for* you—you may have your own reasons and explanations.

Here are mine:

When I see just how far the Lord brought her: from one held completely captive by evil, imprisoned and enslaved by demons—to one of the privileged few who witnessed it all: the healings, the preaching, the miracles—to the first, the one and only, to meet the resurrected Christ at the empty grave.

When I realize what He did *for* and *with* Mary Magdalene, I can hardly bear it! I can't help but praise the God who raises up the low, who wipes away our tears, who forgives every stain—and I can't help but cry out earnestly for myself — "Forgive me too, Lord!"

Because I want to live forgiven too. I want to live with that kind of love—the love that chooses Jesus over my own agenda, the love that presses on in dogged determination even when I feel like I'm given the cold shoulder, the love that doesn't care if a two-thousand-pound gravestone stands in my way, the kind of love that seeks out my Savior even when everyone else is too ashamed or too afraid to claim Him.

I want to live with that kind of love.

I. Want. That.

Forgive me, Lord. I want to love much.

> Our lives can be lived as a prayer, in constant communion with God—a closeness that comes from being forgiven much and results in loving much.

Share a simple prayer time with the Lord:

• Thank God for knowing your name, and ask Him to help you hear His voice.

- Pray for God's forgiveness—thanking Him for paying the debt you could not pay so that you wouldn't have to live in sin and face eternal death.
- Ask God to help you live the kind of life Mary Magdalene lived—in step with Jesus, walking by His side, loving much, being determined, living unafraid, and seeing all God has in store for you.

Takeaway Truth – *"Do not fear, for I have redeemed you; I have summoned you by name; you are mine." Isaiah 43:1*

Friends, do not forget our principal teaching from this week of studying Mary Magdalene:

To pray bold, we beg for God's forgiveness, then live forgiven with love, determination, and confidence.

Pause for Praise: This week as we got a front-row seat to the life of Mary Magdalene, along with some of the other women who encountered Jesus, we got a better view of what it means to cry out, "Forgive us!" and then live forgiven. We learned about loving much, about turning over our calendars to God, about living with determination, and not being deterred by obstacles. And we saw the amazing firsts Mary Magdalene experienced as a result of her closeness to Christ. In Mary Magdalene's life we see the importance of Christ paying our debts so that we can have new life, and it's our sins that lie in the grave. Before you close this book to go on with your day, take a moment to praise the One who forgives, who rose from the grave. I recommend a lyric video for Phil Wickham's "House of the Lord." If you prefer traditional music, try "The Old Rugged Cross." Bask in the freedom that can only be found in Christ burying your sin and death in the grave, and raising you to new life.

This, then, is how you should pray:

Our Father in heaven
hallowed be Your name,
Your kingdom come,
Your will be done,
on earth as it is in heaven.
Give us today our daily bread.
And forgive us our debts,
as we also have forgiven our debtors.

AND LEAD US NOT INTO TEMPTATION
but deliver us from the evil one.

WEEK SIX
MARY
MOTHER of CHRIST
GOD'S HANDMAIDEN

MAIN TEXT:
Luke 1:26-38

DAY 1: SIGNIFICANTLY INSIGNIFICANT

Humble yourselves before the Lord, and he will lift you up.
James 4:10

Humility is an indispensable requisite of true prayer.
- E.M. Bounds

As we cruise into our final chapter, we've come a long way in our study of the Lord's Prayer as illustrated by women in scripture.

We began by seeing God as our Father, as depicted in the beautiful example of the Egyptian slave Hagar, who proclaimed, "You are the God Who Sees Me." We learned from her story that we should boldly run to God with our problems, instead of running away from Him.

Next, we learned the importance of praising our holy, mighty God from the life and song of the first female worship leader and prophetess recorded in scripture, Miriam. We found that praise primes our hearts to boldly pray with the proper perspective— God is the mighty, powerful creator who is both colossal and close.

Deborah the warrior-judge was the next on the list of our praying women. Her story teaches us that God moves heaven and earth to bring victory to those whose lives and bold prayers are kingdom-minded—and that we'd be fools to miss out on it!

Chapter four would follow the story of heartbroken Hannah, who cried out to God the provider in her hour of need. She saw God provide beyond her expectations, turning it right back to the One who owns it all—never outgiving our generous God. We learned to boldly cry out to our Provider for our every heartbroken, desperate need.

Finally, we shifted into the New Testament, looking closely at the story of Mary Magdalene. We saw in her the life and heart of a woman living forgiven—having found deliverance in Jesus, and living a life of loving devotion as a result. We learned to live a life with the heart cry of "Forgive us!" and to love much as a result.

> Mary's life beautifully illustrated her son's prayer, "Lead us not into temptation" as she humbly followed God's lead.

Now, we come to our final chapter, studying the prayers of Mary, the mother of Jesus. We'll see how her life beautifully illustrated her son's prayer, "And lead us not into temptation, but deliver us from the evil one," (Matthew 6:13) as she humbly followed God's lead.

If you've read my Bible study *Significant: Six Ordinary Women, One Extraordinary God*, you know I have an obsession for the unlikely women in Jesus's family tree.

Writing the study about Sarah, Leah, Tamar, Rahab, Ruth, and Bathsheba changed my life big time. I realized that God has a history of using regular women whose lives are devoted to Him for significant things—not the least of which (actually the most of which) was bringing about the much-awaited, desperately needed Messiah.

And the blow-your-mind truth is that God accomplished His rescue mission with the help of ordinary women. These ladies who struggled with lousy life circumstances and messed-up pasts, who came from the wrong side of the tracks and seemed least likely to make an impact, each played a big role in God sending His precious Son as the Savior of humankind.

The Christian life is not about walking according to our own plans and standards, having it all figured out ahead of time, and having all the time, talent, and perfection to give. It's about giving all we've got—no matter how insignificant that seems.

Because with His touch, even the most insignificant woman can be used in eternity-shifting ways. God has a way of shaking things up in ways we don't expect, doesn't He?

Dare To Be a Mary

Mary's story is not much different from the other less-than-perfect foremothers of Christ—in fact, it's the textbook example. Because apart from God, Mary didn't seem to have much going for her.

She was young—strike one.

She was poor—strike two.

And she was a woman—strike three.

Hardly heavy-hitting like the chief priests and the Pharisees of her day—who'd have been well-versed in the scriptures from

> With His touch, even the most insignificant woman can be used in eternity-shifting ways.

²⁹ Mary was greatly troubled at his words and wondered what kind of greeting this might be. ³⁰ But the angel said to her, "Do not be afraid, Mary; you have found favor with God. ³¹ You will conceive and give birth to a son, and you are to call him Jesus. ³² He will be great and will be called the Son of the Most High. The Lord God will give him the throne of his father David, ³³ and he will reign over Jacob's descendants forever; his kingdom will never end."
³⁴ "How will this be," Mary asked the angel, "since I am a virgin?"

LUKE 1:29-34

boyhood, set apart for His work, and trained to follow every law to-a-tee.

But God saw in Mary a heart that was His.

We see evidence of this in her initial reaction to Gabriel's news when he appeared to her in Luke 1. Though she was surprised at the angel's appearance, she also showed a humble confidence in the Lord. She was not terrified, as were the other men Gabriel appeared to.

Gabriel had spoken to greats Daniel (Daniel 8:16, 9:21) and Zechariah (Luke 1:19), and now God sent His messenger to Mary—and Gabriel was just the messenger for the job.

Not too many of us have had a close encounter with supernatural beings. If one of your friends opened a conversation with, "Oh yeah, the other day at Hobby Lobby I shot the breeze with the angel Gabriel," you'd back away slowly ... and probably question her sanity.

But Mary had the honor of speaking with God's angel Gabriel face-to-face.

I mentioned that Gabriel had also appeared to Daniel and Zechariah. Let's compare their reactions to Mary's. You may be surprised with what you find. Circle words that give you clues to their emotions in the following verses:

Daniel wrote, "As [Gabriel] came near the place where I was standing, I was terrified and fell prostrate" (Daniel 8:17).

Earlier in Luke 1, we read, "When Zechariah saw [Gabriel], he was startled and was gripped with fear" Luke 1:12.

"But [Mary] was very perplexed at [Gabriel's] statement, and was pondering what kind of greeting this was" Luke 1:29 (NASB).

Your translation might read that she was "greatly troubled," and at first reading you may imagine her to be terrified at Gabriel's appearing. Me too. But going back to the original Greek and Hebrew texts reveals some deep differences in these encounters with Gabriel.

The Hebrew word translated in Daniel 8:17 as *terrified* means overwhelmed with terror, terrified, and terrorized. And, as you may have noticed, Daniel was so shaken by Gabriel's appearance, he fell on his face. Putting this in context might be even more revealing—Daniel is no coward.

A quick flip back to Daniel 6 will remind us that this mighty man of God defied King Darius's decree not to pray to God, landing himself a date in the lion's den. That's why the children's song "Dare to be a Daniel" is so inspiring.

After his slumber party with the kings of the jungle, Daniel was still frightened enough on meeting Gabriel to fall facedown to the ground—this goes to show just how terrifying his encounter with Gabriel was.

Similarly, the Greek word describing Zechariah's reaction to Gabriel is *phobos*. Perhaps that has a familiar ring to it? Phobias are bone-deep fears. That's why it's translated as "gripped with fear" or "overwhelmed with fear" (NLT) even "terror-struck" (NTE). We're talking panic here—the type of fear that makes your heart race and compels you to flee in terror.

The funny thing is, Mary's reaction was very different. Compared to seasoned priest Zechariah and daring Daniel, she was remarkably composed.

Mary wasn't so terrorized that she fell to the ground. She wasn't so overwhelmed she was ready to turn tail and run. She was really just puzzled. "Perplexed" and "confused" are accurate translations for her reaction. This was a crazy head-scratcher for Mary. In her humility, she wasn't expecting an angelic visitor.

The same type of angel encounter that struck terror in the heart of daring Daniel, and overwhelmed-with-fear Zechariah, didn't trigger a similar reaction in young Mary. Confused? Yes. Petrified? Nope.

What connection do you think there is between Mary's reaction to the news of her upcoming pregnancy and her heart for the Lord? Why?

POOR MARY

It is often said that Mary was poor, but how do we know this? We don't have access to Joseph's budget spreadsheet. What evidence is there in scripture?

One clear sign comes in Luke 2:24. What does this verse say was Mary's offering at the temple? Circle it:

And to offer a sacrifice in keeping with what is said in the Law of the Lord: "a pair of doves or two young pigeons." Luke 2:24

And according to Leviticus 12:8, what would be the reason for offering this particular animal? Underline it:

These are the regulations for the woman who gives birth to a boy or a girl. ⁸ But if she cannot afford a lamb, she is to bring two doves or two young pigeons, one for a burnt offering and the other for a sin offering. In this way the priest will make atonement for her, and she will be clean. Leviticus 12:7b-8

The woman who bore the Lamb of God who would take away the sins of the world, couldn't even afford a lamb for her offering. The mother of the King of kings, Mary, was poor in terms of worldly wealth.

Mary's lack of fear speaks to her heart of faith.

First John 4:18 says, "There is no fear in love. But perfect love drives out fear." Zechariah and Daniel may have been knock-kneed when confronted by Gabriel, but Mary's quiet confidence in God shone through. She knew God was in control—and we'll see evidence of her humble faith as we pick apart her encounter with Gabriel.

But before we do, let's take a moment to approach God in prayer. If Mary can encounter Gabriel without fear, we can certainly face much less, clothed in God's love. And yet, we fear.

So often we fear.

We fear financial ruin, we fear health problems, we fear job loss, we fear rejection by others, we fear uncertain futures, we fear unwanted political outcomes—but we can face them all.

Why? Because of God's perfect love.

If we've learned anything in this study, it's that we can always run to God in prayer. Take a moment to write a sentence prayer in the margin, asking that God's love would cover you in such peace and faith that any fears you carry today would melt away.

Fashionable Strength

Proverbs 31:25 says of a godly woman, "She is clothed with strength and dignity; she can laugh at the days to come."

When we realize the strength Mary showed in her encounter with Gabriel—how composed and God-assured she was, it's inspiring and remarkable. Because, in a paradoxical way, her biggest hardship and embarrassment to come (conception out of wedlock) would also be her greatest honor. It's deeply ironic.

> If a man happens to meet in a town a virgin pledged to be married and he sleeps with her, you shall take both of them to the gate of that town and stone them to death ... You must purge the evil from among you.
>
> DEUTERONOMY 22:23-24

The punishment for a woman in Mary's situation—a betrothed virgin now pregnant (had she slept with a man, that is)—was steep: a death sentence, ordered by law. See the instructions given in Deuteronomy 22:23-24.

Pregnant while engaged, Mary would have been considered an evil worthy of purging. Her guilt would have been assumed. No slap on the wrist for this one, no scarlet letter or second chance—this could be her end.

It had to be a sobering thought—a fearful one, even. And yet, Mary's confidence in God and joy at her newly found position of honor was palpable.

We'll delve into this more deeply as we study her prayer song later this week, but for now, let's take a moment to reflect: that which had the greatest potential to be her utter disgrace—even her demise (her pregnancy) was also her greatest honor, and humanity's only hope.

The Messiah would finally come. Israel's Savior, the Anointed One of God who'd save the people from their sins. The one greater than Moses who'd rescue God's people from their slave master of sin, who'd be the sacrificial lamb once-for-all—all eternity hinged on this!

And it required that Mary looked like a harlot in order to make it happen?!

What a beautiful mystery—and no wonder Mary was puzzled! After all, the Lord works in mysterious ways.

What might make her disgraced among worldly men, would also make her, "most honored among women." But isn't that just how it is in the bizzarro world of God's kingdom? So often things are upside-down and exactly opposite of how this world works.

Just look at me.

I am a mom of 8—and people seem to think I'd be more normal if I had two heads. Raised eyebrows and a loud, "I could never do that!" is the reaction I often get.

Others can't imagine why I'd willingly spend 72 months (6 full years) of my life pregnant, 16 years breastfeeding, enduring morning sickness, slogging through pregnancy discomforts, hours in labor, not to mention temper tantrums, dirty diapers, sleepless nights, teenage attitudes, sibling rivalries, mess after mess (after mess!) and the long days rearing children. Wouldn't something else be easier?

But they also don't know the overwhelming, overpowering, all-encompassing joy I experience when I catch my children in God's word, see the twinkle in my daughter's eye when she's telling a good story, hear the echoes of belly laughter ringing through our home, witness the sisters who know each other so

> That which had the greatest potential to be her utter disgrace—even her demise, Mary's pregnancy, was also her greatest honor and humanity's only hope.

The journey may seem long—no one else may understand—but the view from the top will be all the more worth it for the weary walking.

well they finish each other's sentences, participate in the spontaneous worship dance parties during dinner clean up, perceive the compassion etched on the face of a sibling when another is hurting, listen to the sincere prayers on behalf of the wounded, laugh with the communal whooping celebration when a goal is accomplished by a family member big or small, or snuggle a peacefully limp little one in my arms after a day well-spent. Words don't even come close to accurately describing how satisfying this life is.

So costly, yes—deeply so, my life poured out a living sacrifice—and yet rich beyond my wildest dreams. My soul sings in sync with David's, I will not offer the Lord what cost me nothing (2 Samuel 24:24). And it is precisely because of the cost that the reward is so sweet.

Friend, you likely taste this joy also. In the same way as you spend yourself treading the path God has for your life, rocky and steep though it may be, perhaps you know the puzzling feeling of both exertion and exhilaration as you press into God's ways.

The journey may seem long—no one else may understand—but the view from the top will be all the more worth it for the weary walking. The way to the mountaintop is hard, but it's oh-so good to tread. I wouldn't miss it for the world.

I can cry, "Lead me, Lord!" And I can accept God's call because He leads me well. "He guides me in the paths of righteousness For the sake of His name" (Psalm 23:3 NASB).

That's how good our Shepherd is.

We can humbly follow God's lead without fear because our Shepherd leads us well.

Spend a few moments in prayer:
- Thank God for graciously using humble women (like you!) for His amazing purposes.
- Ask the Lord to give you a heart for Him that can confidently "laugh at the days to come."
- Pray that God would give you the strength and the resolve to follow His lead, no matter how difficult it may seem.

Takeaway Truth – *"Hear my cry, O God; listen to my prayer. From the ends of the earth I call to you, I call as my heart grows faint; lead me to the rock that is higher than I." Psalm 61:1-2*

DAY 2: ENTERTAINING AN ANGEL

MAIN TEXT:
Luke 1:26-38

[God] makes His angels spirits, His ministers a flame of fire.
Psalm 104:4 (NKJV)

We cannot expect a tailor to make us a coat if we do not give him any cloth, nor a builder to build us a house if we let him have no building material; and in just the same way we cannot expect the Lord to live out His life in us if we do not give Him our lives in which to live. – Watchman Nee

Yesterday we learned that Mary, perplexed though she was, did not shrink back in terror during her encounter with Gabriel, but rather showed remarkable composure. Despite her humble status, her heart for the Lord shone through in her quiet confidence. We'll dig more into her angelic encounter today.

What do we learn about Gabriel from the angel's conversation with Zechariah in Luke 1:19?

The angel said to him, "I am Gabriel. I stand in the presence of God, and I have been sent to speak to you and to tell you this good news."

Luke 1:19

Gabriel had spent time in God's very presence and was sent by Him to deliver an all-important message to Mary—one that God's people had been waiting thousands of long, dark years to hear—"It is time."

Let's tear into Gabriel's God-given message for Mary, along with her reaction, to see what all we can learn from these fact-packed few verses:

v. 28 *"Greetings, you who are highly favored! The Lord is with you."* It was clear from Gabriel's first words that his appearance to Mary was all about God's greatness, not hers. Though it was true she was a virgin and from the kingly line of David (v. 27), she was also from Nazareth—not the centrally located, holier city of Jerusalem, a more logical choice—but from the "Galilee of the Gentiles," as some called it. A more heathen place than the holy city of Jerusalem for sure, with the scandalous kind of zip code that raised eyebrows.

It was a place so lowly, some wondered, "Can anything good come out of Nazareth?" (John 1:46). No, Mary's favor was not earned, but a gracious gift of God—the giver of all good things.

Though her details lined up with the prophecies, "a shoot will come up from the stump of Jesse" (Isaiah 11:1, see also 2 Samuel 7:12-16), it was only by God's grace that she would become most honored of women.

Mary had no honor of her own—it was because God was with her that she was honored. It was as if Psalm 46:5 would be her assurance, "God is within her, she will not fall; God will help her at break of day." Just like He was with Gideon (Judges 6:12), He was right by Mary's side.

> When the angel of the LORD appeared to Gideon, he said, "The LORD is with you, mighty warrior."
>
> JUDGES 6:12

v. 29 *Mary was greatly troubled at his words and wondered what kind of greeting this might be.* Mary was confused at this unlikely turn of events. Though every Jewish woman hoped to bear the Messiah, Mary was shocked to find such favor with God—evidence of her humility.

She didn't react to Gabriel's appearance by saying, "Well, it's about time!" Women had longed for millennia to have Mary's position of mother to the Messiah. To be chosen for this role was of monumental, eternal significance—an honor Mary rightly, humbly received.

vv. 30-33 *"Do not be afraid, Mary; you have found favor with God. 31 You will conceive and give birth to a son, and you are to call him Jesus. 32 He will be great and will be called the Son of the Most High. The Lord God will give him the throne of his father David, 33 and he will reign over Jacob's descendants forever; his kingdom will never end."*

> The child would be called "the Lord saves"— Jesus.

Gabriel again reassured Mary of her favor with God. He explained that she would conceive, fulfilling Isaiah's prophecy "the virgin will conceive" (Isaiah 7:14) and that the child would be called "the Lord saves"—Jesus. Like Joshua (Yeshua) had led God's people into the Promised Land, so Mary's son Jesus would lead His people to their eternal promised land—everlasting life.

BOLD: Six Praying Women, One Faithful God

The "Most High" as a term for God harkened back to the days of Melchizedek (Genesis 14:18) and the Psalms (47:2). John the Baptist was a prophet of the Most High (Luke 1:76) but Jesus was greater than a prophet, God's very Son—and He'd reign over a never-ending kingdom. And a poor, young, Nazarene Mary would be His mom.

v. 34. *"How will this be," Mary asked the angel, "since I am a virgin?"* Commentators and scholars write that these statements of Mary's are not evidence of doubt—she didn't ask for a sign, but she had genuine curiosity. In her humility, naivete, and maybe even shock, Mary can't wrap her head around the angel's amazing words. She can't help but blurt out her gut reaction. She had certainty, faith that it would take place as Gabriel indicated, "But how?"

vv. 35-37 *The angel answered, "The Holy Spirit will come on you, and the power of the Most High will overshadow you. So the holy one to be born will be called the Son of God. 36 Even Elizabeth your relative is going to have a child in her old age, and she who was said to be unable to conceive is in her sixth month. 37 For no word from God will ever fail."* Some versions translate verse 37 as, "For nothing will be impossible with God" (ESV).

Mary's baby would be born of the Spirit—because all things are possible with God, no matter how impossible they seem. Her womb would be like the temple's holy of holies, overshadowed by the Holy Spirit.

Just as Sarah of old conceived beyond her years of childbearing (Genesis 21:7) and now Mary's elderly relative Elizabeth also conceived (Luke 1:25)—God would control Mary's womb and make the impossible, possible. This echoed the Lord's words to Abraham from Genesis 18:14, "Is anything too hard for the LORD?"

v. 38 *"I am the Lord's servant," Mary answered. "May your word to me be fulfilled."* And with the humility of Hannah (1 Samuel 1:18), Mary submitted to God's purpose for her life. Her heart for the Lord and His plans were evident in her humble words.

A more fleshly reaction might have been fear—fear of her parents' rejection, or disavowal from her fiancé, or life as a social outcast as an unwed mother, and that is only if she avoided death by stoning.

GOD BECAME MAN

Tradition holds that Luke consulted with Mary herself when writing his Gospel–making her story found in Luke an accurate, firsthand account. The virgin birth is both miraculous, something only God could do, and important–without the stain of Adam's sin (Romans 5:14, 18-19).

Because God stooped down to us, Christ understands our struggles–fully man. Hebrews 4:15 says, "For we do not have a high priest who is unable to empathize with our weaknesses, but we have one who has been tempted in every way, just as we are–yet he did not sin."

And yet, we know Jesus is fully God, not sinful– "He committed no sin" 1 Peter 2:22. Likewise, 1 John 3:5 tells us, "But you know that he appeared so that he might take away our sins. And in him is no sin."

She would certainly have been labelled crazy—after all, the explanation for her condition would be pregnancy via the Holy Spirit—sounds totally realistic, right?

Still she said, "May everything you have said about me come true" (NLT).

When God gave miraculous womb-opening news, Sarah had laughed (Genesis 18:9-15), Zechariah doubted (Luke 1:18), but Mary was all in—no fear here.

Lead Us Not into Temptation

Mary's humble reply to Gabriel's words and her servant's heart reveal that she was willing to follow God's lead—despite any difficulty she might face. A handmaiden (the type of servant Mary described herself as) was the lowliest of all servants—and Mary proclaimed that's just what she was.

As a young, poor, engaged-but-not-married woman, she'd face her share of difficulties. But she was being led by a Good Shepherd. Psalm 23:2-3 says, "He leads me beside quiet waters, he refreshes my soul. He guides me along the right paths for his name's sake."

Mary was wise enough to know that God's paths were the right paths. She knew that life was more than keeping up appearances in Nazareth—that eternity was at stake.

Her son Jesus taught us to pray "Lead us not into temptation, but deliver us from the evil one" (Matthew 6:13). This section of the Lord's Prayer calls upon God for divine guidance. There's more than meets the eye happening in this world (Ephesians 6:12). Satan and his cohorts are prowling.

We must acknowledge that no matter how strong our eyeglass prescription, our earthy vision is limited. We need the Good Shepherd to lead us in the right paths.

Mary's submission to God meant following His lead. Her humble handmaiden heart made the way for our own precious Savior to be born on the earth. What a blessing!

Can you imagine if Mary had resisted? What if she'd become knock-kneed with fear? What if bearing the Savior had seemed too much an inconvenience for her? What if the cost of

> Mary knew that life was more than keeping up appearances in Nazareth— that eternity was at stake.

> Trust in the LORD with all your heart and lean not on your own understanding; in all your ways submit to him, and he will make your paths straight.
>
> PROVERBS 3:5-6

pregnancy and childbirth seemed a burden too great for her to bear?

It's hard to even imagine, so familiar are we with Mary's gracious acceptance of God's will and leading in her life. But how about us? Have we the humility of Mary? Have I?

Cringe.

All too often my teeth chatter in fear at obstacles much smaller than what Mary faced. What if that medical test comes back badly? What if my child strays? What if the paycheck won't cover that bill? What if I've said too much?

All too often my life feels inconvenienced by God's work—the sick baby crying for me at 3:00 a.m. again? Ugh!

A stranger's child shoving mine at the playground—here we go again!

That ministry needs my help—but can't someone else do it?! My attitude of entitlement can smell more rotten than spoiled fish.

Lord, give me the humility of Mary. Give me a spirit that says, "I am your servant! Anything you say, God! As you wish!"

Help me to stop white-knuckling my fears and clinging to my comforts. Help me to follow You in the righteous paths you long to graciously, lovingly lead me, if only I will submit to you.

How about you? Take a moment to reflect. Is there a path the Lord is trying to lead you in, and your pride is bristling in resistance? Write down your thoughts.

> Give me a spirit that says, "I am your servant! Anything you say, God! As you wish!"

It could be as big as a major life decision like a job change or a relocation, or as small as washing the dishes with a good attitude.

Let Him lead you in right paths.

How can we expect to be able to pray bold prayers, if we're not willing to follow the Lord's lead?

> In a dance, only one partner can lead, or else there will be lots of clumsy moves and sore toes. Are you letting the Lord lead you in the dance of life?

We, like Mary, can become vessels for pouring out God's good grace on this earth—if only we are willing to let Him take the lead. We can pray boldly, "Lead us, Lord!" And then follow close in the direction He goes.

In a dance, only one partner can lead, or else there will be lots of clumsy moves and sore toes. Are you letting the Lord lead you in the dance of life?

Lord, lead us not into temptation. Deliver us from evil—both the ugly evil in our hearts that wants to bristle with pride, and the evil that the enemy wants us ensnared in. We're in a spiritual battle; lead us on right paths. We don't want to stumble—but to gracefully dance.

> A crucial part of boldly crying, "Lead us, Lord!" is a humble willingness to accept the Lord's lead.

Spend some time with the Lord in prayer:

- Thank God for the honor and blessing He bestows on you—not for your own glory, but for His alone.
- Praise God for Mary's willingness to follow God's lead, and that He sent Jesus—fully God, fully man—to walk in our shoes.
- Ask God to muster in you a boldness to be able to pray, "Lead me, Lord" along with the strength and resolve to follow His lead in the dance of life.

Takeaway Truth – *"There is a time for everything, and a season for every activity under the heavens … a time to weep and a time to laugh, a time to mourn and a time to dance." Ecclesiastes 3:1, 4*

MAIN TEXT:
John 2:1-11

DAY 3: FOLLOW THE LEADER

For the LORD watches over the way of the righteous. Psalm 1:6

Remember, the shortest distance between a problem and the solution is the distance between our knees and the floor. - Charles Stanley

Right now two of the youngest members of my household are my headstrong three-year-old son and a lovably feisty puppy.

If you've cared for a willful three-year-old before, you may feel some sympathy for me. This is the one who keeps things interesting. I love him fiercely, but he has a way of pushing the boundaries.

At one-and-a-half he had a habit of climbing on the dining room table and swinging from the chandelier as if it were a gymnastics apparatus.

This is the kid who made "papier-mâché" out of toilet water, toilet paper, and press-on nail glue while I was on a Zoom call recording a podcast (and his older siblings were babysitting him—facepalm!). There are still stubborn remnants of the "papier-mâché" on our guest bathroom floor to bear witness to the art project.

This is the child who, when the house is quiet, causes a moment of panic as to what he's found for himself to do.

So you can imagine that such a curious, creative, spunky fellow (schnickelfritz) gets more than his fair share of reprimands and instructions. He has a seasoned mama, two big brothers, and four big sisters, after all.

But oh, is he happy about the puppy.

Why?

Because my schnickelfritz can finally be the boss.

No longer at the bottom of the pecking order, my spunky three-year-old can often be overheard giving the puppy nonsensical orders:

"Tuli! Don't dance!"

"Come bite this!"

"Chase that ball!"

Finally given some power, my spitfire son is in hog heaven.

But as silly as it sounds—taking satisfaction in giving needless commands to a frisky puppy—do we not also ridiculously relish power and control sometimes?

What about how no one else can load the dishwasher just quite right? Can't they see that the forks go tines down?!

Do we not also ridiculously relish power and control sometimes?

> But so many times, the Lord changes us through *not* allowing us control of those things we so desperately want to change. Because the change that needs to happen is first of all in our hearts.

Or maybe you've been called to plan an event, and your co-leader's way of doing things just seems ridiculous. Why would she think that the group would enjoy that silly activity?!

Maybe your husband wants to cook his specialty for supper tonight, but that wasn't on the weekly menu you made up. And it means you'll be having beef three nights in a row. Can't he just stick to the plan?!

And what about our prayer lives? Ever have it all figured out and try to pull God into your plans? Act like He's a genie in the bottle, ready to do your bidding?

What areas in your life right now might you be trying to force God to fit your plans, instead of being ready to follow His?

Your marriage: Your husband has been doing something that doesn't suit you. Can't God change him?

Your career: You can't stand your co-worker. Can't God help the supervisor see how incompetent they are? They should be let go already!

Your ministries at church: You really could use better volunteers. Can't God bring in some fresh talent?

Your extended family relationships: Why does your relative treat you like that? Can't God get them to give you some space?!

Truly we can, and should, take all our requests to God. **We must.** But at the same time, we don't need to cling to unhealthy, ungodly thoughts that aren't from Him.

Yes, sometimes the Lord changes our circumstances in the ways we want—and when He does, hooray!

But so many times, the Lord changes us through not allowing us control of those things we so desperately want to change. Because the change that needs to happen is first of all in our hearts.

Take a quiet moment, asking God to bring to light any place you might be overstepping and trying to control things you should leave to Him.

Sometimes, just like my little boy, we can get too big for our britches.

But we see a better way to relate to Jesus from Mary at the wedding in Cana.

Going To Cana And We're Gonna Get Married

If you haven't reviewed the passage yet, turn to John 2:1-11 and read it. I think you'll be amazed what we find—you'll be delighted with the details.

As we read these verses carefully, a few things jump out.

According to verses 1-2, who was invited to the wedding (list them in the same order as they are found in scripture, please)?

Jesus' mother was there, [2] and Jesus and his disciples had also been invited to the wedding.

JOHN 2:1b-2

Mary is listed first as a wedding guest, followed by Jesus and His disciples. Scholars say this is significant—that Mary is likely listed first because of her close relationship with the wedding host. Jesus and His disciples may have only been invited because of Mary. It is thought to have been Mary's relative, and as the events play out, Mary's deep concern for the wedding hosts is obvious.

If the wedding hosts were relatives of Mary, it is probably a humble affair, as her family was not wealthy. And, as we learn in verse 3, Mary has the inside information when the wine runs out. This is another clue of her close relationship with the hosts—perhaps she was even helping to serve.

Mary's compassion kicked in when the wine supply was exhausted. After all, to run out of wine at a wedding was sheer humiliation. It would be a terrible disgrace to the family. Since Joseph isn't present at this event, he has probably already passed. This means Mary was dependent upon Jesus when she needed help—so naturally to Him she went.

When the wine was gone, Jesus' mother said to him, "They have no more wine."

JOHN 2:3

I chuckle whenever I read her words to Jesus, "They have no more wine."

This reminds me of some of the "information" I give to my children:

"The trash can is full."

"There's a wet towel on your floor."

"You left the milk out."

Requests to "empty the trash," "hang the towel," or "put away the milk" are not spelled out—they're implied. But the expectation is clear. "Take care of it."

Mary's informing Jesus of the lack of wine has the same "Please take care of this" sort of feel. She's not just shooting the breeze here—Mary is hoping for some help.

This is reminiscent of our heartfelt Hannah-type prayers—asking God to provide. We can come to God in our need and ask Him for help. Always.

> His mother said to the servants, "Do whatever he tells you."
>
> JOHN 2:5

Jesus hadn't yet performed any public miracles, so perhaps her request was really just for help finding more wine. She may not have known the glory she was about to see—but one thing she knew: Jesus could handle it.

What happened in verse 5? What did this reveal about Mary's confidence in Jesus?

Mary didn't come to Jesus with an agenda of how the wine would be produced—she didn't even plead and beg with Jesus for more wine. She simply told Jesus the situation, then left it in His hands, confident that He would take care of it. With a "Jesus take the wheel" attitude, she told the servants, "Do whatever He tells you."

There's a meme online that tickles my funnybone. It's a photo of a man driving a car pell-mell. The vehicle looks ready to wreck at any moment, and the driver desperately cries, "Not that wheel, Jesus!" as the back wheel flies off into the ditch. We assume he's proclaimed, "Jesus, take the wheel" in his hour of need, expecting Jesus to help him with steering, only to have one of the rubber tires taken instead! Ha!

A Quiet Miracle

What happened next at the humble wedding is nothing short of miraculous—miraculously personal, that is.

Who realized what had happened when Jesus turned water to wine? Did everyone at the wedding? Look at v. 9 and v. 11 for clues.

At a modest wedding, with only the servants who had drawn the water and His own inner circle even realizing what was happening, Jesus began to reveal His glory for the first time. Because Mary brought her concern to Him and let Him take the lead. And He did.

But Jesus, in His goodness, let others participate in the miraculous. Look up the following verses and see how common people doing common acts of service were used by Jesus to accomplish the miraculous. Do at least three:

John 2:8

Matthew 14:18-19

John 9:7

John 11:39, 41

Jesus took the cooperation of everyday, ordinary people doing everyday, ordinary acts like drawing water, serving food, washing, and moving a stone to accomplish the miraculous: turning water to wine, multiplying food to feed thousands, bringing sight to the blind, and even raising the dead.

Ever think your life isn't glamorous enough? Not with Jesus involved. Think again.

> And the master of the banquet tasted the water that had been turned into wine. He did not realize where it had come from, though the servants who had drawn the water knew ...[11] What Jesus did here in Cana of Galilee was the first of the signs through which he revealed his glory; and his disciples believed in him.
>
> JOHN 2:9, 11

With Jesus, the everyday becomes sacred.

With Jesus, the everyday becomes sacred. The cool drink we give a little one becomes serving Christ Himself (Matthew 10:42). The feeding of hungry souls and hungry stomachs becomes a life of love poured out for Him (John 21:17). We serve others by washing—be it dirty feet or dirty dishes, praying that our acts of service usher spiritual cleansing in the eyes of any who might be blinded (John 13:14), and as we tell stories of God's faithfulness, we stack stones of remembrance so that our children might also know His faithfulness and be raised from death to life (Joshua 4:20-24).

One thing I want to point out in all of these everyday-actions-turned-miraculous is the common theme of unquestioning obedience—following God's lead.

I'm guessing the servants didn't understand why Jesus would want them to fill water jars and draw out water.

I'm guessing the disciples didn't understand why Jesus asked them to feed 5,000 people with only a small lunch.

I'm guessing the blind man didn't understand why Jesus smeared spittle-mud on his face and told him to wash.

And I know people at Lazarus's funeral didn't see the point in moving the gravestone (John 11:39).

But you know what? They did it. And because they followed Jesus's lead, they were able to be a part of something divine—something mysteriously and wonderfully bigger than themselves. Something miraculous.

I've walked that same road—though in my weakness, not as unquestioningly.

When a friend encouraged me to write a Bible study, I thought, "Yeah, right!"

But it wasn't just the friend. As time wore on, it was clear that God wanted me to walk that path—to write in obedience to Him. But it didn't make sense to me. "My plate is full taking care of my kids and being a pastor's wife. Those are important. Isn't that enough? How could I possibly do more?!" I bucked God.

I felt I had so little to offer, but finally I reluctantly gave in. And oh, I am so glad I did!

The richness and sweet moments I've had with the Lord have been well worth any effort and sacrifice on my part! And just like the small lunch feeding the thousands, God has graciously taken my small offering and multiplied it—all glory to Him!

Don't hesitate like me, dive right in!

Allow God to lead you in His paths—even when they don't seem to make sense to you. When we are weak, He is strong (2 Corinthians 12:10). And when you follow God's lead, you get to partner with the divine.

Miraculous Joy

Maybe it's puzzling to you that Jesus would quietly perform this miracle. After all, who cared about the beverages served at a party? It's not as life-changing as a lame man walking or as symbolic as a blind man seeing, right?

I used to be in the "what's the big deal about wine at the wedding" camp, but now I see more clearly what Jesus was doing.

Who cares about the beverages at a party? Jesus. That's who. He cares about sparrows (Luke 12:6) and He knows the number of hairs on your head (Luke 12:7).

And He cared about the wine. It meant something.

Read the following verses, observing the purpose of wine. Circle the common theme:

"... wine that cheers God and men" Judges 9:13 (ESV).

"... wine that gladdens human hearts" Psalm 104:15.

Joy! Wine was a symbol of joy. It cheers. It gladdens.

The joy of the world tastes good at first—it tempts you and baits you and draws you in, then runs out, leaving you empty. Full only of your disappointments, like the first wine at the wedding.

But not the joy Jesus offers.

God's joy never runs out—and it only gets better and better with time! It fills the empty. It never disappoints.

The water to wine was a miracle of grace—demonstrating God's generous gift of enduring joy to undeserving, ordinary us.

WATER TO WINE BUT HARDLY A WINO

Don't be tempted to use Jesus's water-to-wine miracle to excuse compromises in your life. Yes, wine was used during the time of Jesus, and yes, He did turn water to wine. But do not forget that the Bible consistently praises self-control, especially in the area of alcohol. Jesus was hardly a wino.

God's joy never runs out—and it only gets better and better with time! It fills the empty. It never disappoints.

So let's be like Mary—and when the wine runs out, or the car breaks down, or there's a big decision to make, or there's extra money in the bank to give—let's boldly tell Jesus, and stand ready to do what He says.

> When we ask God to lead, and then follow, He turns the ordinary into the miraculous—bringing joy that lasts.

Share a simple prayer time with the Lord:

- Pray for clear conviction in any area you might be overstepping your bounds and trying to "take the wheel" back from Jesus, and ask for the strength to let go.
- Thank God that you can bring any concern to His capable hands.
- Praise the Lord for the ways He allows you to cooperate with Him and be part of the everyday miracles He's doing all around you. Ask Him to give you eyes to see what He's doing.

Takeaway Truth – *"May God give you heaven's dew and earth's richness—an abundance of grain and new wine." Genesis 27:28*

MAIN TEXT:
Luke 1:39-56

DAY 4: ANYTHING-BUT-PROUD MARY

My soul glorifies the Lord and my spirit rejoices in God my Savior, for he has been mindful of the humble state of his servant.
Luke 1:46b-48

The primary goal of prayer isn't instruction—it's intimacy... God knows that if he has our hearts, then our hands will follow.
– Amanda Pittman

Yesterday we looked closely at the water-to-wine miracle at the wedding in Cana. We saw Mary's example of taking our problems to Jesus, and allowing Him to lead the way to the solution. Her deep faith in His leading and His solutions are a beautiful model of how we can humbly allow the Lord to lead.

BOLD: Six Praying Women, One Faithful God

What great lessons we can learn from those who walked with Jesus! They chose obedience in the ordinary things and revealed that when we cooperate with the Almighty, even the mundane becomes sacred. The Lord guides us in right paths for His glory, for His name's sake.

And we see more of the same in Mary's life today. We'll backtrack, rewinding to her beautiful Magnificat—the prayer she prayed glorifying God when she visited her relative Elizabeth after Gabriel told Mary she'd conceive the Messiah.

Not surprisingly, we'll see more mind-blowing humility from this special young woman.

The poor, young girl Mary prayed a heartfelt, scripture-rich song of praise—one that shows a strong resemblance to Hannah's.

We'll do well to emulate her lead-me-Lord mentality, her obedient readiness to follow God's lead, her example of a woman ready to walk in God's paths for His name's sake.

An Encouraging Journey

You'll remember that in our study of Luke 1 earlier in the week, we learned that Gabriel had revealed to Mary that her relative Elizabeth had her own miraculous pregnancy (v. 36). Mary was eager to see "nothing will be impossible with God" (Luke 1:37, ESV) for herself and set out to visit Elizabeth.

The journey took her from Nazareth to Hebron, the priestly town where Elizabeth and Zechariah lived. It was a long journey for a young woman—around 100 miles.

Mary's trip was not a leisurely one—this was not a vacation, but to learn—confirming Gabriel's news and gaining encouragement from Elizabeth.

John Jumps for Joy

You'd expect that after such a long journey, Mary would be ready to collapse upon her arrival. But instead of slumping into her seat, there was jumping for joy all around!

Read verse 41 of Luke 1. Underline or highlight the two things that happened when Elizabeth heard Mary's greeting.

CONCEPTION AT HEBRON?

Some speculate that the Messiah was conceived there—Hebron. It was a location rich with significance—where Abraham had his first land (Genesis 13:18), David his first crown (2 Samuel 2), where the forefathers and foremothers were buried: Abraham and Sarah, Isaac and Rebekah, Jacob and Leah (Genesis 49:31), as well as Adam and Eve (according to tradition).

When Elizabeth heard Mary's greeting, the baby leaped in her womb, and Elizabeth was filled with the Holy Spirit.

LUKE 1:41

For he will be great in the sight of the Lord. He is never to take wine or other fermented drink, and he will be filled with the Holy Spirit even before he is born.

LUKE 1:15

Even Elizabeth your relative is going to have a child in her old age, and she who was said to be unable to conceive is in her sixth month.

LUKE 1:36

Shout for joy to the LORD, all the earth, burst into jubilant song with music.

PSALM 98:4

How was this confirmation of Gabriel's words, both what the angel had told Zechariah about John (the baby) in Luke 1:15, and what the angel had told Mary (see Luke 1:36)? Why might the confirmation matter to Mary?

The supernatural, miraculous, spirit-filled work of God continued in the lives of Mary and Elizabeth with Mary's arrival and greeting. Gabriel's words were proven true: Elizabeth, old though she was, was expecting a son—in her sixth month of pregnancy! And her little one, John, was filled with the Holy Spirit, even in the womb!

And if Gabriel's words about Elizabeth and John the Baptist were true, Mary could surely trust the angel's words about her own pregnancy as well. Let the celebration begin! Mary's faith was bolstered by her visit with Elizabeth. These women and their babes would be filled with God's Spirit and used for His special purposes.

And eternity held its breath.

Elizabeth was filled with the Spirit and knew Mary's privileged position as the Messiah's mother instantly. Her loud proclamation reveals her joy (Psalm 98:4) at this spirit-filled encounter, *"Blessed are you among women, and blessed is the child you will bear! But why am I so favored that the mother of my Lord should come to me? As soon as the sound of your greeting reached my ears, the baby in my womb leaped for joy. Blessed is she who has believed that the Lord would fulfill his promises to her!" (Luke 1:42-45).*

Elizabeth wasn't given a heads-up that she'd be seeing her relative, who also happened to be the Messiah's mother-to-be. But as the Holy Spirit filled Elizabeth, the divine revelation of what was happening caused her to rejoice.

 BOLD: Six Praying Women, One Faithful God

It's worth noticing that though she was the wife of a priest and more notable than Mary herself, we don't see a superior or jealous attitude in Elizabeth.

So often women choose to be unhappy at other's successes or jealous when friends succeed—not Elizabeth! She showed genuine joy, the same attitude reflected in her son John later (see John 1:27; John 3:29; Matthew 3:14)—joy at the greatness of the Messiah to come.

Elizabeth proclaimed that Mary was blessed among women because of her belief in what God would do (v. 45). Elizabeth knew firsthand how easy it was to react in unbelief to such amazing news—she saw an unbelieving reaction in her own husband Zechariah—mute as a result of his lack of faith (Luke 1:20).

What an interesting irony: the old, seasoned priest who had ministered for years, unbelieving of Gabriel's good news, and the young, humble girl whose certain faith rang true.

Mary was hardly mute, as we're about to explore for ourselves. Her prayer of praise—the Magnificat—is called such because she "magnifies" or glorifies God, bringing His praiseworthiness into focus by her scripture-laced words of worship.

Overwhelmed with joy—the same joy felt first by in-utero John and his expectant mother Elizabeth—Mary launched into her beautiful song of praise for the good, mighty, promise-keeping, saving God who exalts the humble and fills the hungry.

Attitude of Gratitude

Mary was well-versed in the word of God, as evidenced by her song echoing many Old Testament scriptures. Like psalms of Thanksgiving, and Hannah's prayer of 1 Samuel 1. Mary thanks God, then explains why she's so thankful—it's really good stuff that we'll dig into in just a minute.

But first, a blast from the past. Here's a quote from our Hannah week, when we studied God as Provider, Our Daily Bread:

> Hannah knew deep down into her very bones that the greatest gift, the greatest provision she could ever receive was God Himself. That's why she proclaimed, "My heart rejoices in the LORD ... for I delight in your

> "Blessed is she who has believed that the Lord would fulfill his promises to her!"
>
> LUKE 1:45

Mary launched into her beautiful prayer of praise.

YOU DO THE MATH

Although we may not want to admit it, often we do calculations when it comes to pregnancies: when was the last cycle? Go back about three months from there and you have the due date. Let's do a few of our own calculations concerning Elizabeth's pregnancy.

Flip back to when Gabriel first told Mary about Elizabeth's pregnancy. How far along was Elizabeth then (see Luke 1:36)?

Elizabeth was six months along when Mary first found out her relative was expecting. Soon after, Mary made her journey to see Elizabeth. How long did Mary stay (see v. 56)?

Add those together and what do you get? Six plus three is nine. Nine months! Scholars feel it is very likely that Mary was able to share not only in the joy of Elizabeth's pregnancy, but likely the birth of John as well.

What a gift God gave to Mary in her relationship with Elizabeth. Those first sometimes-difficult months of Mary's pregnancy, she had the companionship and camaraderie of one a few steps ahead of her. One whose pregnancy was also inexplicably miraculous. What encouragement Mary received from Elizabeth's words and company.

The heartfelt counsel of a friend is as sweet as perfume and incense. Proverbs 27:9 NLT

How kind of God to give Mary this experience, before heading back to the likely gossip and sideways glances of her hometown.

He's so good.

deliverance" (1 Sam. 2:1), a phrase that would be all-but-exactly repeated hundreds of years later by a similarly humble, grateful mother Mary, who said, "My soul glorifies the Lord, and my spirit rejoices in God my Savior" (Luke 1:46-47).

Hannah and Mary both knew that rather than sing of the glory of the gift, they should praise the Giver, the Source of all good things.

Mary's Magnificat glorifies God, not herself. She knew of God's goodness to Hannah and couldn't help but feel the same—God had lifted Mary up, giving her the incredible honor of bringing Christ into the world. But ultimately, her words rang out like the psalmist, "Praise the LORD, my soul; all my inmost being, praise his holy name (Psalm 103:1).

With everything she has and everything she is, Mary sings God's praises. Her heart beat in tune with the man after God's own heart, her own forefather David, who wrote, "Then my soul will rejoice in the LORD and delight in his salvation" (Psalm 35:9).

God saved her and chose her (vv. 47-48) despite her humble state, as she acknowledged, saying, "He has been mindful of the humble state of his servant." God had compassion on those who were despised and lowly, opening the wombs of women like Leah (Genesis 29:31), and Hannah (1 Samuel 1:19), and now Mary. He remembered them.

When Mary proclaimed, "From now on all generations will call me blessed" (v. 48), she acknowledged that God blessed her. This was not a proud statement from Mary. She was receiving God's favor—not taking credit for it as her own, nor acting as though she is deserving—but accepting it, fully intending to receive the blessing for God's glory alone.

This is echoed as she stated, "The Mighty One has done great things for me" (v. 49). Mary makes it crystal clear that it is God who is the Savior (v. 47); He is the One who is great, and He does great things.

In fact, Mary's prayer points to three characteristics of people for whom God has done great things. They are:

- **The hopeful**. Mary proclaimed, "His mercy extends to those who fear him, from generation to generation" (v. 50). Those who fear God realize that without Him, they have no hope at all. He is their only hope. "But the mercy of the LORD is from everlasting to everlasting for those who fear Him, And His justice to the children's children" (Psalm 103:17 NASB). Similarly, Hannah had asserted, "He will guard the feet of his faithful servants" (1 Samuel 2:9) and "I delight in your deliverance" (1 Samuel 2:1). God is merciful to those who fear Him, who put their hope in Him.
- **The humble**. Mary reemphasized the scriptural theme of God lifting up the lowly and bringing down the proud. She said, "He has brought down rulers from their thrones but has lifted up the humble" (Luke 1:52). Hannah had said, "The LORD sends poverty and wealth; he humbles and he exalts. He raises the poor from the dust and lifts the needy from the ash heap" (1 Samuel 2:7-8). God exalts the humble, the low, the meek, the God-reliant. (See also: James 4:6-10; 1 Peter 5:5-6; 1 Corinthians 1:27-31).
- **The hungry**. "He has filled the hungry with good things," Mary said (Luke 1:53). But we know this is not just those with growling stomachs. We know that God fills those who hunger for Him. Mary knew that better than filling our bellies, is filling our innermost cravings—something only God can do. Those who are spiritually hungry are blessed because they're filled by God (John 6:35; Matthew 5:6; 1 Samuel 2:5; Psalm 113:7-8; Revelation 3:17).

He remembered us in our low estate His love endures forever.

PSALM 136:23

The reason Mary's prayer is so magnificent is because it points to a Magnificent God.

HOPEFUL

HUMBLE

HUNGRY

Do you recognize these characteristics in your life and heart? Take a moment to consider: How can you cultivate a greater hope in the Lord? How can you practice greater humility? How can you increase your hunger for righteousness? Record your ideas on the graphics in the margin.

Perhaps you thought of ways to cultivate your hope like memorizing scripture, taking time to worship, or creating some artwork with an encouraging verse.

Maybe your ideas for practicing humility include an apology for a wrong, admitting your guilt, or serving someone cheerfully.

You might have listed ideas for increasing your hunger for God like: finding a godly mentor to glean wisdom from, or committing to a special time of fasting and prayer.

The opposite of these three types of people singled out by Mary in the Magnificat—those who don't fear God, who are proud, who think they are satisfied without Him—are treading on thin ice.

The God-fearing, the humble, and the hungry-for-God are the ones who cry earnestly and boldly, "Lead us not into temptation, but deliver us from evil!" And God listens. He hears. He leads, and they follow.

Keeper of Promises

Mary also made clear that God came through on His promises to his chosen people (vv. 54-55), recognizing that the Messiah she'd bear would fulfill God's promise to Abraham that all peoples would be blessed through him (Genesis 22:17-18).

And the reason Mary's prayer is magnificent is not because she is so blessed or humble or God-fearing or hungry for righteousness (though we know she was all those things).

The reason Mary's prayer is so magnificent is because it points to a Magnificent God—the Savior who has done great things! Who gives mercy freely to those who fear Him. Who brings up the lowly. Who fills the hungry. Who keeps His promises. He's that good.

> Our magnificent God does great thing for the hopeful, He lifts up the humble, and He fills up the hungry—who wouldn't want to follow a God like that?!

Spend some time with the Lord in prayer:

- Look at the graphic organizer you filled out in today's lesson with ideas of growing in hope, humility and hunger. Pray through your ideas, boldly asking our magnificent God to grow them in you.
- Allow your soul to "glorify the Lord" for a few moments and rejoice in God your Savior, echoing the heart-attitude of Mary.
- Thank God for wise friends and mentors to encourage you along the way as you follow His lead—or if you don't yet have any, ask God to provide them.

Takeaway Truth – *"Blessed is she who has believed that the Lord would fulfill his promises to her!" Luke 1:45*

DAY 5: ALL IN THE FAMILY

MAIN TEXT: Matthew 12:46-50

For whoever does the will of my Father in heaven is my brother and sister and mother. Matthew 12:50

It is through prayer that we become friends with Christ.
-Matthew Kelly

Say the Right Thing at the Right Time

I have a terrible habit of mistakenly texting my daughter's soccer coach.

Yikes.

Even more embarrassing is that I've done it multiple times now. Like four times this season.

A friend has told me, "I think my phone needs to check with me before I send each text, 'Are you sure you want to send this to them?'" I think that must be true for me too.

Now there's nothing wrong with asking the coach an appropriate question at the right time—like inquiring about what time the bus leaves for an away game.

But sending her an, "I love you and I hope you're having a great day!" that was meant for my husband right in the middle of practice is highly inappropriate. (Facepalm!)

Or how about the time I texted her: "We just got here and we can't find a parking spot" that was (again) meant for my husband. While she was running through her preparations before the game. Double yikes.

There's something to be said for communicating the right message at the right time. We'll find that in our scripture for today.

First, I want us to take note of the timing of this story. What is it, according to Matthew 12:46?

46 While Jesus was still talking to the crowd, his mother and brothers stood outside, wanting to speak to him. 47 Someone told him, "Your mother and brothers are standing outside, wanting to speak to you." 48 He replied to him, "Who is my mother, and who are my brothers?" 49 Pointing to his disciples, he said, "Here are my mother and my brothers. 50 For whoever does the will of my Father in heaven is my brother and sister and mother."

MATTHEW 12:46-50

Maybe we think, "How could Jesus blow off His mother and brothers!" After all, their motives may have been great—they may have come in love, wanting to encourage Jesus to rest after a long day. Or they may have come in concern, wanting to warn Jesus of the opposition He was stirring up.

But here's the thing—no matter their motives, it was bad timing. Jesus was still teaching. It was like my texting the coach during pre-game warm-ups—it's a no-no. We don't know the reason for Jesus's family interrupting His teaching—only that they did.

Quickly, though, I want you to go back and notice: where were they standing, according to verse 46 of Matthew 12? Underline the answer.

Outside. Hmmm.

Jesus, the long-awaited, much-needed Messiah had finally arrived, after thousands of years of suffering and waiting. The Anointed One Himself—and Mary and her kids were the ones blessed enough to have Jesus in their family! They had the chance to learn from Him. And they were ... outside?

Sometimes familiarity breeds contempt.

We know this was the case among some of Jesus's family members. Look it up for yourself! What does John 7:5 say?

> For even his own brothers did not believe in him.
>
> JOHN 7:5

Can you imagine? Some of Jesus's own brothers didn't even believe him!

Whaaaat?!

It's a glimpse into the drama of Jesus's family. *The Real House Lives of Nazareth*. Wouldn't that have made a good reality TV show! Because they were real people. They made bad decisions—like interrupting Him while He was teaching.

We don't know why, but we do know that even though they were His family members, they didn't always understand what He was up to.

But before we jump to conclusions that Jesus is telling us to forsake our families (vv 48-50), let's hop to a few other places in scripture. Hit the pause button before you read too much into this encounter between Jesus and His attempting-to-interrupt family members, and make sure you don't throw the baby out with the bathwater.

In Matthew 15:1-9 Jesus called the Pharisees hypocrites for neglecting to honor their parents. And in John 19, even as He was dying on the cross, Jesus set the example of ensuring for His own mother's care.

So what's up with the original passage we're studying, where Jesus seemed to blow off His family?

This verse may give you a clue:

"If anyone comes to me and does not hate father and mother, wife and children, brothers and sisters—yes, even their own life—such a person cannot be my disciple." Luke 14:26

Now I know that "hate" is pretty strong language. In fact, it was outlawed in my family growing up.

We don't hate people.

> Near the cross of Jesus stood his mother, his mother's sister, Mary the wife of Clopas, and Mary Magdalene. [26] When Jesus saw his mother there, and the disciple whom he loved standing nearby, he said to her, 'Woman, here is your son,' [27] and to the disciple, 'Here is your mother.' From that time on, this disciple took her into his home"
>
> JOHN 19:25-27.

But Jesus is using strong language to drive home a point here: everything else pales in comparison to loving Him. It's not that we HATE our dad, mom, spouse, kids, siblings, or life—we already reviewed how Jesus called the Pharisees hypocrites for neglecting their families—it's that we love God so much more.

Friends, that's why regularly studying scripture is so important. We must have hearts that beat in tune with God's. We must be able to discern the true meaning of what God is teaching us using *all* of scripture—rather than cherry-picking verses or following empty rules like the Pharisees, we must live a life of love that reflects all of God's word and all of God's heart.

So what was happening when Jesus didn't allow His family to interrupt? Jesus was not giving His obligation to His family precedence over His obligation to God.

In essence—He is following God's lead, instead of His family's.

He didn't dishonor His mother. He didn't leave her high and dry, without what she needed to survive. He didn't neglect her.

He just didn't let her get in the way of doing His Father's work.

And now, the Good Stuff

Oh, how I love being part of a family! My husband's family of origin (the Risners) have so many inside jokes, nicknames, movie quotes they recite, and memories they share that it's a good time whenever we gather. In fact, we've even coined a term for all of our inner circle stuff—Risnerisms.

Admittedly, it took a while for me to understand what they were saying before I became "one of the elephants" (an insider), but now that I've been "trashed in" (hanging around) for over 25 years, I'm getting the hang of it, and it sure is "good, clean fun." Even if I don't have a translator!

Families are fantastic. That's why it's great that Jesus wasn't asking us to hate them for real.

But enough of what Jesus wasn't saying—on to what He did say.

Did you catch it? It's pretty great, especially verse 50. That says, "Whoever does the will of my Father in heaven is my brother and sister and mother."

Luke's take on the verse is very similar, but with just a teensy different angle: "My mother and brothers are those who hear God's word and put it into practice" Luke 8:21.

Doing God's will—hearing His word and living it out—that's how we become part of God's family! What a golden opportunity! It's like winning the lottery, the Superbowl, Publisher's Clearinghouse, Miss America, and going to a waterpark all at the same time! Only better!!

Did anyone else just shout, "Yes!" and do the cha-ching motion with their arm? No? Just me??!

Oh, this is so good, friend. Why?

Because there's a chance for us to join the family. And as much as I like my family, and my husband's family—oh, how I love being in the family of God!

We were designed to be part of a group—God's family. If you are in the church, you get the same protection, deliverance, and close relationship with Christ that His very family had.

Biological relationship is not a necessity—being born of the spirit is. As His body, His family, He will not lead "us" into temptation and He will deliver "us" from evil.

Lest we think this excludes Jesus's family of origin, I'll clue you in—it doesn't. How do I know? Acts 1:14.

This is a fast-forward a few years from the time of the Gospels, when Jesus had already been crucified and raised from the dead. Jesus had appeared to His disciples, then ascended into heaven. Those closest to Jesus were gathered together, and guess who was there? Read Acts 1:14 to find out:

That's right! Jesus's family was there! In the happily-ever-after ending they were both His family by birth and by doing God's will. Pretty cool, huh?

So how about us? Are we hanging out outside? Too busy to really listen to what Jesus is saying, like His family in the Matthew 12 passage?

Maybe you're quick to think, "Oh no! Not me!! I'm not too busy to listen to God!"

> Doing God's will—hearing His word and living it out—that's how we become part of God's family!

> They all joined together constantly in prayer, along with the women and Mary the mother of Jesus, and with his brothers.
>
> ACTS 1:14

> Are the things you're giving your attention to speaking the will of God? Because if not, you'd better be careful.

But take stock for a minute: What is it you've been listening to today? What music? What voices? What people? Take a moment to reflect and jot down your thoughts.

Are the things you're giving your attention to speaking the will of God? Because if not, you'd better be careful. How are you going to hear the word of God and obey it if you're too busy listening to something else?

What's the point of boldly calling to God, "Lead me!" and then listening more intently to the newscaster? Or your best friend? Or your spouse? Or that novel you've been reading to escape from your stress?

If what you're listening to isn't helping you hear God, then take a good hard look at ditching it.

Seem too radical?

Maybe it is extreme, but I don't want to end up like Mary when she was outside—interrupting what Jesus was trying to do, getting in the way instead of jumping in and being part of it. I don't want to miss out on the good stuff, and if you knew how good the good stuff was, you wouldn't want to miss out on it either.

> If you knew how good the good stuff was, you wouldn't want to miss out on it either.

So, without further ado, boldly ask Him to lead you—not into temptation, but away from evil.

Why?

So that you can be part of the family. So you can know the inside jokes and the joy of being so close you finish each other's thoughts. So you can make eternal memories with the Lord, walking with Him, laughing with Him, and sometimes crying with Him.

What more could you want?

> The joy of being part of God's forever family includes boldly asking Him to lead, listening to Him closely, and following Him.

Spend some time with the Lord in prayer:

- Pray that God would help you to know if you're listening to voices that aren't helping you follow His lead, so that you can stop listening to them.
- Thank God for the amazing opportunity to be in His family—and ask Him to help you hear His word clearly so you can obey it.
- Ask God to help you, like Mary and Jesus's siblings, learn to be in constant prayer.

Takeaway Truth — *"He replied, 'Blessed rather are those who hear the word of God and obey it.'" Luke 11:28*

Friends, latch onto this important point we've learned from the life and prayers of humble and wise Mary, mother of Christ:

To pray bold, we ask for God to lead us, and then follow Him—finding abundant, blow-your-mind blessing where He leads.

Pause for Praise— By looking at the life and prayers of Mary we make an important realization: that humility and honor go hand-in-hand in following God's lead. In her encounter with Gabriel and in her Magnificat there is beautiful evidence of her willingness—her desire even—to follow God's lead, giving Him the glory and honor He deserved. In both Mary's life and the miracle at Cana we learned that when we allow God to lead us, He lets us partner with Him to do the miraculous! And when we cry out for Him to lead, then faithfully follow Him, we get to be part of His forever family. Before you close these pages, pause for some special time praising the One who longs to lead you well. Magnify God's name, like Mary the mother, watching a lyric video for Brooke Fraser's "A Thousand Hallelujahs." If your tastes tend toward hymns, choose a lyric video for "Savior, Like a Shepherd Lead Us." And as you worship, lift Him up and humbly look to Him to lead you well, committing to follow His path where you find real life.

CONCLUSION

Here is the conclusion of the matter: Fear God and keep his commandments, for this is the duty of all mankind.
Ecclesiastes 12:13

True prayer is a way of life, not just for use in cases of emergency. Make it a habit, and when the need arises you will be in practice. – Billy Graham

A Broken Body, and a Broken Heart

God's so good—He gives us exactly what we need, right when we need it.

This study was no different for me.

I had been cruising along, researching and drafting the pages of this book—digging through commentaries, poring over scriptures, looking up Hebrew and Greek words—the whole nine yards. And it was incredible (it always is). God was revealing Himself to me in new ways, taking me deeper than I had gone before.

Then it happened.

The worst day of my life.

My husband, John, had always struggled with back pain as long as I'd known him. It would range from everyday nagging discomfort to knock-you-to-the-ground-for-a-week agony.

It had flared up at some of the most inopportune times in the past—just after the birth of a child, right before a family vacation or a ministry trip, or days before a big move—you get the picture.

Over the years, I often had seasons of carrying heavy loads—both literally and figuratively—while watching my husband struggle with limitations. I felt the burden of bearing every physical responsibility for my family: loading and unloading suitcases and groceries, moving furniture, mowing, raking leaves, trimming, cleaning, organizing, snow shoveling, mulching, packing boxes for our move, trying (and usually

I will sing the Lord's praise, for he has been good to me.

PSALM 13:6

God gives us exactly what we need, right when we need it.

failing) to repair any and every broken thing around our home—you name it, and if it was physical, I did it.

There were days he couldn't even lift our children, bend to take out the trash, pick up a toy off the ground, or even tie his own shoes. It was rough.

He had learned to live with the pain—even as we cried out to God for John's healing.

And through the pain, despite the difficult days, we chose to see God's goodness. John is a pastor, after all, and able to work lying on the floor with a laptop and a cell phone. If he'd been a builder or a postman or a plumber, we'd have been sunk. We were (and are!) so grateful for God's provision financially, keeping our family afloat.

And God had provided so many lessons through the struggle. He'd taken John deeper in prayer, and taught John that His grace was sufficient—that His power was made perfect in weakness.

God had taught me that with His help I could do things that didn't seem possible, that the body of Christ was a beautiful blessing when it came to burden-sharing, and that—when it was all said and done—the only thing I needed was Him.

But just like that, it seemed the world came crashing in.

Against his better judgement, John helped unload an 800-pound basketball goal and injured his back again. But this was different; this pain was worse than ever before. So. Much. Worse.

He couldn't sit; he couldn't move—he was in agony. His pain was off the charts, and I felt so very helpless. I remember begging John to let me call the squad to get him to the ER, but he was convinced they'd hurt him getting him on the stretcher. I remember pleading with John to let me drive him to the hospital, and him telling me that he thought he'd pass out from pain if he tried to make his way downstairs to the vehicle.

I was so desperate.

I remember the lowest-of-the-low moment as I had finally convinced him to let me take him to the hospital. Inching together down the staircase was heartbreaking. He was in so

> But just like that, it seemed the world came crashing in.

much pain, tears streamed down his face—and by the time we made it to the bottom step, tears streamed down my face too.

The pain persisted for 22 days.

But here's the incredible thing—I had just the tools I needed, freshly placed in my own prayer toolbox. I was ready-as-I-could-be for the hurricane-force storm I was about to face.

In the weeks that followed, and the hardship we endured, I reminded myself:

- "God sees you, Rachel. You're not alone in this. He's so close. Run to Him—He's your Father."

- "God is holy and mighty—He's so powerful that He parts the waters, making a way when there is no way. Praise Him for it, Rachel."

- "God has kingdom purpose in this battle, Rachel. Lean into it! Pray His Kingdom come and His will done and see the stars fight on your behalf, and the heavens rain down to bring victory."

- "God can handle your heartbreak, Rachel. Your brokenness isn't too much for Him. Bring your pain and your struggle and your need and lay it at His feet. He will provide."

- "God wants you to live forgiven, Rachel. Bask in all He's done for you, loving much, clinging to Him with courage. Be confident in His love for you."

- "God will lead you, Rachel. Dig into His word for comfort and direction, instead of relying on yourself. Follow His lead, even in the ordinary, and expect to see miracles in the everyday."

And you know what? It was absolutely true. Every single bit of it.

As my heart cried out these truths to God in desperation—praying with every breath, it seemed—He met me there. And He saw me through.

Was it easy? Absolutely not. It was the hardest thing ever. And in some ways, my heart still bears some bruises and scars—but

But here's the incredible thing—I had just the tools I needed, freshly placed in my own prayer toolbox.

if He hadn't carried me, I don't know where I would be. I would probably be bitter, broken, and utterly defeated.

But because God taught me these truths about how to pray bold, I didn't sink when the storm came. With my eyes on Him, I walked on the water until He calmed the seas.

> Not because I am so strong, or so holy, or so good. Hardly. But because He is.

Not because I am so strong, or so holy, or so good. Hardly. But because He is.

And then, the healing came.

It wasn't fast, and it wasn't flashy. It wasn't even something that can be explained—the doctors never pinpointed John's injury, nor could they explain why the pain went away, but it did.

And now, here I am on the other side—so grateful for these truths God graciously gave me, just in the nick of time, right when I would need them most. So grateful to share them with you.

Friends, cling to these things we've learned. Hold fast to these prayer principles—they bring life!

Whether the seas of your life are calm, or the winds feel hurricane-force, with these truths on your lips, God will see you through. I am living proof.

Grab on to the One who won't let you go.

What Next? What Now?

At the end of a time of intense study, there's always a sense of "So what?" or "What next?"

Substitute your name for mine in the bulleted list, and read it through, allowing these precious lessons to penetrate your spirit. Let them wash over your weary soul on difficult days.

You heard my story of how these truths equipped me to weather a storm—now it's your turn to consider, how will they help you? How is God calling you to lean in during this season of life? Where do you feel particularly weak, or lacking?

Take a few moments to review the six main truths we've covered in this study, based on the Lord's Prayer and the lives and prayers of the six women we've studied, asking God to make your heart soft to His voice and leading. Circle or star the truths you need to hear most today. Hold them tight, and don't let go:

BOLD: Six Praying Women, One Faithful God

Hagar: To pray bold **we must run to our Heavenly Father**, who sees us and knows us by name.

Miriam: To pray bold **we must glorify our Holy God**, who fights for us and delivers us.

Deborah: To pray bold prayers of victory, **our hearts' cry must be, "Your Kingdom Come**, Your Will Be Done."

Hannah: To pray bold we must **pour out our heartbreak** to God, and watch in amazement as He provides our deepest need.

Mary Magdalene: To pray bold we **beg for God's forgiveness**, then live forgiven with love, determination, and confidence.

Mary, Mother of Jesus: To pray bold we **ask for God to lead** us, and then follow Him—finding abundant, blow-your-mind blessing where He leads.

Father, Holy One, King, Provider, Forgiver, Leader— pray *bold* to Him today. Pray *bold* to Him always.

Not to us, Lord, not to us but to your name be the glory, because of your love and faithfulness.

PSALM 115:1

This, then, is how you should pray:

Our Father in heaven
hallowed be Your name,
Your kingdom come,
Your will be done,
on earth as it is in heaven.
Give us today
our daily bread.
And forgive us our debts
as we also have forgiven
our debtors.
And lead us not into
temptation,
but deliver us
from the evil one.

for yours is the kingdom and the power
and the glory forever.

Amen.

Truths to Help You Pray Bold

(Fill your name in the blanks)

God sees you, _____. You're not alone in this. He's so close. Run to Him—**He's your Father.**

God is holy and mighty—He's so powerful that He parts the waters, making a way when there is no way. Praise Him for it, _____.

God has kingdom purpose in this battle, _____. Lean into it! Pray His Kingdom come and His will done and see the stars fight on your behalf, and the heavens rain down to bring victory.

God can handle your heartbreak, _____. Your brokenness isn't too much for Him. Bring your pain and your struggle and your need and lay it at His feet. He will provide.

God wants you to live forgiven, _____. Bask in all He's done for you, loving much, clinging to Him with courage. Be confident in His love for you.

God will lead you, _____. Dig into His word for comfort and direction, instead of relying on yourself. Follow His lead, even in the ordinary, and expect to see miracles in the everyday.

Sources consulted:

Arthur, Kay. *Discover the Bible for Yourself*. Eugene: Harvest House, 2000.

Atlas of the Bible. Pleasantville: Reader's Digest, 1985.

Bible Gateway (website), biblegateway.com

Bible Project (website), bibleproject.com

Bible Study Tools (website), biblestudytools.com.

Bible Works 8 (software program), 2008.

Biblehub (website), biblehub.com.

Bibleref (website), bibleref.com.

Blue Letter Bible (website), blueletterbible.org.

Bock, Darrell L. *The IVP New Testament Commentary Series, Luke*. Downer's Grove: IVP, 1994.

Complete Guide to Christian Quotations. Uhrichsville: Barbour, 2011.

Dockery, Karen, and Johnnie and Phyllis Godwin. *The Student Bible Dictionary*. Uhrichsville: Barbour, 2000.

ESV Study Bible. Wheaton: Crossway, 2008.

Geldenhuys, Norval. *The New International Commentary on the New Testament, the Gospel of Luke*. Grand Rapids: Eerdmans, 1988.

Hallesby, O. *Prayer*. Minneapolis: Augsburg, 1994.

Halley, H. H. *Halley's Bible Handbook*. Grand Rapids: Zondervan, 1965.

Henry, Matthew. *Matthew Henry's Complete Bible Commentary*, 1706.

Karssen, Gien. *Her Name Is Woman*. Colorado Springs: NavPress, 1975.

Life Application Study Bible, New Living Translation. Carol Stream: Tyndale, 2007.

Lockyear, Herbert. *All the Men of the Bible*. Grand Rapids: Zondervan, 1958.

Lockyear, Herbert. *All the Prayers of the Bible*. Grand Rapids: Zondervan, 1959.

Lockyear, Herbert. *All the Women of the Bible*. Grand Rapids: Zondervan, 1967.

Miller, Stephen M. *The Complete Guide to the Bible*. Uhrichsville: Barbour, 2007.

NKJV Study Bible. Nashville: Thomas Nelson, 2018.

Pittman, Amanda. *Stand in Confidence*. Colorado Springs: David C. Cook, 2022.

Torrey, R. A. *How To Pray*. New York: Revell, 1900.

Tozer, A. W. *The Quotable Tozer*. Minneapolis: Baker, 2018.

Wiersbe, Warren W. *The Bible Exposition Commentary*. Colorado Springs: David C. Cook, 2008.

Also available from Rachel Risner

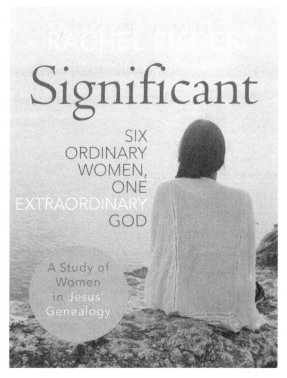

HOW CAN YOU WALK BY FAITH
IN THE FACE OF UNCERTAINTY?

This study will help you learn from scripture how to:

- **Dig in your heels** with tenacity when you feel like giving up.
- **Worship instead of worry** when life throws you curve balls.
- **Quit living skin-deep** by cultivating the inner beauty of trust in God.

Walk alongside real women of the Bible through their struggles and successes, and discover how to become a woman of **significance**.

Get your copy at: https://rachelrisner.com/books/

More Resources

ADD ONS FOR
NEXT-LEVEL BIBLE STUDY

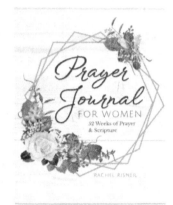

- Prayer Journal for Women – Nab my beautifully-designed Prayer Journal for Women with thoughtful prayer prompts to keep your prayer times focused.

 Get your copy at: https://rachelrisner.com/books/

- Video teaching — Stream six free lessons (one per week) with lesson notes online anytime at: www.rachelrisner.com/boldvideolessons

- Promotional goodies — Grab attractive, ready-made images and catchy blurbs for promoting your own *Bold* study group at: www.rachelrisner.com/boldpromogoodies

- Women's Ministry Pro-tips — Nab my free e-book on leveraging the powerful tool of social media for your local women's ministry at: www.rachelrisner.com/facebookforwomensministry

- RachelRisner.com — Find encouraging posts, book giveaways, shareable images, a chance to subscribe (yay!), pics of my family, and more goodies on my blog at www.rachelrisner.com

Been blessed? Pass the blessing on!

If you've been blessed by the *Bold* Bible study, please spread the word. After all, who doesn't love good news?! Here are five specific ways you can catch the vision and help other women learn for themselves how to pray *Bold*.

1. Word of Mouth—one of the most powerful ways you can let others know about this study is also the simplest—talk about it! Whether in person, by text, or on social media, you can spread the word to other women in your circle of influence. If the study helped you, it's likely to help them. **Let them know**.

2. Leave a Review—reviews at online retailers are worth more than their weight in gold. **Leaving yours would be a huge boost**. Reader reviews lend credibility and visibility to books. If you leave a simple review (even just one sentence), it helps online shoppers find this study, and have a better idea if it's right for them. Go to the *Bold* book page on Amazon to leave your review. Simple as that! (If you can't figure it out, reach out to me at www.rachelrisner.com/contact/ and I'll help). Seriously—if you leave a review, I will be on Cloud 9!

3. Lead a group—leading your own group study of *Bold* is an awesome way to pay forward what God has taught you through the study. **Prayerfully consider if God's calling you to this step today.**

4. Give feedback—I would be glad to hear any feedback you have after doing this study. I am all about giving our best to God, and that means being willing to hear it all—the good, the bad, and the ugly. If you let me know feedback on your experience in this study it gives me the chance to tweak it and make it better. It also helps me learn and grow as a Bible study writer and be better equipped to write the next one. Use the contact form at www.rachelrisner.com/contact/ **I love to hear from my readers!**

5. Pray—Best for last! My heart and prayer is that everything about this study gets women closer to God through His word. I'm thrilled and blessed with the impact it's had so far. Will you pray that God would continue to use it? *"So is my word that goes out from my mouth: It will not return to me empty, but will accomplish what I desire and achieve the purpose for which I sent it." Isaiah 55:11*

Thanks to each of you for walking with me on this journey!
I can't wait to see the hand of God move
as we keep praying *Bold*.

Week One: Hagar
VIDEO VIEWER GUIDE

Streaming video lessons is easy!

Go to:
rachelrisner.com/
boldvideolessons

or Rachel Risner's
YouTube channel

Jesus began his famous Lord's prayer (Matthew 6:9-13) by calling out to "Our _____ who is in heaven."

Hagar fled when problems came. (Genesis 16:4)

1st truth:
We don't have to _____ when problems come our way.

We don't have to play hide-and-seek. How much more does the God who sees deep into our hearts long to hold us when we've tried to run and hide?

2nd truth:
You can be bold in prayer because _____!

John 1:43-51 *Jesus and Nathanael - "I saw you while you were still under the fig tree"*

3rd truth:
You can boldly embrace your place as a _____.

I'll never forget the moving true story of a devoted father seeking his son in the midst of disaster.

When we give God our past, when we give Him our future, we no longer need to run away from our problems. We can run *to* the bright future God has for us. We can situate ourselves squarely and boldly on the lap of our loving Heavenly Father, positioned to humbly follow His course correction. And when we do, we're ready to be part of his kingdom, and to pray bold. After all, Jesus said the kingdom belongs to us when we receive it like children (Luke 18:16-17).

For printable discussion guides, go to: rachelrisner.com/ boldvideolessons

Answers: Father, run from God, God sees you, child of God

269

Week Two: Miriam
VIDEO VIEWER GUIDE

In Matthew 6:9, Jesus teaches us to pray, saying, "_____ be your name."

Miriam is a prime example of praising God for his holy power and might. (Exodus 15).

1st truth:
Put aside your _____.

Don't struggle against the only way that you can really find peace.

2nd truth:
Because He is a great God we can _____.

"yeshuw`ah." -our salvation

Be still, and know that I am God; I will be exalted among the nations, I will be exalted in the earth. Psalm 46:10

3rd truth:
Don't hold back your _____!

When we remember the power of God who saved us from our sins, how can I not sing his praise? How can I not adore Him? Friends, let's pray bold with the power of praise.

It's not that we won't have problems—just look at the Hebrews on the shores of the Red Sea, Just look at me with my failed epidural and baby whose heart wasn't beating well — the problems will come and the pain will be real—but our God will be bigger.
He'll fight for us, if we can only be still.

For printable discussion guides, go to: rachelrisner.com/ boldvideolessons

Answers: hallowed, power struggle, be still, praise

Week Three: Deborah
VIDEO VIEWER GUIDE

In Matthew 6:10, Jesus teaches us to pray, saying, "_____ come, your will be done."

The story of Deborah can help prepare us for our own spiritual battles. (Judges 4-5).

1st truth:
Be _____ ready.

Drive out the idols. Whatever it is that's causing your focus and heart to be led away from God needs to be put firmly in its place.

2nd truth:
Step _____ battle.

In Luke 12 Jesus taught about the foolishness of choosing to seek other things over seeking God's kingdom.

3rd truth:
Our _____ is sweet!

Even though we're still in the throes of battle, we see glimpses of the victory ahead.

When we boldly pray, "God your kingdom come" and live like we believe it – readying ourselves for battle and stepping right into the spiritual combat God is calling us to face, then God comes alongside for a victory we wouldn't want to miss!

For printable discussion guides, go to: rachelrisner.com/ boldvideolessons

Answers: your kingdom, battle, into, victory

Week Four: Hannah
VIDEO VIEWER GUIDE

In Matthew 6:11, Jesus teaches us to pray, saying, "_____ our daily bread."

The lesson we learn from Hannah's life story is that God provides. (1 Samuel 1-2).

1st truth:
You can _____ to God.

Not only can He handle it. He wants to handle it. God desires us to bring all our cares to Him
1 Peter 5:7

2nd truth:
No matter how much we give to God, we can't _____.

Give, and it will be given to you. A good measure, pressed down, shaken together and running over, will be poured into your lap (Luke 6:38).

3rd truth:
God's greatest provision is _____!

Jesus declared, "I am the bread of life. Whoever comes to me will never go hungry." John 6:35.

If Hannah's heart cry brought about God moving among His people and providing a leader like Samuel, just imagine what God will do if you and I cry out to Him in our need. Just imagine what leaders He'll raise, just imagine what mountains He'll move, just imagine what hearts He'll change, just imagine what brokenness He'll heal, just imagine how much life He'll give.
Give us today, our daily bread, Lord. Give us You.

For printable discussion guides, go to: rachelrisner.com/ boldvideolessons

Week Five: Mary Magdalene
VIDEO VIEWER GUIDE

In Matthew 6:12, Jesus instructs us to pray, "_____ our debts."

At the tomb of Christ, like Mary Magdalene, we find new life. And because we've been forgiven so much, we love much.

1st truth:
We must _____ in asking God's mercy.

Last at the cross, and first at the grave (Matthew 27:56, 61)—even when Jesus's other disciples fell away, Mary Magdalene shows us an example of the dogged determination in the life of one who's been forgiven.

2nd truth:
God _____. He responds to our diligence in seeking Him

Mary Magdalene was the privileged first to find her own Atonement between two angels in the mercy seat himself, Jesus Christ (Hebrews 9), when she came to the empty grave.

3rd truth:
Because of God's forgiveness we can _____ with mercy and grace!

When we encounter the life-changing forgiveness that God offers, it spills over from our lives into the lives of others.

For printable discussion guides, go to: rachelrisner.com/ boldvideolessons

Week Six: Mary
VIDEO VIEWER GUIDE

The last line of Jesus's prayer from Matthew 6 says, "_____ not into temptation, but deliver us from evil" (v 13).

We see this same spirit of following God's lead in Mary the Mother of Jesus — in her quiet faith, her gentle humility. Her heart was His.

1st truth:
We must _____ even when it doesn't make sense.

The Messiah would finally come—all eternity hinged on this! And it was up to Mary to look like a harlot to make it happen.

2nd truth:
I can accept God's call because He_____.

Who cares about the beverages at a party? Jesus. That's who. (John 2).

3rd truth:
When we allow God to lead us, the everyday _____!

Jesus took the cooperation of everyday, ordinary people doing everyday, ordinary acts like drawing water, serving food, washing, and moving a stone to accomplish the miraculous.

The joy of the world tastes good at first—it tempts you and baits you and draws you in, then runs out, leaving you empty. Full only of your disappointments, like the first wine at the wedding.
But not the joy Jesus offers.
So which way will you go at the crossroads of life? The way that makes sense, seems easy, or feels good? Or will you dare to follow God's lead—the righteous path—even when it takes humility and even though it might not make sense, because you know it leads to joy in the end. The decision is yours.

For printable discussion guides, go to: rachelrisner.com/ boldvideolessons

Answers: Lead us, boldly follow God's lead, leads me well, becomes divine

Made in the USA
Las Vegas, NV
08 April 2024

88372296R00151